THE GLOBAL FLOW

OF INFORMATION

EX MACHINA: LAW, TECHNOLOGY, AND SOCIETY
General Editors: Jack M. Balkin and Beth Simone Noveck

The Digital Person: Technology and Privacy in the Information Age
Daniel J. Solove

The State of Play: Law and Virtual Worlds
Edited by Jack M. Balkin and Beth Simone Noveck

Cybercrime: Digital Cops in a Networked Environment
Edited by Jack Balkin, James Grimmelmann, Eddan Katz,
Nimrod Kozlovski, Shlomit Wagman, and Tal Zar

Law on Display:
How New Media Are Transforming Persuasion and Judgement in Law
Neal Feigenson and Christina Spiesel

The Global Flow of Information: Legal, Social, and Cultural Perspectives
Edited by Ramesh Subramanian and Eddan Katz

THE GLOBAL FLOW OF INFORMATION

Legal, Social, and

Cultural Perspectives

EDITED BY

Ramesh Subramanian

and Eddan Katz

NEW YORK UNIVERSITY PRESS
New York and London

NEW YORK UNIVERSITY PRESS
New York and London

www.nyupress.org
© 2011 by New York University

Library of Congress Cataloging-in-Publication Data

The global flow of information : legal, social, and cultural perspectives /
edited by Ramesh Subramanian and Eddan Katz.
p. cm.
Includes index.
ISBN 978-0-8147-4811-4 (hardback : alk. paper) — ISBN 978-0-8147-4896-1 (e-book)
1. Information networks—Law and legislation 2. Internet—Law and legislation.
3. Law and globalization. 4. Information society. I. Subramanian, Ramesh. II. Katz, Eddan.
K564.C6G58   2011
343.09'944—dc22   2011007757

New York University Press books are printed on acid-free paper,
and their binding materials are chosen for strength and durability.
We strive to use environmentally responsible suppliers and materials
to the greatest extent possible in publishing our books.

Manufactured in the United States of America
10 9 8 7 6 5 4 3 2 1

Contents

Contents

Preface and Acknowledgments

ON APRIL 1, 2005, a group of leading experts from academia, industry, and the nonprofit sector met in New Haven, Connecticut, at the Yale Law School, under the auspices of the Yale Information Society Project (ISP). For the next two and a half days they discussed, presented, and argued the implications of global flows of information that were rapidly transforming the global society. The Conference on the Global Flow of Information featured lively panels and presentations on topics as varied as governance, economics, culture, politics, science, and warfare—how the global flows of information affect these areas, and how these in turn affect global flows. At the end of the conference it was decided that the best articles would be chosen to be compiled and edited into a book, to be published by New York University Press. Accordingly, fourteen papers were selected by the editors, and the respective authors were invited to revise and resubmit their work for the book.

That was the beginning of this volume. It has been five years in the making. Unfortunately, a variety of circumstances conspired to slow down progress on the book. But finally, thanks to the persistence of the Yale ISP's founder-director, Jack Balkin, and executive director, Laura DeNardis, we (the editors) made a determined push in 2009 to get the book finished within a year. Of course, by then some of the papers had become dated and had to be returned to the authors for further revision. The authors of one of the articles pulled out. One of the authors unfortunately suffered an untimely death. But despite these setbacks, almost all of the original authors remained committed to the process—a testament to the temporal relevance of the topic. The revised chapters began arriving, and the final book began to take shape by the end of 2009. What you hold in your hand is the result of this long process.

A book such as this does not happen just as a result of the efforts of its editors. Numerous actors have played critical roles in the final outcome and should be recognized. First, we thank all of the authors for their unstinting support, understanding, and patience; without them, there would be no book to speak of. Also, without the constant support and encouragement of Jack Balkin and Laura DeNardis, the book would never have made it to the publisher. Thank you both. We also thank Deborah Gershenowitz, senior editor at NYU Press, for her patience through all the years this book was in the making. We appreciate her efforts at shepherding it through the editorial process. Finally, we thank all the fellows and staff of the Yale ISP—a truly dynamic combination of pragmatists, idealists, and thinkers who offered constant feedback and other support throughout the book's development. Thank you all, once again, and we hope you enjoy reading this book.

Ramesh Subramanian
Eddan Katz
New Haven, 2011

Perspectives on the Global Flow of Information

Ramesh Subramanian and Eddan Katz

PATTERNS OF INFORMATION FLOW are one of the most important factors shaping globalization. The sheer scope of these flows is vast, encompassing global intellectual property, scientific research data, political discourse, brand names, and cultural symbols, to name just a few. Digitally networked environments subject information to ever newer methods of distribution and manipulation. Today, individuals, groups, countries, and international organizations actively promote and try to control the flow of different kinds of information across national borders. Conflicts over control of information flows help define who holds power in the global information economy. The information infrastructure—which includes methods of production, reproduction, and transmission and transformation of information symbols and artifacts—as well as economics, politics, and culture, determines who does and who does not have the power to control access to information.

Globalization's biggest enabler is the Internet, which began as a government-funded, mostly academic project and has now become the single most important network facilitating most, if not all, global information flows. In doing so, it has also become the single most profound transformative force that informs today's conduct of commerce, culture, education, politics, and war. Transformations wrought by the Internet, both massive and swift, show no signs of abating. Rather, they continue to accelerate exponentially as they have over the past decade and a half, strengthening and confirming the ever-expanding extent and reach of the global networked society.

From the ARPANET to the "Network Society"

The evolution of the Internet, starting from its ARPANET beginnings in the late 1960s to the colossal global "network society" that it is today, is a fascinating story of collaboration among computer scientists (seeking better, bigger, and faster networks), sociologists (seeking to use this new network to enhance human collaborations), and entrepreneurs (seeking to provide newer, more innovative services). A bit of this history is worth more than just a mere mention.

In 1971, just a few years after the "birth" of the Internet, Murray Turoff, a computer scientist working in the Office of Emergency Preparedness, Executive Offices of the President of the United States, was tasked with developing an electronic information and communication system to aid the U.S. government's response to emergencies. The resulting system, EMISARI (Emergency Management Information System And Reference Index), is considered to be the first computer-mediated, multi-machine communications and conferencing system and an early precursor to many of today's chat, messaging, conferencing, and collaboration systems.[1] Throughout the 1970s, sociologists, noticing the promise of social transformations emanating from networked communities, began actively studying the phenomenon. In 1978, collaboration between Turoff and the sociologist Roxanne Hiltz resulted in the earliest and brilliantly prescient seminal work on the emerging networked nation, described in their book *The Network Nation*.[2] The book became a defining document and a standard reference in computer-mediated communications. In her 1993 review in *The Village Voice*, the Pulitzer Prize–winning author Teresa Carpenter said the book contained:

> . . . a fascinating vision. In it home computers are as common as the telephone. They link person to person, shrinking, as the authors put it, "time and distance barriers among people, and between people and information,

to near zero." In its simplest form, the Network Nation is a place where thoughts are exchanged easily and democratically and intellect affords one more personal power than a pleasing appearance does. Minorities and women compete on equal terms with white males, and the elderly and handicapped are released from the confines of their infirmities to skim the electronic terrain as swiftly as anyone else.

Around the same time *The Network Nation* was published, Barry Wellman, a University of Toronto sociologist, was also studying the emerging network society, but from a purely sociological angle, arguing that societies are best seen as networks of people rather than as hierarchically organized social structures. He developed this theory in his 1979 article "The Community Question" and then expanded that idea substantially in his 2001 article "Physical Place and Cyber Place: The Rise of Personalized Networking"[3] to include technological advancements that enable individuals to expand their individual networks temporally and spatially.

The early 1990s saw a major escalation of the networked society. The nascent Internet, which had maintained a predominantly academic presence through the 1980s, suddenly became a household presence with the development of the World Wide Web (WWW). A network that connected all of global humanity became a clear possibility, prompting more scientists and sociologists to study the shape of things to come in this new environment.

One of those attracted to this area of research was Jan van Dijk, a Dutch professor of communications science, who, in a seminal 1999 book, *The Information Society*, noted the rise of the networked society and the inherent dualities that existed in it:

A combination of scale extension and scale reduction marks all applications of the new media in the economy, politics, culture and personal experience. This combination is the prime advantage and attractiveness of these media. It explains their fast adoption in what was considered to be a communications revolution. A dual structure returns in several oppositions described in the former chapters: centralization and decentralization, central control and local autonomy, unity and fragmentation, socialization and individualization.[4]

Van Dijk foresaw the tensions that such networked flows would cause:

> The main actors designing and introducing this advanced and expensive technology are at the top of corporations and governments. They are the investors, the commissioners and the decision makers. It is to be expected they use it to strengthen central control, be it in flexible forms, and to limit personal autonomy and free choices at the bottom of the organization not matching their interests. In this book it was noticed several times that ICT [Information and Communications Technology(ies)] enables better means of advanced and intelligent forms of central control than old technologies. It is a matter of social and organizational struggle whether the (other) opportunities of ICT to spread decision making will be utilized.[5]

He also predicted that the changes wrought by the networked society would be evolutionary rather than revolutionary, and that the networked society would not be an altogether *different* type of society.

Of the many works of this period, perhaps none has so comprehensively catalogued the coming networked society as that by Manuel Castells, a sociologist from Barcelona, Spain, working at the University of California, Berkeley. In his voluminous 1990s trilogy *The Information Age*,[6] he presciently portrayed the advent of a hyper-networked society, terming the new mode of development "informationalism"—paying tribute to Max Weber, who published his classic essay "The Protestant Ethic and the Spirit of Capitalism" in 1904–5 and whose ideas Castells used as a guideline in his theory of informationalism. Castells addressed many topics in his trilogy: the promise of a new networked world in the development of communications among peoples, the economic benefits and the cultural changes that this networked world would herald, the crisis of identity that it could lead to, and the real possibility of disintegration of societies "left behind" by the fast-moving train of globally networked economies. Even though Castells did not specifically focus on the power and expanse of the Internet, he nevertheless noted its enormous influence on the ongoing "network age"—the "microelectronics-based, networking technologies that provide new capabilities to an old form of social organization: networks."[7]

The most impressive aspect of Castells's work is the depth of empirical data he deployed to explain informationalism's connections to numerous apparently unconnected phenomena—such as the economic successes of Southeast Asia; Russia's capacity to retain a healthy civil society after the fall of communism; the future likelihood of Japan's regaining a leadership role in the Asia Pacific region; and even cocaine-trafficking networks around the globe. Castells also noted that new networking technologies are fundamentally different from older networking technologies by virtue of their being more adaptive and flexible and by their enabling decentralized structures to flourish, whereas older networks were characterized by their focus on the private life and vertical organizations such as "states, churches, armies, and corporations that could marshal vast pools of resources around the purpose defined by a central authority."[8]

Castells's trilogy covered the three sociologic dimensions of production, power, and experience. His real feat was in synthesizing these dimensions with the emerging network technologies and offering a theory of cyberculture that stresses the role of the state, social movements, and business. He observed that each of these entities has a competing agenda and interests, and there exists a permanent tension among these entities in controlling the flow of information.

Castells is often the most-cited socioinformation theorist and is often compared to Karl Marx and Max Weber in his analysis of modern production, its destabilizing effects on capitalism, and the meaning and role of identity politics, which in turn determine social relations among classes, all within the context of the networked society. As noted by Andrew Calabrese[9] in his extensive review of Castells's trilogy, the areas that Castells focused on in the most sustained manner are the nature and status of sovereignty, citizenship, and democracy in light of the globalization of information flows—which are also the topics of focus in this book.

Effects and Consequences

All of these early scholars of the information society—from Turoff to Castells—easily recognized that the network age is characterized by global flows of information. The flows shrink the spatial and the temporal and have the effect of exhilarating, aweing, and shocking their global participants. For better or for worse, network-enabled global information flows are here to stay, and here to change. Changes include cultural assimilation, unified standards of governance, massive decentralization of all matters commercial, global access to goods and services, and global projection of power. To critics, the network age aids and speeds up monoculturization, imposes particular governance standards (such as democratization) on all regions of the globe, increases global outsourcing leading to massive shifts in jobs, and forces unneeded products and services on countries that don't need them. Even modern terrorism conveniently places its *raison d'être* on the alleged threats to culture and values—posed by global information flows—mostly from developed Western nations. And distressingly, terrorists use the same global networks and network flows to promote their philosophy, propound their propaganda, gather recruits, and plan and implement their destructive agendas.

But the criticisms have come not just from the developing world. Many experts and commentators from the developed world—those that have advanced well into the network age—have also been equally strong in criticizing many of those governments that initiate, support, and extend policies that seek to impose a cultural hegemony on the rest of the world. Of course, some extreme critics of these practices (e.g., anti–world trade activists) have sought to neutralize the effects by commandeering the same technologies that enable the functioning of the network age (and thus global flow) to pursue (sometimes) violent and asymmetric struggles against those whom they perceive to be perpetuating globalization. An excellent example of this was the anti–World Trade Organization protests in Seattle in 1990. The primary agenda of anti–world trade activists is to negate, neutralize, or just strenuously oppose what they consider systematic efforts by developed economies—especially the United States and to a slightly lesser extent the European Union—to dominate the world economically through international IP laws and agreements. While it is easy to categorize these activists as belonging to fringe groups, it should be noted that impediments to free global flows of information orchestrated by developed countries are most often the cited reasons for such protests.

Impediments to the Free Global Flow of Information

Impediments to free information flows have also been extensively studied and catalogued by scientists, activists, lawyers, and humanists. Peter Drahos and John Braithwaite catalogue the impediments to free global flow by developed countries and call it a form of "information feudalism." They argue:

> Information feudalism is a regime of property rights that is not economically-efficient, and does not get the balance right between rewarding innovation and diffusing it. Like feudalism, it rewards guilds instead of inventive individual citizens. It makes democratic citizens trespassers on knowledge that should be the common heritage of humankind, their educational birthright. Ironically, information feudalism, by dismantling the publicness of knowledge, will eventually rob the knowledge economy of much of its productivity.[10]

Such proponents of truly free global flows of information have further sought to focus on the economic efficiencies, not to mention global equity, that could arise out of free flows of information unrestricted by stringent and often self-defeatist forms of copyright and other control regimes that seem to stifle, not further, innovation. Lawrence Lessig, the "American academic and political activist"—according to Wikipedia—and an ardent advocate of free culture, notes that the Internet is a prime answer to those who suggest that innovations can take place only in a controlled sphere. He notes:

> . . . always and everywhere, free resources have been crucial to innovation and creativity; that without them, creativity is crippled. Thus, and especially in the digital age, the central question becomes not whether government or the market should control a resource, but whether a resource should be controlled at all. Just because control is possible, it doesn't follow that it is justified. Instead, in a free society, the burden of justification should fall on him who would defend systems of control.[11]

Yochai Benkler of Harvard Law School goes further in explaining the networked information economy (NIE) and the challenges it faces from entrenched economic interests. He argues in favor of creating appropriate social structures (by the mechanism of public policies) by governmental bodies that would promote and help retain the "commons-based peer production." However, these "free flow" arguments face constant challenges from various fronts—the content providers, service providers, intellectual property guardians (mostly consisting of industry lobbyists, who effectively pressure governments and influence more protective laws).[12] Jonathan Zittrain, also of Harvard Law School, notes that industry pressure to enact and retain control over copyrights all over the globe is killing the "generative" characteristic of the hitherto "free" Internet, causing it to become fractured into smaller and smaller components, each governed by its own technological walls, rules, culture, and laws. Unfortunately, governments have only aided this unwelcome development, seeing that it would eventually provide them with more control over their own vested interests. This, argues Zittrain, is much to the detriment of free global information flow.[13]

Global Flow of Information: Current Perspectives

This book, coming a full twelve years after Castells's trilogy was published, aims to provide more contemporary perspectives to the nature, effects, and consequences of global networks and corresponding information flows. It takes a multidisciplinary approach to examining current facets of the Internet and the patterns that it weaves, be they political, economic, social, or cultural. The plurality of views expressed here covers international law, culture, global inequities, modern practice of war, governmental actions, and culture—all touched by current global information flows. Consequently, the book features essays from key experts from a variety of disciplines—from sociology, law, and culture to technology and economics. Given its preeminent role in the world today, the Internet—and its effects—forms a constant undercurrent in most, if not all, of the chapters. Many discussions focus on how the Internet is shaping the forces of globalization and, in turn, how the Internet is itself being continually reshaped by the politics of globalization in areas ranging from culture to commerce to warfare. The essays, taken together, focus on five key questions:

- Can the flow of information across national borders be controlled? If so, how?
- Whose interests are going to be affected by flows of information across borders? Who will be empowered and who will lose influence and authority?
- What role can or should international law play in securing freedoms, rights, and democratic accountability as individuals, groups, and nations struggle over access to and control of information flows?
- What are the cultural impacts of such global information flows?
- What lessons can we learn about how to regulate information flow from experience with other kinds of flow across borders—for example, flows of goods, services, people, and capital?

Three Models of Globalization

Following this chapter, the book starts with an introduction of the global phenomenon by Victoria Reyes and Miguel Angel Centeno (chapter 2). They offer three models of globalization—the "Corner Deli" model that illustrates a completely unstructured form of globalization wherein the "local" completely intertwines and coexists with the "regional" and "global"; the "Wienerwald" model akin to the restaurant chain in Germany and Austria, which offers a regional perspective focused on a specific region or culture, also known as "clustered globalization"; and the "hegemonistic globalization" model exemplified by the global restaurant chain McDonald's, which closely resembles a rimless bicycle wheel—a strong center with ever-expanding spokes in all directions.

Reyes and Centeno observe that despite much theoretical scholarship, there is a striking lack of empirical work in studying globalization—which limits our determination of "the structure of participation in this global net," which in turn affects our ability to truly determine the political, economic, and cultural ramifications of the same. They then use data from the Princeton International Networks Archive (INA) and the Mapping Globalization Project (MGP) and network analysis to map global network connectivity to locate various nations within their three models.

Starting from this perspective of globalization, the rest of the book is organized into thirteen chapters thematically categorized into five parts:

Culture, Politics and Law, Science and Medicine, War, and Power. This categorization is neither mutually exclusive nor collectively exhaustive. It does, however, provide different and interesting perspectives on the phenomenon of the global information society and corresponding information flows. We describe here each of the sections along with the essays contained within them.

Part I: Culture

Pervasive interconnection is the hallmark of the global information society—everyone is linked to everyone else. A new potential global audience has shaped the production of movies, music, books, and other cultural works, and these, in turn, have penetrated local and national cultures. Multinational corporations seeking ever new markets have spread images and ideas through branding and advertising campaigns. Sometimes existing cultures successfully integrate this influx of new forms of global culture, but sometimes they may also try to resist or reject it.

The essays in Part I focus on the capabilities and limitations, the benefits and detriments of new forms of global culture in the digitally networked environment. They discuss the effect of information flows on the production and evolution of culture and how nations and local communities adapt to the global flow of cultural information while attempting to control it. Some countries, for example, discriminate against foreign cultural products and promote national works, or try to keep out what they consider harmful or dangerous forms of culture. Intellectual property rights, the broadcast flag, and anticircumvention laws help facilitate control over culture and provide new forms of control over its dissemination.

One promising development arising from the global spread of the Internet is the global flow of filmed entertainment through Internet TV. Of course, critics of globalization have immediately jumped upon this as another example of colonization of the world by (mostly) American cultural artifacts. The same arguments and attributions that preceded this development—namely, the success of Hollywood in exporting American culture to the rest of the world—have been advocated in this case, too. Eli Noam (chapter 3) takes each one of these "causes" and argues that none of them is the real reason for the success of Hollywood productions in the world. He thus pours cold water on such causes as market capture emerging from the destructions of war; dumping movies cheaply that have been primarily paid for by American audiences. Rather, Noam argues that the success is attributable to other factors, some well known—namely, Hollywood's high productivity and industry structure. He argues that it is managerial responses to the concept of globalization, manifested through such strategies as extensive outsourcing of production (e.g., animators from Japan, special effects software programmers from India, venture financing from London, postproduction in Shanghai, and marketing and advertising in New York) and the free-agent culture of Hollywood, that prevails in the end, in spite of cultural criticism and political protectionism from the rest of the world's detractors to this global spread of digitally transmitted entertainment.

In chapter 4, Lawrence Liang provides an intriguing insight into how copyrights are perceived in emerging economies. This is the only chapter in the book whose author represents an emerging economy—that of India. In looking at how copyrights have been handled in emerging economies, Liang sees a dichotomy of approaches. By and large, governments in emerging economies adhere to international laws and treaties in the hopes that they may benefit from increased trade with developed economies on which they depend on for exporting their products. On the other hand, their private citizens exuberantly participate in a parallel, gray economy almost entirely devoted to creating pirated versions of movies and music in complete contravention of all existing international laws. Liang focuses entirely on this phenomenon—the people involved, their motivations, and the infrastructure. Much has been said about the detrimental effects of copyrights. But even champions such as Lawrence Lessig eventually concede the argument that pirating involves no creativity, and thus profiteering from such copying is, and should be, illegal. Lessig's arguments, however, do not gain much ground with Liang, who frames the whole issue of copyright violations in the emerging world context as one pertaining to access to knowledge and right to livelihood, arguing that piracy actually increases the visibility of the works and thus may actually promote future sales of such works even in emerging economies. Liang convincingly argues for an equitable pricing of books and other copyrighted works in developing countries vis-à-vis the developed countries, employing a pricing strategy that uses percentage pricing based on disposable income, rather than the current practice of pricing that uses simple dollar-to-rupee or euro-to-rupee conversions.

In chapter 5, Stanley N. Katz addresses the preservation of and access to digital cultural artifacts.

When it comes to the issue of preserving and making accessible cultural artifacts using the new digital environments, many age-old contradictions seem to reemerge with greater emphasis and significance. Katz offers numerous examples. For instance, the new digital environments have been used and abused to the fullest extent by terrorist organizations like Al-Qaeda, yet use of the similar telecommunications and social computing infrastructure by American soldiers blogging from the battlefields of Iraq has been frowned upon. The new copyright and IP battles between rights holders and consumers make one wonder whether technology shapes the law, or whether the law shapes technology. The Google Books project, which ostensibly seeks to open up orphaned and other hard-to-get works to consumers, has heightened resistance from authors, publishers, and especially academics, who would, at first sight, only stand to gain from the project. Members of the European Union, especially France, are wary of Google Books because of fears that it may foment cultural imperialism, wherein (to take one example) French masterpieces might be controlled and made available by Google to world audiences.

Not to be outdone, the UN has also immersed itself in this argument, and the United Nations Educational, Scientific and Cultural Organization (UNESCO) has convened a committee to draft a statement on "the Protection of the Diversity of Cultural Contents and Artistic Expressions." The committee has issued preambles that confuse, rather than clarify, the issue of how to use digital technology to enhance the global reach of cultural artifacts while at the same time protecting the cultures whence such artifacts emerge. Katz concludes that his point is not to showcase the inconsistencies but rather to raise questions that will have to be addressed in the future, where much global flows of cultural significance will take place in the digitized environments.

If there is one thing that new telecommunications technology does exceedingly well, it is in the realm of communication between and among people. Technology is the biggest enabler of interactions between people and cultures. It facilitates the "doing of," and the consumption of culture. Given that cultural interactions "produce meaningful personal experiences and increase not only personal but also collective capacities that are beneficial to members of the community beyond the individual actor,"[14] it is useful to explore the nexus between technology and culture. The late Edwin Baker (chapter 6) explores the economic and cultural aspects of products whose costs of reproduction, once the first copy is made, are almost zero. This, however, poses problems—on the one hand, a product with zero marginal costs of production would swamp the entire market and prevent other comparable, and sometimes better, products from seeing the light of the day. But sometimes the larger audience could also encourage new innovators to enter the field and deliver alternative products. The trick, then, is to determine a way to measure these phenomena to determine which actually works.

The fact that technology enables cultural transactions is not without its detractors, who believe that technology-enabled cultural exchanges could somehow dilute their own culture or hasten cultural colonization of some nations by others. Some of these actors propose cultural isolationism as a solution, through "strong" protectionist measures—despite the fact that such measures may not be economically beneficial. Baker proposes an alternative concept: "weak" protectionist measures that would tax imports to fund local products within a democratic framework. Baker in general seems to imply that weak protectionist measures have a beneficial effect, overall, to society.

Part II: Politics and Law

The essays in Part II discuss how global information flows affect national and international politics, and, conversely, how global politics affects information flows. Information flows can change the political dynamics both intranationally and internationally, and they can reinforce or destabilize governmental and nongovernmental power structures. Information flows made possible by digital networks can support new political coalitions, form new communities, and reshape the public sphere. At the same time, traditional politics, through governments and international organizations, often defines how information, and what kinds of information, will be permitted to flow across borders. Governments establish regulatory frameworks for information flow, control the various layers of networks and communications systems, and impose filtering strategies to control information flow. Some of these strategies are fairly successful, while others fail. Some help their societies, while others help oppress people within them.

The tussle, tension, and distribution of power between global civil societies and governments are the subject of Daniel W. Drezner's essay (chapter 7), which takes a politicoeconomical view of the development. Ever since the Internet became a global, commonsense phenomenon, civil society groups such as NGOs and other activist/watchdog groups have been very quick to adapt to the new communications technology. They have successfully used it for political purposes to organize protests, to inform the community, and to direct actions against the government. Drezner attributes these successes to the fact that the nature and structure of the Internet resemble those of global civil society. However, such success is just one part of the story. There is a second view of the spread of the Internet—one in which governments have sought to gain control either by blocking entire swaths of the Internet's content or by skillfully infiltrating citizen groups with a view to exposing them, as well as scare them away through laws, as well as "requests" to cooperate. The primary question Drezner attempts to answer in his chapter is "Does the Internet empower the coercive control of governments at the expense of citizen activists, or vice versa?"

Drezner first addresses the rise and spread of smart mobs and their initial successes in a variety of international negotiations as varied as human rights advocacy to the Landmine Convention. He then juxtaposes this against the reactions of the state's seeking to regain control and neutralize such movements. He uses a transaction cost approach to explain why ICT affects the tussle between the state and civil society groups. It seems that the same ICT which helps reduce the transaction costs of the citizen by shrinking the hierarchy of his global organization, thus allowing for more rapid communication, also empowers the state to reduce its own hierarchy, thus nullifying the effects.

Governments use this effect not just to control but also to enable citizen participation to the extent they deem appropriate. In some cases, countries such as the United States have actually begun to invest resources to enhance citizen participation. It has sent even teams to other countries ostensibly to aid and educate other governments in their quest to reach their people through Web 2.0 technologies, while at the same time teaching the nuances of maintaining secure systems with high levels of data integrity. However, Drezner warns that the positive actions of the governmental and civil groups organizations will go only so far, and it is a fallacy to think that the Internet will aid only "good" groups. He points out that the Internet is also currently infiltrated by illiberal elements who may want to control and negate the efforts of the government to support legitimate groups.

These ideas gain further traction in John G. Palfrey Jr.'s essay (chapter 8). Notwithstanding several gains made by global citizen groups and individuals as a result of the rise of the Internet, it is disappointing that the Internet still faces considerable censorship and control by states. As the phenomenon of control rises, world governments have started to debate the issue at "Internet Governance Forums." However, meetings such as the World Summit on the Information Society (WSIS) have and the Internet Governance Forum (IGF) have not resulted in any substantial improvement on the censorship issue because of the participants' reticence to indulge in hard conversations on thorny topics. The OpenNet Initiative has undertaken research to determine the depth and breadth of Internet filtering in various countries and concludes that some form of filtering takes place in almost every nation. While much of the most determined filters focus on stopping access to pornography and "anonymizing" sites, many countries filter content for political reasons, with a view to retaining control over their citizens.

Palfrey suggests that Internet Governance Forums have focused more on mundane topics such as port number assignments and spam while avoiding issues of Internet censorship and controls practiced by member nations. Palfrey emphasizes that such discussions should be much broader in nature, so that these thorny issues can actually be discussed in the open.

Dan L. Burk (chapter 9) considers the intriguing possibilities and con-sequences of treating law like a product, much like a commercial prod-uct, governed by market economics and affected by phenomena such as Tiebout's application of interjurisdictional competition theory to pub-lic services, and "cartelization" effects. Burk suggests that just as citizens and businesses migrate to jurisdictions or cities that have laws and codes favoring them, and away from jurisdictions that are not favorable to them, purveyors of "protected" informational products such as copyrighted books, music, and other media forms would also be inclined to move to locations where the existing laws favor them and are less obstructive to their endeavors.

In response, developed nations (where a majority of information products are developed) may resort to international-standards agree-ments and "laws as products," combined with a "cartel" approach—that is, entering into agreements with similar nations to impose laws and restrictions on lesser developed countries and thereby maintaining their stronghold over such products. This approach may again break, as car-tel members may resort to bilateral agreements or rent-seeking "quid pro quo" arrangements with politicians of certain emerging economies. In discussing these issues, Burk successfully details the interactions and connections between technology-based standards setting and interna-tional law and illustrates some of the problems that may arise from these.

Part III: Science and Medicine

Nowhere is the conflict between the radical potential of globalized infor-mation flow and the profound consequences of the interruption and regulation of this flow more apparent than in the domain of science. This is especially true in the life sciences: From traditional medicine to the map of the human genome, the processes of science are increasingly globalized. But the AIDS epidemic has highlighted a crucial disconnect between the possibilities of global science and the realities of the distri-bution of its production and consumption.

In the name of more and better science, treaties such as TRIPS and regulatory bodies like WIPO are ratcheting up intellectual property pro-tection around the world. These changes are affecting the conduct and progress of science, controlling the flow of scientific information internationally and changing models of scientific research and production. A key debate in science policy is the extent to which science will be "open" or "closed" and the role that intellectual property rules should have on the shape and direction of future scientific research.

Frederick M. Abbott addresses the issue of what global flows of information could do to the whole notion of right to medicines and the global pharmaceutical industry in his insightful and highly informative essay (chapter 10). While it can be argued that enhanced global flows of information would also enable easier flow of information products such as pharmaceuticals, Abbott notes that this is sadly not the case. Pharmaceutical companies from developed economies have made it difficult for citizens of emerging economies to have access to the medicines, but often the medicines are prized unrealistically high for anybody in the developing world. Efforts by the developing countries to resist and overcome the problems are being challenged and frustrated by developed pharmaceutical companies through various means, including pushing unpalatable international treaties that safeguard patents by these companies, lobbying domestic governments to offer additional protections, controlling distribution channels, and, finally, acquiring pharmaceutical companies in developing countries. Given this, the only solution for the developing countries seems to be to mount a concerted attack through affirmative action, placing legal limits on foreign acquisitions, and protectionist measures.

Part IV: War

Modern warfare and diplomacy would be impossible without global flows of information, but at the same time, both war and diplomacy must try to control these flows and turn them to their own purposes. Current national security policies attempt to construct a unified information warfare plan to handle the various aspects of the "information front." These include influencing public opinion, defending the nation from harmful information, maintaining the quality of information used to make important decisions, and initiating offensive strategies targeted at the enemy's information systems. In the modern world, military and political strategy is inseparable from concern with patterns of information flow.

The essays in Part IV examine the strategic use of information flow: the use of misinformation and disinformation techniques, accreditation and disaccreditation of sensitive sources, control over informational access to the battlefield, and the use of manipulative techniques to dominate information search and retrieval access points. "Information warriors" filter traffic, reroute and channel flow or block information nodes, and attempt to reshape patterns of information flow. Through this process, they create innovative defense methods that seek to interfere with the flow of information by polluting the environment or subverting the architecture of flow and, in the process, actually change the global information ecosystem. But information warfare is a tool of offense as well as of defense: Information warriors try to penetrate, demolish, or undermine the enemies' information infrastructure, using methods such as hacking into information sources, inserting malicious code, jamming traffic, and attacking information systems to harm critical infrastructure or to amplify a physical attack.

Jeremy M. Kaplan poses several questions in his essay (chapter 11): What is the connection between the global flow of information and wars of the future? Kaplan notes that the same developments and technologies that enable the information flows among citizens of the world can also be used for conducting future wars. Indeed, this notion of open flows of information in the conduct of a nation's wars is counterintuitive at first. For instance, how can a nation open up its information infrastructure with a view to providing just-in-time information to a soldier in the battlefield? How can the information from that soldier about possible enemy targets be sent to appropriate weapons platforms without any information leakage to the enemy? How can the battlefield's operational and supply needs be transmitted to the suppliers and how can the suppliers tap into the needs on the battlefront seamlessly, through interoperable, interconnected networks? What will be the future of such "net-centric" wars?

More important, Kaplan raises critical issues that emanate from such open net-centric military structures and compares them to net-related security, privacy, and information assurance issues that exist in the civilian and commercial world today. The issues seems to be the same, but the concerns of the military are radically different, more critical, and more urgent and could result in more devastation if mishandled. Kaplan addresses possible solutions to the problems that might arise as a result of global information flows and their use in the conduct of modern warfare.

From fighting wars of the future, we focus next on the structure, role, and function of information flows in war and peace. James Der Derian (chapter 12) argues that global information flows have brought with them a world of enhanced communication, transparency, and productivity (the "good side" of information). But unfortunately, the same have also brought about surveillance, terror, and war (the "bad side" of information). Instead of focusing on one or the other, it is useful to analyze both aspects of information, recognizing that the "good" and the "bad" are simply symptoms of the stresses induced by the information revolution. Tackling the notion that global flows enhance the ability of the terrorist, Der Derian avers that it is very difficult even to identify and define terror—as one man's terrorist could just as easily become another's freedom fighter. So instead of wasting time and effort in trying to define who is a terrorist, and what actions and uses of information constitute terrorism, he suggests that the whole notions of "information age" and "information revolution" should be studied using a multidisciplinary lens. An interesting observation that Der Derian makes pertains to the transmission of images rather than words in influencing people around the world—a technique used very effectively by terrorists.

In order to study the information revolution, Der Derian proposes a framework in the form of eight propositions that will form the basis in studying "infoflows." He describes the concept of information as one that exists in a continuum, with the extreme positions being "infowar," categorized by the use of information to wage war, terrorize, demonize, target, and even kill the enemy; and "infopeace"—which is focused on the reduction of personal and structural violence, thereby enhancing the mediation and resolution of wars.

Part V: Power

The book concludes with two wide-ranging chapters about information flow as power, and how control over information flows becomes a central source of power in a globalized world. The first chapter considers how individuals and nation-states wield many different types of information flows strategically to enhance their power over others. It treats information as a kind of power that people can consciously use to achieve their goals so that as globalization proceeds, it will amplify the strategic and instrumental uses of power.

Dorothy E. Denning (chapter 13) looks at the notion of power and its effects on information flow. As she notes, current information flows are dictated by two powers that are often in conflict with each other—the power to enable the flow of information, and the power to block such flow. These powers manifest themselves at all levels—that of the individual users as well as that of the government infrastructure. Individuals and organizations enable, and often desire to exert control over, information, whether it is to enable the flow or to block it. And sometimes, entities act in cross-purposes. While an individual may seek unfettered access to information, government may seek to block the information or prevent it from leaving or reaching the individual. Governments may also use pressure on individual citizens and make sure that only "approved" information is accessible to the individual. To this scenario a third entity could be added—that of the malware creator and digital attacker. Malware and attacks can occur in the form of computer viruses, worms, or attacks using various techniques. Sometimes the perpetrator is a lone thief, and at other times the attack is the result of an organized group effort. Sometimes, it is also the government apparatus itself aiming to control another country or to spy on its own citizens.

Denning notes that localized rules, laws, and regulations enable governments as well as individuals to exercise more control over the digital information "new west" while also enabling some information flow deemed appropriate by either party. But she also notes that in the end, "it is not the ability to control flows that matters as much as the ability to influence decisions and actions."

The second chapter, by contrast, begins with the assumption that information creates forms of power that may transcend anyone's grasp or use. It asks how the development of increasingly interconnected global networks of power ensnare individuals, groups, and nations in ever-proliferating networks of power that they do not control and that, in fact, are in the control of no one in particular.

Thus power is at the heart of Jack M. Balkin's theorization of global information flows (chapter 14). He offers a different, antihumanist perspective on the whole notion of power, its effects on global flows of information, and the effect that such flows have on people. Instead of looking at the Internet and accompanying global flows as a strictly human creation that is completely under human control, he proposes an interesting theory: that the Internet actually projects its own power to a human race that may, or mostly may not, even be aware of, much less be able to counter or control, such projection of power. He develops the theme by looking at three theories to explain the flow of information: memetics, Gaia, and the proliferation of information power.

The memetic theory speaks to the reproduction of memes—a cultural reproduction, aided by the technologies that humans willingly and almost unwittingly develop. From the memes' point of view, humans and their technologies are simply means to aid the reproduction and proliferation of memes. The Gaia theory considers the entire globe as one "system" whose quest is continually to learn more about itself. Thus the global flow of information—in all directions—is simply a means for Gaia to learn more about itself. The "proliferation of power" theory takes as its bases those of Marx, Weber, and Foucault and proposes that technology gradually evolves bureaucracies and various forms of subordination that eventually regiment and subjugate human behavior. Balkin cites the spread of pornography and spam as examples to illustrate his theories and suggests that while we as humans promote human rights, we should also be aware of these alternate forces of nature that work orthogonally to human rights. Such awareness, in the end, would enable us to "divert this new form of power toward human ends."

Balkin's powerful antihumanist theorization about global information flows provides a fitting conclusion to the overall theme of the book. Along with everything else in this world, information is also an evolving phenomenon. Over eons, it has been created by humans, disseminated by humans, and controlled by humans. However, over time, a profound change may have taken place—information may have gained a life of its own, and all our attempts to use information simply plays out in its own playbook of spreading itself to every corner of the human mind's reach. Humans, thus, can no longer claim complete control of information, or the way information flows and spreads around the globe. We hope that this book will give the reader a plurality of current perspectives on the multifaceted nature of information flows, their use and misuse, and the future they are likely to bring.

Notes

1. See Stewart, Bill, "The Living Internet," http://www.livinginternet.com/r/ri_emisari.htm. In 1971, EMISARI was put to one of its first practical uses to coordinate policy information for U.S. President Richard Nixon's wage and price control program to fight high inflation. Users of EMISARI accessed the system through teletypewriter terminals linked to a central computer through long-distance phone lines. The EMISARI chat functionality, called the Party Line, was originally developed to replace telephone conferences that might have thirty or so participants and in which no one could effectively respond and take part in a meaningful discussion. Party Line had a range of useful features familiar to users of modern chat systems, such as the ability to list the current participants and the invocation of an alert when someone joined or left the group.

2. See Hiltz, S. R., and M. Turoff. 1978. *The Network Nation: Human Communication via Computer.* New York: Addison-Wesley. [Revised Edition. Cambridge, MA: MIT Press, 1993.]

3. See Wellman, Barry, "The Community Question: The intimate networks of East Yorkers," AJS Volume 84, No 5, March 1979, pp 1201–1231.

4. See van Dijk, Jan, "The Network Society: Social Aspects of New Media" (1999, 2nd edition 2005), pp 220–223.

5. Ibid.

6. See Castells, Manuel (1996, second edition, 2000), *The Rise of the Network Society, The Information Age: Economy, Society and Culture Vol. I.* Cambridge, MA; Oxford, UK: Blackwell; Castells, Manuel (1997, second edition, 2004), *The Power of Identity, The Information Age: Economy, Society and Culture Vol. II.* Cambridge, MA; Oxford, UK: Blackwell; Castells, Manuel (1998, second edition, 2000), *End of Millennium, The Information Age: Economy, Society and Culture Vol. III.* Cambridge, MA; Oxford, UK: Blackwell.

7. See Castells, Manuel, "The Network Society: From Knowledge to Policy," © Center for Transatlantic Relations, 2006. Pp 4.

8. Ibid.

9. See Calabrese, Andrew, "The Information Age according to Manuel Castells," in the Journal of Communication, Summer 1999, pp 175–176.

10. See Drahos, Peter and John Braithwaite, Information Feudalism: Who Owns The Knowledge. Economy, Earthscan Publications, London, 2002, p. 219.

11. See Lessig, Lawrence, *The Future of Ideas,* Random House, 2001. P 14.

12. See Benkler, Yochai, *The Wealth of Networks,* Yale University Press, 2006. Chapters 11 & 12.

13. See Zittrain, Jonathan, *The Future of the Internet and How to Stop It,* Yale University Press, 2008. Chapters 4 & 5.

14. See Balkin, Jack M. "Digital Speech and the Democratic Theory of Culture: A Theory of Freedom of Expression for the Information Society," 79 *NYU L. Rev.* 1 (2004).

2

McDonald's,
Wienerwald, and the Corner Deli

Victoria Reyes and Miguel Angel Centeno

GLOBALIZATION IS EVERYWHERE.[1] States, economies, and societies are increasingly integrated, with flows of goods, capital, humans, and cultural objects forming a global web. There is little doubt that we are undergoing a process of compression of international time and space. Globalization is also nowhere. Although lacking a coherent empirical or theoretical underpinning, the concept has become a catchall phrase in academia and the mainstream media, simultaneously meaning everything, and nothing at all. In order to understand the global flow of information, we first have to examine the various meanings of "globalization."

Our title hints at three dominant perspectives.

The "Corner Deli" phenomenon describes interdependent globalization. The nice elderly couple still owns the store, but they now offer Belgian chocolates, flowers from Kenya, and Japanese novelty soda. This shape of globalization resembles that of the Internet—a network without hubs and with low variance in the probability of any node's being connected to any other node.[2] In this way, the model may be described as a noncentric spider web without stratification or hierarchy. In many ways, it is the utopian vision of classic liberalism and *laissez-faire* policies.

"Clustered globalization" is exemplified by the Wienerwald chain. This group of German and Austrian restaurants imposes a culinary and managerial model (similar to what opponents of globalization claim happens on a global basis) but is limited by region. Similar multinational, but nonglobal, chains can be found in different parts of the world, such as the Jollibee fast-food chain in the Philippines. This large chain captures clustered globalization in a different sense—restaurants are found in the countries of Saudi Arabia, Vietnam, Hong Kong, Brunei, and the United States. While Jollibee is "global" in the sense that it transcends a specific region, the locations are marked by historically large Filipino migration patterns. A third type of clustered globalization can be seen through the creation of ethnic-specific enclaves—such as "Little Senegal," "Little Manila," "Little Italy," and "Chinatown"—in cities marked by historically large immigrant populations. This model, then, sees the global system as consisting of cliques or subgroups linked by culture, history, and/or geography. The most ominous view, of course, is Samuel Huntington's clash of civilizations. Not so dissimilar is an Orwellian vision of an Oceania and a Eurasia engaged in perpetual struggle. Less ominously, we may also expect to find vestiges of old empires or regional cooperatives—a good example of this may be the European Union.

McDonald's exemplifies hegemonic globalization. A less polite or less politically correct term might be "empire." In such a case, we do have a spider web, but now it has a very distinct and clear center. Another image is that of a bicycle wheel without a rim, possessing a strong center and spokes unconnected to one another. In this instance, a single taste and organizational regime is imposed on the world, and it becomes impossible for local actors to survive.

These three distinct perspectives represent ideal types of globalization, and overlap may, and does, occur. For instance, the global chain of McDonald's displays regional variation through localized menus. The now (in)famous dialogue between two of the main characters in the Oscar-winning American movie *Pulp Fiction* demonstrates this variation.[3] Despite these localized changes on the menu, McDonald's may still be viewed as a hegemonic model because of the American-based institutional and management-related patterns enforced in each chain. The restaurant is marked by a brand that is wholly and distinctly American, and despite localized features, these structural and cultural meanings are influential in changing local societies.[4]

We can imagine parallel versions of these perspectives outside of restaurant management. There is the locally owned TV broadcast station as opposed to Al Jazeera and CNN. The *International Herald Tribune* has a global footprint, while the *South China Morning Post* has a regional one and *El Clarin* is read only in Argentina. Hollywood actors are known worldwide, Bollywood actors in the subcontinent and Indian diaspora (although it may be argued that the Bollywood milieu is fast becoming a global phenomenon because it was featured in the multiple-Oscar-winning movie *Slumdog Millionaire*), while Moscow TV stars are not recognized outside of Russia.

Each of these models carries with it not only images of what "globalization" means but also assumptions regarding power asymmetries and influence flows. The most optimistic of them see each participant in the global system as being able to access a much broader scope of information and culture while simultaneously maintaining his or her identity relatively intact. Not accidentally, the closest parallel to such a vision is of an unencumbered mass market—a global eBay of ideas. The most pessimistic predicts monopolization of information and the standardization of tastes—a Microsoftization of the world. Although information-embedded goods such as pharmaceuticals or agri-biotechnology can be used to explore these relationships of (a)symmetrical flows, this chapter specifically highlights cultural media because it is an example of something with which most people have experience and of which they have an intimate understanding. Additionally, although institutional structures shape and modify culture—and vice versa—rapid changes in globalization may be more readily apparent in media exchanges than in modifications within economic or social structures. Therefore, if globalization is a democratizing force, we would expect cultural patterns to appear randomized, with no central hub(s) directing flows. If it is nothing more than the intensification of already existing regional ties, then we will see cultural clusters. Finally, if globalization has a single center, then we will expect to note an overall homogenization.

While much has been said in favor of or against each of these perspectives, the major obstacle to our understanding of globalization has been that theoretical treatments outpace empirical evidence. Key distinctions between globalization and internationalization, for example, lack a concrete basis. Despite the ubiquity of the term "globalization," we have remarkably little data on increasing international integration. For example, little research has examined the structure of "global" brands such as Coca-Cola or Starbucks and their relations to their country of origin (which can help determine structural inequalities and its relation to culture); tracked Internet usage and most-often-visited sites by country; collected widespread global data on the number of television shows and their national origin; conducted qualitative studies on people's perceptions of countries; or analyzed the content and form of countries' popular entertainment. Essentially, because of the dearth of empirical evidence, we lack the capacity to determine how the structure of participation in this global net affects and helps determine political, economic, or cultural outcomes.

The limited empirical work that has been done shares a series of faults. Most relevant for this essay, studies of globalization have not defined an appropriate and systemic unit of analysis. How do we measure its extent? How do we define the relevant geographical and substantive areas that have been affected? Has globalization had the same reach across the globe and all fields? How should we study the effects of globalization: in the aggregate (that is, on global totals)? Are regions more appropriate? Should we count countries as the relevant units for measuring results or persons?

Since 1999 and 2006, respectively, the Princeton International Networks Archive (INA) (www.princeton.edu/~ina) and Mapping Globalization Project (MG) (http://qed.princeton.edu/main/MG) have endeavored to answer these questions by focusing on the production of empirical data. The work of these two entities is based on two critical assumptions. The first of these is that the relevant unit in globalization and the one that can provide the best grounding for a global definition of the concept is the transaction. This can be interpreted as an exchange (be it social, cultural, or financial), an international trip, or a simple phone call. The important aspect is that transactions are the basic units through which the world is connected—they represent the basic links defining the global web. However, the world's becoming more integrated is a double-edged sword for the measurement of transactions. Although many transactions take place in a given day, these are increasingly difficult to track as technology changes; for example, the rise of cell phone use makes it exceedingly difficult to track telephone usage, and increased black market–produced and –sold media complicate measures of cultural consumption.

Our second assumption is that to appreciate the particular qualities of globalization, the metaphor of a network may be most appropriate. Most literally, networks are arrangements of connections into nets, or open-work systems linking groups of points and intersecting lines. Obvious examples are the human body's circulatory network of veins or a country's arteries of rivers, canals, railways, and roads. They may also be interconnected chains or systems of immaterial things, events, or processes. A focus on networks allows us to examine the integration of economic, social, political, and cultural regimes as a process in and of itself. Viewing globalization as a network allows us to combine different forms of interaction (e.g., trade, migration, conflict) into a cohesive portrait of international integration. Finally, network methods operate under the assumption that structural position and associated characteristics are determinant. This assumption allows for a clearer analysis of the consequences of globalization for individual societies over and above endogenous factors.

Network analysis is particularly important because what is new about this contemporary phenomenon is not necessarily its reach but rather its velocity and complexity. Thanks to new technologies, the speed with which transactions take place has astronomically increased. Perhaps more important, we can no longer speak of a globalization based on a few commodities or imperial projects. Instead, contemporary globalization consists of broader sets of exchanges. The interdependence upon which these exchanges rest upon is what makes examining contemporary globalization so complex and meaningful.

By focusing on the structural map of transactions produced by globalization, we can also better understand the *relational* aspect and the relative (in)equality of exchanges. We are more interested in the "who/whom" questions rather than in how much has been produced, transported, and bought across the world. Who has called whom, in what frequency, and who else participates in, and is isolated from, this emergent group of contracts are critical aspects for understanding the impact and consequences of globalization.

Mapping Information Flows

If we are to understand the implications of the flows of information, we must first seek to map them and locate where in the process of global transmission different countries and societies may lie. Who are the senders and receivers? Do they face monopolies or monopsonies? Who is close to the center of the network and who is at the periphery? Only with such a map can we begin to measure what the costs and benefits may be of such positions.

Based on our data on international Internet routes, student transfers, trade, and other global exchanges, there is no question that there has been a revolutionary shift in the flow of information across the globe, in terms of the amount, the breadth of information, and the overall structure of exchanges. There has been a constant growth both in terms of absolutes and in terms of acceleration in global communications since 1970, particularly speeding up after 1990 and continuing to do so in the 2000s. The Internet revolution is only one part of this as we also observe dramatic increases (in both quantity and acceleration) in every possible form of communication: travel, media exchanges, Internet use, and the like. The manner in which this growth has occurred, however, is *not* random or uniform but reflects and also helps create global relations of prestige.

The network analysis of these transactions reveals a very different model from a simple "all talking to all":

- We see little evidence of Huntingtonian civilizations. Although countries with similar cultures and languages do tend to communicate more with one another, there is no structural evidence of cultural cliques or subnetworks.
- There is clear evidence of diasporic communities. Whether through strong Turkey–Germany telephone links or the export of Bollywood films to zones of Indian migration, these communities are important carriers of globalization and need to be further examined.
- The residue of empires is rapidly eroding with "Franco" and "Anglo" zones still present but not overdeterminant. The erosion of Russian cultural centrality from Eastern Europe after 1989 took perhaps less than a year.

- There are regional (not cultural in the Huntingtonian sense) networks, each developing significant subnetwork centrality. We see this in study-abroad destinations, media exchanges, and other forms of global exchange.
- Overall, one clear pattern emerges from this data: In all measures there is increasing centrality of the global rich. Network analyses of World Bank categories, for example, show that the "Global South" does not establish links within itself but concentrates on making connections to the rich.
- Not only do the developed countries enjoy multiple ties around the globe while developing ones have a single dominant partner, but we also find that even many of the "haves" are not communicating with one another—only their "have not" satellites *and* the United States.

The United States lies at the heart of this "global rich clique." This is illustrated by looking at trends in international trade.[5] In this instance we note regional concentrations not only around NAFTA, the European Union, and China/Japan but also the predominance of the United States as first among the rich. We find a similar pattern for global mergers and acquisitions.[6] Here we see that the vast majority of mergers and acquisitions occur between North America and Europe (e.g., wealthy regions), with North America having ties to Latin America and Australasia, and Europe connected to Sub-Saharan Africa, Eastern Europe, Central Asia, Australasia, and, to a lesser extent, the Middle East, North Africa, and South Asia. Despite wealthy regions' enjoying ties with many parts of the world, virtually all the developing regions are connected to one dominant, high-income region rather than to one another. Additionally, we know that in East Asia and the Pacific there are a plethora of mergers and acquisitions, yet these areas remain isolated from other regions in a pattern that mimics economies even much less developed than the ones in East Asia. One way to interpret this pattern is through a Huntingtonian point of view wherein this is evidence of a deep divide based on culture and civilizations. We believe, however, there is another, perhaps more valuable interpretation—that this pattern reflects the ability of East Asian countries to build autonomous and intraregional networks that reflect their unique (1) institutional patterns of finance and (2) informal and formal regulations.

This pattern holds for practically every single type of transaction that we wish to analyze. For example, the United States remains a central global destination for postsecondary education, with only a handful of OECD countries dominating the rest of the student exchange market.[7] Similar concentrations may be seen in maps of transport and distribution networks. But the flows of cultural products may best illustrate the relative influence and centrality of some global actors and the marginality of the vast majority.

Mass media is, theoretically, one of the most fluid and malleable forms of globalization given its speed and distribution. However, what we find is the continued domination of the United States in a variety of media formats. For example, in 2001, 90 percent of feature films shown on television globally came from the United States; while some local programming was growing (and news remained a fairly privileged sector), Hollywood to a large extent still ruled the airwaves.[8] Not surprisingly, U.S. distributors' foreign syndication revenues rose from $500 million in 1984 to $6.5 billion in 2005.[9] The cultural domination of U.S. and Western European programming may actually be understated as even when produced locally, many shows directly borrow concepts from the richer countries. For example, "Who Wants to Be a Millionaire?" is licensed to more than sixty countries, while "Big Brother" and "Deal or No Deal" are produced by forty-two and sixty territories respectively.[10] Most of these countries simultaneously make use of graphics, sound effects, and questions from the original show while incorporating local cultural mores. There is indisputably some "localizing" that occurs, but the "global rich" cultural footprint is quite large.

Estimates of television viewership have become increasingly problematic with the advent of Web 2.0 and sites such as YouTube, Hulu, and others that allow you to download or view television shows. Web 2.0 sites have exploded in the past five years, and not just in connection to television shows. In 2006, the globally popular YouTube was estimated to have 100 million video views and 65,000 video uploads in one day, and it accounts for 60 percent of all videos watched online—making it the largest video-sharing site on the Internet.[11] With YouTube, we do witness a more democratizing cultural flow with international videos. A prominent example may be when the recording of Filipino prisoners dancing to Michael Jackson's "Thriller" went viral.[12] The "Playing for Change" viral phenomenon is another.[13] Yet, note that even these examples show the predominance of Western cultures because in the first, the Filipinos are reenacting an American hit, while in the second, the management and direction of the video are clearly American. Rarely does one see the reverse phenomenon of American or Western Europeans reenacting something made popular in a non-Western nation, or Western performers under non-Western direction.

The United States continues also to dominate the film industry—comparing all-time non-U.S. and U.S. box office figures, the list consists solely of U.S. films, many of which overlap.[14] In total, Hollywood films account for about the majority of total industry revenues by value, with filmed entertainment serving as a major export sector for the United States—Hollywood studios now depend on overseas revenue from more than half of the returns on any investment.[15] While the music industry, coupled with Web 2.0 technology, allows for greater local product, it continues to be dominated by giants from the OECD—particularly the United States. For example, thirty-one of the fifty bestselling albums of 2008 were from U.S. artists,[16] and 2003 global market shares for music companies were as follows: BMG 11.9 percent, EMI 13.4 percent, Sony 13.2 percent, Universal 23.5 percent, Warner 12.7 percent, and independents 25.3 percent.[17] The American domination is perhaps clearest in the nomenclature used: Artists from the United States and the United Kingdom are categorized by genre; practically all others are under the generic rubric of "World Music."

Social networking sites such as Facebook, MySpace, and Twitter have also revolutionized the Internet and global communications, but the disparities between users and sites are evident.[18] Although there is regional variation among the less frequently used networking sites, among the two most popular sites—MySpace and Facebook—we see the dominance of North American and European use. In fact, one 2008 study found that 77 percent of MySpace users were from the United States, with 5 percent from the United Kingdom, 2 percent from Canada, 2 percent from Australia, 1 percent from the Philippines, and 1 percent from Mexico. Among 2007 Twitter users, we continue also to see this familiar Web 2.0 global distribution—the increasing use and connectedness of the United States,

Europe, and Japan, and the virtual non-use and isolation of Africa, South America, and parts of Asia.[19] Regarding Internet links, the map of major international Internet routes reveals an almost dictionary definition of dependence.[20] Thanks to the work of TeleGeography and its mapping project, we can clearly observe three patterns: the marginalization of much of the world; the concentration on links among the "global rich," and the central role of the United States within this Internet elite.

Data on other media is much more difficult to find for recent years, except on an anecdotal basis. Two of the most obvious cases of global publishing phenomena are, of course, the "Harry Potter" and "Twilight" properties—one a U.K., the other a U.S., young adult fantasy series. Increasingly, computer software is the critical medium for accessing global information. Here, Google serves as the number one global Web parent company,[21] while Microsoft (as the parent company to Internet Explorer) accounted for 79.79 percent of global user shares in March 2009.[22] Again, the centrality of the United States is fixed in the nomenclature of global usage because only its domains do not need to specify their geographical location with a two-letter country code—this indicates both political power in Internet governance as well as dominance in information and Web pages.

We may also use both brand awareness and brand ratings as a proxy for the flow of information. The 2009 annual listing by *BusinessWeek* of the top global brands reveals the strong position of the United States, with eight of the top ten and sixteen of the top twenty-five brands being American while the remaining brands originate from top OECD countries.[23] Additionally, the top ten countries in the 2009 Anholt-GfK Roper Nation Brands Index—which measures the nature and power of a country's brand—are all OECD countries, with the United States in first place.[24]

Finally, the distribution of officially recognized cultural capital is extremely skewed. UNESCO's program to preserve "heritage sites," for example, appears to affirm European cultural superiority through its designation of places worth preserving.[25] Half of these are in Europe and North America. If we exclude "natural" sites where it is the landscape and not human creation that requires special preservation, the overrepresentation of Europe is even more extreme. The same applies for the distribution of heritage cities and of "modern" sites worthy of special attention. The sites of the Global South, particularly those of Africa and South America, are overwhelmingly not cultural or, when they are, usually products of civilizations long gone. The message is clear: Of the past five centuries, only the "culture" produced by Europeans is worth preserving.

Consequences

Whether one divides the countries of the world into emergent groups or network cliques, one finds that the United States is the only one that communicates with all groups. It occupies the critical role of a structural hole, serving as the bridge between different regions and groups.

The next obvious question is what could be the consequences of this network structure. Let us take NAFTA as an example. Over the past fifteen years, all the members of NAFTA have seen dramatic increases in their international integration. What is remarkably different, however, is that while for Mexico and Canada, NAFTA has become more central to their international network, for the United States it has become arguably less so. If network dependence is power, then the relative position of the United States vis-à-vis its partners is increased. The United States now needs Mexico and Canada less than those countries need it, and this has become even more so over the past decade.

This is not to deny the rise of non-American globalization. A favorite example of this is the ubiquity of sushi restaurants and other national cuisines, in which the rise of these foods is associated with both diasporic communities as well as increases in cultural capital—for example, the rise of Japan's social and cultural standing and the rise of sushi popularity. While it is a cliché to remark on the McDonaldsization of global diets, sushi presents a case of globalization from other sources. Similarly, globalization—and increased travel between countries—provides opportunities for aspects of previously isolated cultures to be shared globally. As mentioned above, the very success of U.S. media on the global markets means that non-American tastes have to be factored into production; we may also be seeing the development of a dual market structure for global information and entertainment products, where one (mostly consisting of the global "North") purchases the project, while the other consumes the same, but pirated, media.[26] We would still argue, however, that the central strands tying these globalization processes together are American.

Many have spoken of the critical importance of this American "soft power" and the importance of consolidating and institutionalizing this influence in noncoercive ways. While there have been travel restrictions post-9/11 and anti-American reactions toward U.S. foreign policy in Afghanistan and Iraq, we also have observed the global celebration of President Barack Obama's election, the subsequent (and almost immediate) rise in America's image, and the Nobel Peace Prize's being awarded to Obama shortly after his assumption of the presidency. We are also seeing the rise of competing educational centers in Western Europe and East Asia (particularly China). But even in the fluctuations of anti-/pro-American attitudes and in the educational threat to American "hegemony," the depth of America's centrality is evident: The books and sources used in these alternative centers of relearning tend to be American, and the global impact and influence of America—its political, social, and military policies—are evident, despite fluctuations in popularity. The evidence we have indicates that American centrality is quite robust. This may be permanently altered by the spectacle of the economic failure of 2008, but in the absence of any global competitor, American dominance appears safe.

What are the consequences of this network for inequality between countries? The empirical debate has divided those who use each country as a single and equivalent unit and those who weigh values by populations. Utilizing the former, there is considerable evidence for growing inequality between the already rich nations and the more developing countries. If we assign the rapidly growing economies of India and China their appropriate population weight, the trend is reversed. The rise of these economies and the economic catastrophe that began in the United States may signal the beginning of a reversal of American cultural hegemony. But despite the increasingly important roles assumed by the new economic players, their roles are still constrained.

The INA and MG are particularly interested in assigning specific quantitative values to network position so as to test statistically the relationship between network position and economic growth. Here, the critical test is to what extent the differing economic outcomes for East Asia and

Latin America may be explained by their network position and regional structure—though it's not inconceivable that these factors are decreasing in importance.

What about inequality within countries? Once again, position within the network is critical. The creation of a global brand or standard and possibilities to re-create a nation's image are opening up opportunities for fortunate members of all societies (no matter their geographical location) to participate in the global marketplace. The possession of the cultural capital—the right university degree and the mastery of the appropriate languages—provides many the unheard-of opportunity to be a "global" citizen, something that we have seen is, in fact, rooted in American centrality and necessarily requires technological access. The question is whether these opportunities are available in such a manner as to reduce domestic inequality. Here the outlook is not optimistic. The disparity between those with access to the global marketplace and those without it can only exacerbate existing divisions.

The skill and technical costs of entry into this global marketplace are ever deepening the gulf between the haves and the have-nots, both *between* and *within* societies. Two measures of this include Internet connectivity and English literacy. The chances of one's being able to become a citizen of the world without access to English, or to the Internet (and the two may, in fact, be equivalent), are quite low. Despite improvement in the "digital divide" within the rich countries, we see no evidence of its being reduced in the Global South—particularly in Latin America. There, phone—much less Internet—penetration remains stubbornly low. What we do see is perhaps the creation of a dual system of global citizenship. The dominant class travels legally in comfort and manages the global system of flows of information while enjoying the benefits of life with the rich; the lower classes also travel the world—if only to escape the poverty of their countries—but they travel in search of employment that allows them to send home remittances to sustain their families.

Thus, international flows of informational resources produce inequality on two levels:

- It has consolidated nation-level inequality between the "center" and the "periphery."

· Within individual countries, including those in the North, it has also exacerbated inequalities between those citizens able to participate in the global economy and those not able to do so.

The consequences of globalization may be even more complex. Precisely because of the massive flows of information and media, we live in a unique moment in history. Neither globalization nor inequality is new, but the ability of the poorest to witness the lifestyle of the global rich and, conversely, the inability of the rich to isolate themselves leave the future of the global system uncertain—will inequality at this level of visibility continue to sustain itself, or will increasing knowledge of how the "other side" lives be a catalyst for sustained political, social, and cultural change?

Notes

1. One search through the ProQuest Research Library database found 11,110 scholarly articles whose topic was globalization. If you include magazines, trade publications, newspapers, and reference/reports, the search yields 21,510 documents.

2. In actuality, we realize that the Internet does, in fact, contain hubs; however, the image of a randomized Internet network best exemplifies the idea of a corner deli society.

3. The dialogue is as follows:

VINCENT VEGA: [Y]ou know what the funniest thing about Europe is?

JULES WINNFIELD: What?

VINCENT VEGA: It's the little differences. I mean they got the same shit over there that they got here, but it's just, just there it's a little different.

JULES WINNFIELD: Example.

VINCENT VEGA: Alright, well you can walk into a movie theater and buy a beer. And, I don't mean just like a paper cup, I'm talking about a glass of beer. And, in Paris, you can buy a beer in McDonald's. You know what they call a Quarter Pounder with Cheese in Paris?

JULES WINNFIELD: They don't call it a Quarter Pounder with Cheese?

VINCENT VEGA: No, man, they got the metric system, they don't know what the fu** a Quarter Pounder is.

JULES WINNFIELD: What do they call it?

VINCENT VEGA: They call it a Royale with Cheese.

JULES WINNFIELD: Royale with Cheese.

VINCENT VEGA: That's right.

JULES WINNFIELD: What do they call a Big Mac?

VINCENT VEGA: Big Mac's a Big Mac, but they call it Le Big Mac.

JULES WINNFIELD: Le Big Mac. What do they call a Whopper?

VINCENT VEGA: I don't know. I didn't go into Burger King.

4. James L. Watson writes, in his article "McDonald's in Hong Kong" in *The Globalization Reader* (2008) about how the sanitation and cleanliness of McDonald's bathrooms raised consumers' expectations, thus changing local rivals' bathroom standards, and how its marketing to children transformed aspects of familial patterns in Hong Kong.

5. Centeno, Miguel, Abigail Cooke, and Sara Curran. 2006. "NetMap Combined Studies." Princeton University and University of Washington. http://qed.princeton.edu/images/b/b5/BriefIntro_042006.pdf

6. Brakman, Steven, Gus Garita, Harry Garretsen, and Charles van Marrewijk. 2008. Unlocking the value of cross-border mergers and acquisitions, pp 10. *CESifo Working Paper No. 2294.*

7. Atlas of Student Mobility, data period: 2008; retrieved on November 20, 2009: http://www.atlas.iienetwork.org/page/Country_Profiles/;jsessionid=3dhoromqp56uf

8. Havens, Timothy. "Window on the West: Foreign television programming in Hungary and the future of U.S. domination of global television," Working Paper cms.mit.edu/mit3/papers/havens.pdf

9. Havens, Timothy. 2006. *Global television marketplace*. Pp. 28 Bfi Publishing: London.

10. Hastings, David. 2002. Global Television Scenario: Part 5 (Cross Country Viewers). http://www.xtvworld.com/tv/global/global_vision.htm; Endemol. http://www.endemol.com/programme/big-brother; Endemol. http://www.endemol.com/programme/deal-or-no-deal

11. USA Today. July 2006. YouTube serves up to 100 million videos a day online. http://www.usatoday.com/tech/news/2006-07-16-youtube-views_x.htm

12. http://tinyurl.com/26au9r5

13. http://www.youtube.com/watch?v=4xjPODksIo8

14. IMDB. 2009. All-time non-U.S. Box Office http://www.imdb.com/boxoffice/alltimegross?region=non-us; IMDB. 2009. All-time U.S. Box office http://www.imdb.com/boxoffice/alltimegross

15. focus 2009—World Film Market Trends, http://www.obs.coe.int/oea_publ/market/focus.html

16. IFPI. 2008. http://www.ifpi.org/content/section_statistics/index.html

17. IFPI. 2003. http://www.ifpi.org/content/section_news/20040616a.html

18. comScore World Metrix. http://www.comscore.com/Press_Events/Press_Releases/2007/07/Social_Networking_Goes_Global

19. UMBC ebiquity. 2007. http://ebiquity.umbc.edu/blogger/2007/04/15/global-distribution-of-twitter-users/

20. Source: TeleGeography research, retrieved November 19, 2009: http://www.telegeography.com/ee/free_resources/figures/gig-03.php, data excerpted from Global Internet Geography 2006 and includes only routes with at least 9 Gbps of aggregate capacity.

21. Nielsen NetView. October 2009. Top 10 Global Web Parent Companies—Home & Work. http://en-us.nielsen.com/rankings/insights/rankings/internet

22. OneState.com, 2009. http://www.onestat.com/html/press-release-global-browser-market-share-april-2009.html

23. BuisnessWeek. 2009. http://bwnt.businessweek.com/interactive_reports/best_global_brands_2009/

24. Nation Brands Index. 2009. http://nation-branding.info/2009/10/07/nation-brands-index-2009/

25. UNESCO World Heritage Centre. 2007. *World Heritage—Challenges for the Millennium* http://whc.unesco.org/en/news/306

26. O'Brien, Timothy. August 28, 2005. "King Kong vs. the pirates of the multiplex" New York Times, http://www.nytimes.com/2005/08/28/business/media/28movie.html?_r=1&scp=9&sq=market&st=nyt

I

Culture

3

Internet TV and the
Global Flow of Filmed Entertainment

Eli Noam

IT'S BEEN NOW ABOUT NINETY YEARS that American films and video media have predominated globally, and despite many efforts, despite many government-supplied francs, marks, and now euros, despite various restrictive rules and regulations going all the way back to the 1920s, not all that much has changed. Yes, there is always some hopeful news every year—some film or reality TV series that has been successful, some production company that lights the imagination—but somehow this hopeful news has not diminished the basic dominance of Hollywood.

In 1998, of the forty most successful movies worldwide in terms of box office, Hollywood films constituted the top thirty-nine. Britain's *The Full Monty* was number 40. In 2004, of the fifty highest-grossing films worldwide, forty-seven were American. In 2009, of the fifty highest-grossing films worldwide, forty-nine were American.[1]

This is not a supply issue. Whereas the United States produced 520 theatrical films in 2008, the European Union produced 1,145 films, while Japan and China produced 418 and 400 films, respectively, that year.[2]

Yet in 2008, European films had a 28 percent share in the European Union, whereas U.S. movies had a share of 63 percent.[3] Even in France, the world's first movie nation, audience share for domestic productions dropped below one-third of total theater audiences.[4] The share of British movies in their domestic market was 31 percent[5] in 2008, and German films had 27 percent[6] of their domestic market.

At the same time, the global audience for European films has declined. In the 1960s and '70s, there were decent-sized audiences for quality European films. Truffaut, Godard, Fellini, Antonioni, Bergman, Fassbinder, Pasolini, Wertmüller, Richardson, and Tanner were icons. But the audience for such films has been steadily graying. In 2002, French films' total box office in the United States was an anemic $36 million for the films of a country that makes about 200 films a year. In 2008, French films' total ticket sales on the North American market including francophone Quebec were 14.2 million,[7] which translates to approximately $30 million in the U.S. market.

The worldwide dominance of Hollywood has been especially hard for Europeans to take. For several centuries, culture had been flowing largely in one direction: out of Europe, and into the rest of the world. Then, before World War I, the flow reversed direction for the young and populist medium film. Around the world, audiences flocked to American movies. European cultural elites promoted government protectionism. Already in the 1920s, Germany's near-monopoly producer Ufa advocated the protection of "European films" and established European cartel collaboration together with the French film trade association, in a rare alliance across the Rhine. Various restrictive contractual arrangements were agreed upon with other countries, supplemented by import quotas enacted by governments.

Today, various forms of film protectionism abound. In Canada, the government subsidizes film production directly, and 60 percent of the TV schedule must consist of Canadian content, an indirect regulate subsidy. In Australia, government money makes up around 37 percent of overall investment, plus the lost tax revenues from a 100 percent tax deduction for film investments.

In Europe, Brussels provided in 2002 subsidies of $850 million for films that generated box office revenues of around $400 million. More recently, the EU media program was budgeted at €755 million over seven years.[8] In 2008, according to the European Commission, the twenty-seven member states spent about €1.6 billion in direct support of films each year.[9] Some

European countries provide subsidies for more than 50 percent of a film's budget.[10] And on top of that, there are generous tax shelters for rich investors to entice film production. In addition, there is substantial support for production through public service TV, whose budgets derive from a substantial quasi-tax. In Germany this compulsory levy amounts to about €18 per month per TV household.[11] Germany's public ARD network service TV in 2008 invested €190 million in the production of theatrical films.[12] Furthermore, there are ceilings on TV's showing of non-European (e.g., U.S.) productions.

But even with all of these generous direct and indirect subsidies, non-Hollywood films are rarely an international success. Domestic films are watched in Europe by about 20–30 percent of audiences. But those audiences rarely watch the films of neighboring countries. European films, outside their national market, got only 8 percent of audiences in other European countries in 2006, and 7 percent in 2007. They got a worldwide audience share of less than 5 percent.[13]

Why has Hollywood's dominance occurred? And what are the implications for the next generation of film distribution, over the Internet? Many cultural observers, whether abroad or in American academe, rail about "American cultural imperialism" as a substitute for an analysis, or they invoke, tautologically, the symptoms as cause, such as dominance over "distribution channels" or over "intellectual property rights." "Cultural imperialism" is a term vague enough to project onto a lot of inkblots, from those of the left to those of the right, but historically Hollywood was dominant already before World War I, before America's ascendance to a superpower status.

Hollywood's success is remarkable insofar as it is, by far, the high-cost producer. It has also been astonishingly lacking in foresight and vision. At almost every juncture, Hollywood misjudged the future and fumbled its own actions. It fought television, then pay-cable, and then home video. In each case, the technology it unsuccessfully tried to suppress soon turned out to be hugely profitable to itself. But despite high cost and low vision, Hollywood rides high in the saddle.

Vilification does not provide the kind of understanding that is the precondition for successful remedial action. If ninety years of well-financed, politically well-supported, and benignly reported efforts have failed to dislodge Hollywood, maybe something is wrong with the underlying analysis of the problem.

To analyze this, we start with the most frequent explanations, which turn out to be impressive. From there, we will proceed to stronger explanations.

Market Size

For a time, Europeans attributed the problem of Hollywood's strength to the destructions of war. But those wars happened a long time ago. Another explanation was the large size of the American market. But actually, more films per capita are made in the United States than in many countries, which mean that they divide up the domestic audiences into narrower slices.

The domestic population per feature film produced in 2008 in the United States is 593,000, whereas it is 435,000 in Europe, a modest difference that cannot explain the disproportionate dominance of American films. And, in any event, in a global economy, the size of the home market is not the determinative factor. Otherwise, Swiss watches or Belgian chocolates, hailing from small markets, would never make it internationally. One could even argue that the more a film can support itself in a big domestic market, the less it must try to enter foreign markets in order to survive. India's film industry is an example.

A related explanation is that of English as the global lingua franca. True, but most people watch films dubbed or subtitled, and it's not more expensive to do that from Italian into Spanish than from English into Spanish.

Dumping

Another frequent explanation is that because American films are already produced and paid for by American audiences and then dumped cheaply onto the world market, displacing domestic films would require expensive production. This argument confuses sunk cost with new-project costs. By this logic, nobody would ever buy a car because taking a taxi is always cheaper. For this dumping argument to hold water, one must also assume that Hollywood does not factor foreign markets into its production decisions, while at the same time foreign producers do not export to other countries and must subsist on domestic revenues alone.

Distribution

Another frequent explanation is that Hollywood distribution companies are vertically integrated and favor their own content and suppress that of others. Such advantages of joining distribution with content production are also stressed by empire-building American CEOs and by investment bankers in search of deals, and these are commonly called "synergies." One must observe that film-oriented firms which engrossed themselves by M&As (mergers and acquisitions) have been splitting or tottering: Viacom, Vivendi, Kirch, Time-Warner, Disney, and GE/NBC-Universal. All had well-publicized dysfunctionalities and were barely able to contain their centrifugalism. In economic terms, for vertically integrated firms, discrimination in favor of one's own product is sensible only as long as that product is not inferior. It rarely makes sense for a distribution organization to push its own inferior films into theaters and to reject other producers' potential blockbusters. Ultimately, the market power of Hollywood distributors depends on their access to attractive films, not vice versa.

Popular Culture

In many countries, films are controlled by directors and their artistic vision. Popularity with audiences is not a goal in itself and can even be a source of unease about "selling out." Celebrated French film *auteur* Jean-Luc Godard expressed his attitude: "Who is the enemy? The audience!" In contrast, in America films are controlled by commercially minded producers and distributors. This dichotomy is of long standing. Already in the early nineteenth century, Alexis de Tocqueville, commenting on American culture, observed:

In aristocracies a few great pictures are produced; in democratic countries a vast number of insignificant ones. In the former, statues are raised in bronze; in the latter, they are modeled in plaster.[14]

This distinction between popular culture and high culture has been commented upon frequently by less sympathetic observers than de Tocqueville. It became a comforting notion that it was the uncompromising integrity of European filmmakers which limited their popularity, in contrast to Hollywood's pandering. But actually, most European (and Japanese, Korean, Indian, Mexican, Brazilian, Egyptian, and Chinese) films are not artsy at all. Those films outside the public TV axis are mostly commercially oriented and have adopted Hollywood's style elements. They are typically produced by big and established domestic media firms, often centered on commercial TV operations. In Italy, Berlusconi; in Germany, Bertelsmann. In France, Vivendi. In Brazil, Globo; in Mexico, Televisa. In Japan, Shoshiko and Toho. All try to be popular in their home markets. Most of their films never reach American audiences, and usually deservedly so.

Conversely, statistical studies have shown that Hollywood producers seem to accept somewhat lower profit margins in order to be associated with "edgy" projects that enhance their prestige.[15] They want not just the money success but also the prestige success. And on top of that, American independent film production is alive and vibrant. For the 2008 Sundance Film Festival, the mecca of American indies, there were 3,624 feature-length submissions, 10 percent more than the year before.[16] This is the pool of Hollywood's next generation of talent. Thus, the self-image of culture versus commerce might be comforting, but it is not really an explanation.

If so, what is? To me, the main success factor for content production is the efficiency of Hollywood.

Productivity

This seems counterintuitive. Hollywood movies are vastly more expensive than European or Indian ones. To produce a film in Hollywood costs about ten times as much as in Europe, and fifty times as much as in India. The budget for two minutes of a Hollywood film pays for an entire feature film in India.

TABLE 3.1. *Film Productivity*

	Investment/ Film	# of Films	Worldwide Tickets/ Film (mil)	Worldwide Tickets/$ Invest	Overall Rev/ Investment
US	70	543	5.5	0.61	1.27
Europe	7.5	752	0.6	0.08	(.08)
India	1.5	843	3.5	2.3	1.19

But Hollywood is more productive. That may be a bit surprising given its high costs. But it all depends on how one defines the product. Table 3.1, prepared by the author with 2006 figures, compares costs and revenues, and shows this in its first column. A Hollywood film costs on average $70 million to produce, versus $7.5 million per film in Europe and $1.5 million in India. But if one defines the product as "tickets sold," then Hollywood is almost eight times more productive than European producers. ($0.61 versus 0.08 tickets per dollar investment). India's Bollywood, on the other hand, generates four times more tickets per dollar than Hollywood. But even that gap vanishes when one looks at overall revenues generated. Now, given the disparity in ticket prices, Hollywood has a slight advantage over India (1.27 versus 1.19), whereas European films have, on average, a *negative* return.

Lower Risk

Most other production centers have a weak financing structure to generate investment for movies. In contrast, Hollywood has established numerous ways of raising funds. Efficiency is gained by superior risk reduction strategy: portfolio diversification. Film projects are enormously risky. Eighty percent of films, it is said, lose money. Hollywood has managed to create a portfolio of investments, each with certain riskiness, that achieve a lower risk than any individual part of the portfolio. A studio pools many risky projects, making its aggregate cash flow reasonably safe for the lenders. And this in turn facilitates investments in film projects. In contrast, missing in Europe and other production centers are strong financing structures to invest significant capital into movies. In India, a good part of film financing, for a long time, was through organized crime cartels that liked its glamour and money-laundering potential. European films rely on the public TV system and on direct governmental support. This tends to require a greater emphasis on national culture and hence often reduces global appeal.

Industry Structure

Perhaps the most powerful advantage of Hollywood is the structure of its industry. Most people think of Hollywood as six major studios and two or three mini-majors. And that was the way it was up until the 1950s, when studios were vertically integrated mass producers. But when TV emerged, it forced Hollywood to "re-engineer" itself earlier than other industries. One strategy was to create high-end products in terms of production budgets. But, just as important, the major film studios radically lowered overhead costs by shifting to a project-based structure. Most of the actual production is done not by the handful of studio companies but by hundreds of small independent production companies, which in turn use thousands of specialized firms, with tens of thousands of specialized freelancers. The six major studios provide back-office support for production teams, coordinate advertising, and provide financing and distribution.

More than two-thirds of the Los Angeles–based film industry's workers are freelancers or work for tiny companies. Collectively, they create an industry structure of project-based ad hoc organizations with low fixed costs. The result is an industry characterized by two factors:

· oligopolistic distribution
· competitive creation

The remarkable thing about this structure is that it did not emerge by design or strategy. Rather, it was a case of organizational Darwinism. The relentlessly competitive and risky nature of each film project led to the emergence of such a structure.

The significance of such a model of the project-oriented, almost "virtual" production firm is that it is perhaps the forerunner for many business firms and industries in general. It is an organizational model that integrates creativity with business in a way that functions better than anyone else's model. It is decentralized, networked, virtual, freelance, global, and disaggregated (not integrated), and it draws on diverse creativity. It combines the creativity of small organizations with the economies of scale of large ones.

We can see similar developments reaching consumer electronics, IT, and automotive industries. Specialist firms do the design. Others produce the components. Still others assemble. Still others do the marketing. The major firms then are mainly becoming integrators of the specialist firms and the branders of the final products. This might be, for many industries, the business model of the future.

It would not be the first time that media have led the way for a general business transformation. The printing press pioneered the industrial mass-production system. Today, the film industry model, created in the Darwinian process described, is a forerunner for the next stage, the postindustrial production system and economy.

And now, a new medium is knocking—film over the Internet—and the question is how it will affect this system. Will it be a multicultural richness of many national sources, or will it be just more of the same old Hollywood?

The knee-jerk response to this question is to invoke the usual platitudes. Anybody can enter. You can't tell who's a dog on the Internet. The Long Tail. The Internet community, staunchly internationalist and multicultural by outlook and background, does not want to face the very question of whether it contributes to the further ascendancy of American mass culture.

How then does Internet distribution affect this system? Will it enable other production centers to thrive? To answer this question, we need to look at the same economics of content production and distribution, as they relate to the Internet.

True, Internet film content includes a lot of low-budget, experimental, and user-generated production. At the same time, the high-speed Internet enables much more than standard, linear, and cheap video. Internet film will create content that goes far beyond conventional TV and film: specialized, archived, interactive, asynchronous, immersive, 3-D, multimedia, and globally delivered. Such content requires many additional technical features beyond just video. After some initial low-budget amateur period, providers of Internet film will have to offer content of high technical and design features.

To produce such interactive content is expensive. It requires creativity, lots of programmers, significant testing, and many new versions. It might be a bit like "Dungeons and Dragons" meets "Baywatch" meets "Survivor" meets Harry Potter. Such content exhibits strong economies of scale on the content production side, and network externalities on the demand side. Both favor content providers that can come up with big budgets, can diversify risk, distribute also over multiple other platforms, create product tie-ins, and establish global user communities.

Even for nonpremium programs—such as creative small productions, or sex shows and games—where the absolute production costs are lower, the economic advantages of a large user base still apply.

At the same time, the distribution costs for films over the Internet are high, because the individualization of transmission requires significantly larger transmission resources. Individualization requires transmission capacity that is at least forty times higher than that of a cable channel. It is a common mistake to argue that as transmission is becoming cheaper, it will overcome such a gap. But technological progress leads transmission cost to drop just as much for cable TV distribution as it does for Internet distribution. The relative cost of shared (synchronous) transmission is still much lower than that of nonshared, asynchronous transmission. What the drop in cost means, however, is that the impact of distance becomes much lower. National TV and film lose the protection of distance, and satellite and cable TV lose the protection of limited spectrum on licensing.

Thus, both content and distribution costs for Internet film are high, but distance-insensitive. Therefore, commercial Internet video can function economically best as a premium medium or a specialized medium, delivered globally.

These characteristics favor American companies when Internet distribution emerges as a mass medium. The United States has a large base of an Internet community; significant hardware and software entrepreneurial energy barely contained by the recent downturn; a financial system that provides risk capital; big content-producing companies with worldwide distribution and with experience in reaching popular audiences; talent in content creativity and technology from all over the world; efficient geographic clusters in production and technology; the cultural prowess of the world's superpower; language; a diverse culture; and a university system that generates technology and entrepreneurship. Thus, the medium of Internet film distribution combines the strengths of U.S. firms in entertainment content, in Internet, and in e-transactions. Add to that economies of scale, and scope, and nothing on the horizon can match it.

The broadband Internet means that programs can be distributed globally, at relatively low cost. People in Peru, Panama, and Portugal can select, click, and download. The protection of distance is thus giving way. And the content itself exhibits strong economies of scale. This means that the content of Hollywood, adapted for interactivity, can be all over the world.

Many of these specific factors are also available elsewhere, but probably nowhere quite in such combination. On the other hand, the United States lacks the supportive mechanism of public TV that exists in Europe and Japan for quality content.

Companies and public service organizations from other countries will also participate either domestically without much global reach or as global players who will provide basically American-style commercial content to the world, like British ITV sitcoms, Dutch Endemol reality shows, and the Italian "spaghetti Westerns" of the past. There will also be opportunities for other producers to create and distribute specialized programs for niche and general audiences. And those needs could be met by providers from other countries. And there will also be a community-based, collaborative production environment of user-generated and wiki-style low-budget content.

But the main audience will still be attached to big-budget, technically sophisticated productions that combine Hollywood glitz, Silicon Valley tech, and New York finance. And that means that Hollywood will be even stronger, because it now has a more direct relation with global audiences. It does not have to go through the intermediaries of TV networks and pass through the regulation of governments. It has the ability to fine-tune prices. And it can deploy in its network of specialists also the talent and creativity from everywhere—animators from Japan; special effects software in India; postproduction in Shanghai; venture finance in London;

advertising companies in New York. Thus, Hollywood will become, even more than before, the entertainment content integrator to the world.

A century of history should teach us some lessons. Artistic creativity is not enough. The only way for other countries' film industries to attract the attention of global audiences is for them to resort to managerial responses rather than to find comfort in cultural criticism and political protectionism.

Notes

1. Box Office Mojo, "Yearly Box Office 2009 Worldwide Grosses," http://boxofficemojo.com/yearly/chart/?view2=worldwide&yr=2009&p=.htm, visited: December 15, 2009.

2. The European Audiovisual Observatory, "Marche du Film 2009, FOCUS," http://www.obs.coe.int/online_publication/reports/focus2009.pdf, visited: December 15, 2009.

3. European Audiovisual Observatory, "EU film production reached record high in 2008 as admissions to European films remained strong," May 2009, http://www.obs.coe.int/about/oea/pr/mif2009_cinema_pdf.pdf.en, visited: December 15, 2009.

4. cineuropa.org, http://cineuropa.org/cfocus.aspx?lang=en&documentID=89394&treeID=1618, visited: December 17, 2009.

5. Screendaily.com, "British films bank $4.2 billion worldwide last year," http://www.screendaily.com/british-films-bank-42-billion-worldwide-last-year/5003671.article, visited: December 15, 2009.

6. Cineuropa.org, "Positive 2008 results show rise in admissions" http://cineuropa.org/newsdetail.aspx?lang=en&documentID=89890, visited: December 15, 2009.

7. The European Audiovisual Observatory, "Marche du Film 2009, FOCUS," http://www.obs.coe.int/online_publication/reports/focus2009.pdf, page 19, visited: December 15, 2009.

8. Casey, Zoë, "EU executive backs film subsidies," Europeanvoice.com, http://www.europeanvoice.com/article/2008/10/eu-executive-backs-film-subsidies/62834.aspx, visited: December 15, 2009.

9. Ibid.

10. EUbusiness, "EU extends rules for supporting film industry," http://qa.eubusiness.upfronthosting.co.za/news-eu/1233155821.47, visited: December 15, 2009.

11. Spiegel.de, "GEZ-Pflicht für PC, Smartphone & Co. geplant," http://www.spiegel.de/netzwelt/web/0,1518,665970,00.html, visited: December 15, 2009.

12. ARD, "ARD Jahrbuch 2009," http://www.ard.de/intern/publikationen/-/id=1292634/property=download/nid=8080/sbs2wv/index.pdf, visited: December 15, 2009.

13. Lumiere, "Methodology—Limitations of the Lumiere Database," http://lumiere.obs.coe.int/web/sources/metho.html, visited: December 15, 2009.

14. De Tocqueville, Alexis, "In What Spirit the Americans Cultivate the Arts," in Rosenberg, Bernard, ed., *Mass Culture: The Popular Arts in America*, London: The Free Press of Glencoe, 1957.

15. De Vany, Arthur & Walls, W. David. Does Hollywood Make Too Many R-Rated Movies? Risk, Stochastic Dominance, and the Illusion of Expectation. *Journal of Business*, 2002, vol. 75, no. 3. The University of Chicago.

16. Sundance Film Festival Press Release, "Sundance Film Festival announces films in competition," http://www.sundance.org/festival/press_industry/releases/2008_films_in_competition.asp, visited: December 17, 2009.

4

Piracy, Creativity, and Infrastructure

Rethinking Access to Culture

Lawrence Liang

Prologue: Once upon a Time in Malegaon

Approximately an eight-hour bus ride from the bright lights of India's finan-cial and film capital, Mumbai, is a small, nondescript town called Malegaon.[1] The town is populated mainly by migrant Muslim laborers from North India, who work in the power loom sector. Malegaon became infamous in 2006 after a series of bomb blasts. Serious communal riots broke out after the destruction of the Babri Masjid (a mosque in Ayodhya, in the state of Uttar Pradesh, that was demolished by Hindu zealots in 1992). The town has however been in the news recently for another reason. It has emerged as the center of a parallel film industry that churns out remakes of Bollywood hits, contexualizing them to address local issues and to cater to local tastes. Thus, one of the biggest blockbusters of India, *Sholay* (*Flames of the Sun*, 1975), is remade as *Malegaon ki Sholay*; and the Oscar-nominated *Lagaan* (*Taxes*) is remade as *Malegaon ki Lagaan*, and instead of opposition to colonial taxes, the film addresses problems of civic amenities. All the actors in the films have become stars within the local community, and one of the reasons cited for the popularity of these remakes is the fact that the local people get to see people they recognize on the big screen.

The average budget of a Malegaon production is around Rs. 50,000 ($1,000US) and runs in one of the fourteen local video theaters in the town. It all started when Naseer, a local videographer who shot wedding videos, decided to borrow money to make his own film. He shot the film on video and used two videocassette recorders to edit the film in real time. The film turned out to be a surprise hit and thus started the Malegaon film industry. Local people working in the various small-scale industries double as actors, and the filmmakers try to stay as close to the original as possible, including camera angles, lighting, and other production details. Understandably, it is difficult to emulate a large Bollywood film with its mega-budgets in a small town like Malegaon, so the Malegaon crew has learned to adjust and innovate using local resources to re-create these films.

So a cycle stands in for a dolly, and a bullock cart is used for crane shots. While remaking an expensive Hindi film, *Shaan*, the director realized that with a total budget of Rs. 50,000, there was no way he would be able to hire a helicopter, so his crew simply made do with a toy helicopter and shot it in a way that made it look as authentic as possible.

In the past few years, the Malegaon films have created a market of their own, and now there are film distributors who are willing to buy such films for nearby towns and cable operators who regularly get requests from their customers to screen a Malegaon film. The director of *Lagaan*, one of the films remade in Malegaon, when shown the remake said, "It is remarkable, what they have managed to achieve. Using video theatres as a film school, they have managed to create an alternative to the Hindi film industry in the Hindi language [*sic*]" (Sukhija, 2003).

The Malegaon phenomenon is very similar to the emergence of Nollywood, the film industry in Nigeria (Hausa, English, and Yourba films), which emerged through a creative history of appropriation and localization of Bollywood films. What was remarkable about the rise of Nollywood was that it arose in the absence of either private or state investment in cinema, and it started out as a cottage industry and has now emerged as a significant film industry in the African region (Larkin, 2008). There are a number of similarities between the Malegaon film industry and that of Nollywood, but one significant difference between them is that Malegaon remains a very local industry that serves as a counter to the more well-established Hindi film industry, which is often seen as the "national cinema" of India.

We read the Malegaon phenomenon in many ways. It is on the one hand a story of local creativity that uses remixes as a mode of appropriating dominant culture. It could also be read through the prism of copyright to see how creativity relies on pastiche and quotation, and how a regime of copyright would inhibit such forms of creativity. But it has to be stated that despite using copyrighted material from films to music, the question of copyright has thus far been a nonexistent one in Malegaon. Like Nollywood, the Malegaon film industry arose out of an infrastructure created by media piracy. The proliferation of video stores, video theaters, the availability of video cassettes and now VCDs and DVDs for the distribution of these films, have all contributed to the Malegaon success story.

I have chosen to begin with the Malegaon story because it illustrates for me the relationship between quotidian media piracy and the creation of an infrastructure for cultural production. When thinking of cultural production, we tend to focus on what gets produced, or the content, and we do not pay sufficient attention to the conditions of its production, circulation, and reproduction. Thus infrastructures of cultural production could include video cameras, computers, cars, Internet bandwidth, cycles, printing facilities, sound mixers, and, as we have seen, even toy helicopters and bullock carts. In a number of developing countries the biggest hurdle to access to knowledge and culture is the question of poor infrastructure. The aim of this chapter is to look at the relationship between infrastructure and creativity—not as distinct domains, but to see how they inform each other and to introduce a materialist understanding into our understanding of creativity.

The innovativeness of the Malegaon films, for instance, lies as much in their remixing of narratives as it does in the ways in which low-cost infrastructure is recycled to make the films possible. Working with extremely low budgets and yet wanting to emulate the big-budget blockbuster, these filmmakers use everything from cycle rims to bullock carts as replacements for expensive equipment. The mode of production of the Malegaon films reminds us that the materiality of knowledge and cultural production cannot be ignored in any examination of process of creativity.

In many debates on the politics of intellectual property and access to knowledge, much of the focus is on the availability of content, whether it is in the form of books, software, or cultural objects. This is undoubtedly an important area, and the battle over the control and dissemination of knowledge and cultural goods will keep us busy in the years to come. But in these debates there is often a lack of any discussion on the infrastructure that enables the creation and dissemination of knowledge and culture. By "infrastructure," I refer both to a range of things, from computers to photocopiers and from cameras to cycles, but equally to a network of services and support systems that either provide these goods or provide services in relation to these goods.[2] Infrastructure has always been the key to the expansion of global capital, enabling the movement of people and goods across space and time. One of the markers that distinguish developed from developing countries has had to do with the state of infrastructure in the latter, where often infrastructure is seen to be either missing or in a state of collapse.

With the shift to the knowledge economy, and the coalescing of value around intangibles, intellectual property emerges as the new cluster of primary commodities made up of culture and information. These are also brought into the world through transcontinental networks and through infrastructure consisting of telecommunication networks, such as broadband cables that traverse the seas, much as the ships of maritime capitalism did, carrying spices, tobacco, and silk to many continents. It is important to locate the transformation to the information economy across different temporalities, where countries marked by historic inequalities are invited to enter the information economy of the twenty-first century as though it were an equal playing ground. It is also important to bear in mind that even in countries like India that are linked to the global economy, only a very small section of the population finds itself "wired in," and for large sections of the population, access to information and technology is as distant as access to basic infrastructures of housing, water, and health care.

When thinking about access to knowledge, it is vital to keep in mind the fact that for populations largely ignored by the state or corporations, the building of infrastructure becomes a self-organized and organic task involving kinship networks. This is well documented in the ways in which cities have incrementally developed, and it is perhaps time to start looking at how a similar form of informal infrastructure, built through piracy, enables the entry into the information and knowledge economy of a large of number of "entrepreneurs" from developing and underdeveloped countries.

Another challenge that the Malegaon story presents for us is in terms of how we think beyond ideas of access when we think of knowledge and culture. While the idea of access has been central to the imagination of the Access to Knowledge (A2K) movement, it is the argument of this chapter that ideas of access cannot be examined without simultaneously looking at issues of desire and subjectivity. There has been a tendency to frame the issue of access to knowledge via the trope of "development," and the history of developmentalism has tended to favor a top-down approach wherein the needs of people are defined in pedagogic terms.

There is a tendency toward a kind of division of labor in the progressive circles looking at information politics. People working with initiatives like the Creative Commons tend to speak a universal language of creativity while glossing over issues of political economy, development, and equity. There is an assumption, for instance, that most people across the world have access to technologies that enable the process of ripping, remixing, and sharing. At the same time, people in the A2K movement tend to focus on issues of equity and access but rarely look at questions of creativity and curiosity. They thus speak of more equitable access to lifesaving medicines but deemphasize the joys of storytelling and music-making that make life worth living.

By reframing the way in which we look at the relationship between piracy, development, and creativity, I hope to be able to question some of the existing assumptions in the debate on IP and public interest, as well as suggest ways in which we can move forward.

Introduction

> In civilizations without boats, dreams dry up, espionage takes
> the place of adventure, and the police take the place of the pirate.
> Foucault, *Of Other Spaces*

Over the past decade and a half, technological changes have significantly altered the ways in which we create and disseminate knowledge and culture. These developments have been accompanied by the expansion of intellectual property and its transformation from an esoteric legal subject to a topic of daily conversation. The aggressive expansion of property claims into every domain of knowledge and cultural practice has inserted almost everyone, from the academic to the musician, into the heart of the debate. No account of our contemporary times would be complete without an examination of the dominance of the copyright sign or the small print of the trademark on our lives. In many ways, the mere act of looking at, reading, listening to, making, understanding, or communicating any objects that embody thought, knowledge, or feeling is as fraught with danger and anxiety today as the appropriation of material wealth or the trespassing into private property has been through much of human history.[3]

While the anxiety and conflict over IP may be universal, the nature of the conflict gets configured differently as we move from the United States and Europe to parts of Asia, Latin America, and Africa. In the United States the crisis is represented in terms of the shrinking of the public domain and the commons by the extension of copyright. In South Africa the main concern has been the availability of cheap generic antiretroviral drugs. And in many parts of Asia the proliferation of cheap technologies of reproduction has created a parallel economy that threatens the monopoly of old media players.

The concern over the expansionist tendency of intellectual property has also motivated a rearticulation of the importance of the commons of knowledge and cultural production. In many ways this is exemplified by various processes and through the important scholarship that has arisen on the public domain and the increasing popularity of nonproprietary modes such as free software, open content, and so on. A number of these concerns have historically emerged from the experience of Europe and the United States and traveled to the rest of the world. But when one attempts to translate the terms of the IP debate into the contemporary experience of countries in Asia, Latin America, and Africa, it is not easy to locate any easy indexical reference to ideas like the "digital commons." There are challenges ahead of localizing the language of the commons through an exploration of ways in which cultures have shaped their relationship to knowledge and culture, and how such practices may inform contemporary sensibilities toward intellectual property (Liang, 2007).

The ways in which IP unfolds in many of these countries are through the dual tropes of a triumphalist fantasy of harnessing IP to "catch up with the West" or being perpetually condemned as pirate nations by the U.S. Trade Representative (USTR) in the Annual Special 301 reports (Mertha, 2007). Pressures from the USTR, backed by the threats of trade sanctions, have translated on the ground to an increase in criminalization of piracy, rise in police and private raids, the hyperprofiling of piracy in mainstream media, and the emergence of the figure of the pirate as one of the key defining figures of criminality in the twenty-first century. One of the challenges for us as critical scholars of IP will be to question the dominant narrative of criminality that marks the contemporary discourse on piracy and look at the relationship between piracy and the democratization of knowledge and culture. It may, however, be useful first to lay out a broad map of the kind of IP scholarship and activism that have emerged in the past few years, before examining how they play out in Asia.

- The most visible research thus far has sought to look at the expansion of IP and its impact on creativity and innovation. Public domain scholars have argued that this expansion has resulted in a world in which information is increasingly privatized, and hence threatens the public domain of knowledge and the possibility of creativity in the future. The work of scholars like Boyle, Benkler, and Lessig, to name just a few, is important here as they strive to make an argument for a stronger understanding of the public interest that underlies IP policy.[4] There is also a convergence between research and activism as evidenced in the Creative Commons initiative and the bourgeoning A2K movement.
- The second strand that can be identified would broadly fall under a political economy critique of IP. Scholars like Peter Drahos, Carlos Correa, Susan Sell, and others have been looking at context in which IP has been globalized, critiquing the unequal north–south character of IP. Their targets are often the institutional players such as WTO, WIPO, and the TRIPS agreement, charging them with "information feudalism" or of neocolonialism.[5]
- The third critical strand has been shaped by the coming together of literary theory and legal theory in the form of the critique of the myth of authorship in copyright law and theory. Inspired by the works of poststructural thinkers like Barthes, Foucault, and Derrida, scholars like Peter Jaszi and Martha Woodmansee have been highly critical in inaugurating

a critical interrogation of the figure of the author as an isolated romantic genius, through a historical identification of the emergence of the author function, as well as problematizing the idea of the romantic author in the age of digital production.[6]

· A fourth strand that can be identified would broadly be the historical approach, which looks at the emergence of particular strands of IP in its historical context and especially the context of the history of industrialization. This strand has been very important in countering the usual claims made by IP proponents such as those who argue that that without a strong patent regime there would be no innovation.[7]

· The response to the question of IP from "developing countries" has generally been framed around the "epistemological question" or the "nationalist approach." In the former, the argument made is that IP is not a universal mode of relating to knowledge and that it emerges in the specific history of the Western enlightenment discourse, carrying with it presumptions such as originality and authorship. IP therefore faces an epistemological problem when it encounters other forms of knowledge production such as traditional knowledge and aboriginal art and when it seeks to translate the latter into the terms of a modern IP framework. The second strand that developing countries have adopted is a more strategic and instrumental one that looks at whether IP is beneficial to developing countries, and this approach has often produced contrasting results.[8]

The sheer diversity of the responses to the question of IP poses interesting intellectual questions and challenges for us. First, it is clear that it would be a mistake to presume an absolute uniformity that exists between these different strands. The idea of these various strands' being united by a "single enemy"—namely, intellectual property—may actually conceal more than it reveals. In fact, a number of the strands, far from being complementary, may have contentious relationships with one another, and the challenge for us would be to look at the kind of questions that we can raise when we look at the different registers in which the critical debate on IP operates.

What do these differences reveal in terms of the intellectual project that lies ahead of us? What are the intellectual and philosophical fault lines that exist between the different approaches, and in what way can questions asked by a particular strand be extended or enriched when it encounters a competing vision of the commons or the public domain? What are the limitations even within such an array of ideas of the discourse of intellectual property, and what new terms may have to be introduced to the debate before we can attempt to construct a theory of knowledge practices that interlinks the historical, the ethnographic, and the normative imperative? What are the critical cultural resources that we have to build and draw on to provide new alternative accounts?

The Problem of Piracy

A quick survey of the range of debates reveals the relative absence of any serious engagement with the world of quotidian nonlegal media consumption and circulation, or piracy. This is surprising, given that the everyday life of IP plays itself out through an extraordinary focus on the pirate. What is it about the nature of piracy that creates this uncomfortable silence around it? Scholars like Lessig and others have been responding to a debate on IP by looking beyond the binaries of legality/illegality that are set up by traditional copyright, but yet when it comes to piracy, there is still a problem of accommodation.

What then is the exact problem of piracy and why can it not be accommodated within the terms of public domain theorists? Surely, it cannot be just the fact that it is tainted by illegality, because many other acts, including downloading music, are also tainted by illegality. There are ways in which these acts find redemption, which the pirate just cannot. Is it a problem peculiar to the precise nature of the illegality, the domain that it operates in and the subjectivities that it interpellates?

Or is it possible that there is instead something about the way in which the critical responses to IP have been framed that makes it impossible for it to deal with piracy, or for piracy to redeem itself? Perhaps we will have to start asking different kinds of questions if we are to move beyond the impasse.

Lawrence Lessig, a copyright scholar and one of the founders of the creative commons, has this to say:

All across the world, but especially in Asia and Eastern Europe, there are businesses that do nothing but take other people's copyrighted content, copy it, and sell it—all without the permission of a copyright owner. The recording industry estimates that it loses about $4.6 billion every year to physical piracy (that works out to one in three CDs sold worldwide). The MPAA estimates that it loses $3 billion annually worldwide to piracy. This is piracy plain and simple. Nothing in the argument of this book, nor in the argument that most people make when talking about the subject of this book, should draw into doubt this simple point:

This piracy is wrong . . .

The copy shops in Asia, by contrast, are violating Asian law. Asian law does protect foreign copyrights, and the actions of the copy shops violate that law. So the wrong of piracy that they engage in is not just a moral wrong, but a legal wrong, and not just an internationally legal wrong, but a locally legal wrong as well [Lessig, 2004].

Piracy poses a representational problem in the contemporary discourse on law, public goods, and creativity. Piracy seems to allegorize *an impure* transgression, tainted by commerce and an inability to produce a discourse on itself. Pirate production of commodities and media objects fits neither a narrative of resistance nor normative critique, nor does piracy seem to fit received models of creativity or innovation. Piracy produces a series of anxieties: from states, transnational capital, and media industries, and even—as the Lessig quote suggests—amongst liberal scholars critical of IP's excesses. The efflorescence of nonlegal media production and circulation exists as a series of publicly articulated facts, constantly referred to in media panics, national security discourses, and everyday conversations. A serious reconsideration of the relationship between piracy and democratization of knowledge and culture can present new questions that challenge our assumptions about creativity, subjectivity and transformation, commodification, and social life.

Let's try to identify the ways in which piracy seems to be "tainted" before offering different ways of reframing the question of piracy.

First, because piracy operates within the logic of profit and within the terms of commerce, it gets tainted as an activity that cannot claim a moral ground in the way that other nonlegal media practices can. For critics of copyright working with the paradigm of legal reform, it would be an embarrassment to support any nonlegal commercial enterprise. Within copyright law, there is a history of allowing forms of uses in fair dealing provisions that are primarily noncommercial in nature, and hence it becomes easier to justify noncommercial piracy, such as that which is done via P2P networks.

The critics' stance against piracy may therefore stem from either a strategic or an ethical position. The strategic stance against piracy may, for instance, be adopted by people who do not per se have any serious objections to piracy but recognize that it would be counterproductive for them, in their struggle against stricter IP regimes, to be seen as espousing commercial piracy. On the other hand, a number of people, including Stallman and Lessig, would argue that if a certain law exists, and we do not agree with it, then we either reform the law or create an alternative legal paradigm. However, so far as the law exists, then we cannot encourage the violation of such a law. We shall, however, see that this division between commercial and noncommercial piracy breaks down when you look at it through the prism of infrastructure, and the vital role that commercial piracy plays in creating forms of access that would just not exist otherwise.

Another reason for the suspicion of commercial piracy, in relation to entertainment, stems from the fact that it pertains to the domain of pleasure. Unlike access to affordable medicines and access to learning materials, it seems that there is very little possibility of redeeming piracy that provides people with low-cost films and music. Access to films and music is seen as frivolous and not in the realm of the real-world concerns of the A2K movement. In the world of knowledge and culture there seems to be a very clear demarcation between essential and nonessential goods. The suspicion of pleasure and curiosity stems from an older history wherein the development discourse constructs the subject of development as a wretched figure that then enables all kinds of top-down interventions to improve their lives. But if we are to reverse the assumption of what are the essential needs of people, these divisions between the essential and nonessential needs get a little more complicated.

Finally, a major critique of commercial piracy is that unlike instances wherein people remix content, commercial piracy is unable to redeem itself by an act of creativity. Thus, while young people illegally download music, they then remix the music to produce new music. In the case of commercial piracy, there is a slavish making of copies without any trans-formative redemption. Thus, Lessig says, "Efforts at justifying commer-cial piracy simply don't cut it. This kind of piracy is rampant and just plain wrong. It doesn't transform the content it steals; it doesn't transform the market it competes in. It merely gives someone access to something that the law says he should not have. Nothing has changed to draw that law into doubt. This form of piracy is flat out wrong" (Lessig, 2004).

I shall argue that this understanding of transformative use, while important, has to be expanded if we are to understand creativity across countries where access to infrastructures of creativity are not the same.

Whose Public Domain?

Having set up the conceptual problems posed by piracy to public domain theorists, let us try and understand the terms of representation that public domain scholarship sets for itself. While the public domain has emerged as the most viable alternative to the expansion of IP, the ques-tion is whether the public domain is the only way through which we can understand contemporary conflicts around IP, and what are the limits of the "public domain" approach when you attempt to provide an account of piracy. Do we use the same conceptual and descriptive terms while attempting to narrate these two worlds? Can the world of the "public domain" and the world of the pirate be narrated as though there were a seamless web that should necessarily tie the two?

In many ways, the public domain argument deploys classical terms of representation that borrow from either political or cultural theory, and some of these include categories of citizenship, resistance, and creativity. I think it is important to take a slight detour into a debate about the his-tory of citizenship to understand why certain classes of people always get left out in the imagination of the liberal public sphere.

One of the problems we have when we try to understand piracy is that it often does not fit within any of these existing categories, and there is a "positivity or excess" in the body of the pirate that cannot be disavowed (Dhareshwar, 1996). Dhareshwar uses this phrase to understand the emergence of the modern Indian citizen.

In the Indian context, the history of the citizen is clearly tied to the project of the nation,

the largest imagined space which claimed the nomenclature of the new, or at least with the Utopian projection of the ideal community, freed from colonial domination, and free to create a world untainted by inequalities of caste-class, community or gender. It was a community, however, only of those who were eligible to be citizens, and the question of how citizenship was conferred is in many ways the same question as how the nation was imagined. Nationalism was a marker of the readiness to enter the "modern" age, and the modern person produced as "Indian" was also the free, agentive, romantic subject of liberal humanism.[9]

Dhareshwar claims that the citizen emerged as the juridical category that would erase older histories of caste, religion, and gender, and the occupation of the space of the citizen simultaneously implied a movement from older identities. His claim is that certain forms of historic inequalities make it impossible for most people to occupy the space of the unmarked citizen, and the histories of violence and oppression writ large on their bodies.

In a similar manner, the idea of the public domain imagines a free, open space wherein people can participate in the world of ideas and cultural production. And when this space is threatened by the taint of illegality caused by copyright law, there arises a need for a theory that redeems the illegal act and inserts it within the terms set up by the normative ideas of the public domain.

One way in which the copyright infringer is rescued from the accusation of being an illegal pirate is through an act of redemption, for instance by showing that his or her acts of infringement actually result in an increase in creativity, and this is often done through doctrines such as the idea of transformative authorship. But then what happens to entire realm of nontransformative authorship or the "Asian piracy" that does not necessarily transform but merely reproduces ceaselessly using cheap technologies? How do we read this account of the public domain? While one can understand that Lessig would have to be careful about the ways in which he pitches a reform of copyright law within the context of the United

States, it is also a little difficult not to miss the linkages in this paragraph to older accounts of illegality in which Asia, where many accounts of the urban experience in Asia and Latin America have been narrated in terms of its preponderant criminality and illegality. This, for instance, is particularly true not merely in the context of the colonial imagination but also in the ways that cities and everyday life in Asia are understood. While the United States has always narrated itself through the tropes of constitutionalism and the rule of law, the crisis arrives when all of a sudden the very language of criminality and illegality that accounts for much of the world arrives home in the form of the criminalization of students downloading music. But clearly one cannot have an account of illegality in a country that prides itself on its constitutional tradition and its emphasis on the rule of law.

One of the narrative strategies is then to redeem the acts of "ordinary" American citizens, and what better way to do this than through the discursive construction of an "other," in this case an Asian other. The categories of the public domain serve as the neutral ground over which the two kinds of pirates are pitted against each other, and the terms of reference of this public domain are creativity and innovation. This kind of framing is a bit misleading because it relies on the presumption that creativity and transformation are only at the level of content, and, when it is framed thus, we are delivered a *fait accompli* when we encounter quotidian media piracy.

Underlying much of copyright's mythology is a certain understanding of creativity that draws on ideas of creativity, innovation, and progress. These specifically emerge within the history of modernity and have served as the foundational reasons for the existence of copyright itself. The idea of creativity as a universal good is shared by advocates of stronger copyright as well as advocates of the public domain. Our having established the progress myth of copyright, the question of dispute is whether we arrive at the ultimate public good through the route of more copyright or through more freedom. By setting themselves up as alternative accounts of the idea of progress and creativity, public domain arguments nonetheless share the assumption of copyright theory that the end goal is to maximize creativity. Advocates of the public domain argue that while copyright aspires to promote creativity, it actually fails to do this, and excessive protection has actually resulted in a decrease of creativity or a threat to creativity.

The difference between public domain scholars and copyright advo-cates lies in their understanding and interpretation of the idea of the creative. Lessig insists that we should protect *some* illegal works—based on "transformativity"—and distinguishes the Asian pirate as the other of creative transformation. But the creative subject invoked here is in fact a very particular *kind* of creative subject—a liberal, disembodied one. The difference between the idea of an embodied and disembodied way of understanding of creativity can be stated in the following man-ner: When creativity is seen as a transcendental virtue, it acquires an ability to move beyond time and space and can in fact be used to mea-sure practices that may be situated in local histories. On the other hand, if we do not see creativity in a universal sense but attempt to draw it out by situating it historically in time and in particular spaces, we have an idea of creativity that may be far more open-ended and flexible and able to accommodate not just similarities in processes of creativity but dif-ferences as well.

Returning to the point of the close link between ideas of public domain and the realm of political representation, we could say that the public domain is bracketed as a space of equal participation in which everyone can participate as equal rights-bearing citizens. The linking of public domain theories to freedom of speech and expression is not accidental, and the very model of the public domain as the sphere of rational communication borrows from existing accounts of the public/private divide.

Many postcolonial scholars have seriously contested the category of the citizen as the universal bearer of rights, and the representa-tive capacity of the citizen to participate in the public sphere as an unmarked individual remains mythical at best. In India, for instance, the creation of the citizen subject category demanded a move away from the oversignified body of the individual marked by religion, gender, and caste into an unmarked subject position, "the citizen," a category based on equality and access and guaranteed rights within the constitutional framework. But the majority of people in India are only precarious citizens who often do not have the ability to claim rights in the same manner as the elite in India do. Instead, the manner in which they access institutions of democracy and "welfare" is often through complex negotiations and networks, often marked by their illegal status.

In their work on citizenship, Dhareshwar and Srivatsan suggest that the discursive figure of the citizen always throws up its other, the denizen, and in fact the denizen may be essential for the definition of the citizen itself. Thus, while citizenship and modernity are normatively constructed as highly desirable, and the grand project wills everyone into a state of modernity, there arises from the start a clear lack or inability for the bulk of the population to occupy this space. So what happens when people fall off these official maps and plans? How do they find their way back into official memory and create for themselves avenues of participation? I suggest there lies a great deal of work to be done on engaging with how people create vibrant spaces outside of official plans through which they participate, and more often than not these spaces are marked by their high degree of illegality.

One way of understanding the place of the "illegal" in the India context is through Partha Chatterjee's notion of political society. From the very beginning of the independent career of the Indian nation-state, he argues, there was a contradiction between its modernizing aspirations and its commitment to democracy, which was sought to be managed on the terrain of political society. This was the large and muddled field on which compromises had to be made, from point to point, moment to moment. Political society, he says, constituted a field which lacked the clarity of moral language and legal concepts that were supposed to define the relations between state and civil society. It meant bending the rules, recognizing that the legal fiction of equal citizenship did not always apply, that the laws of property and contract might sometimes need to be overlooked. It meant speaking in both languages—of rights as well as policy—often using the one to overcome the limitations of the other.

Similarly, pirates who merely reproduce without producing are unable to shed the illegal excesses to enable them to play a role or become a part of the reconstituted public domain. The pirates contribute nothing and cannot play a role in the public domain, because they cannot claim the representative status given to the transforming creator within the productive public domain. There are very few possibilities of the pirate occupying the normative terms set up by the public domain of the creative citizen. And yet despite the expulsion, a look at history and at the present seems to indicate that there is a certain stubbornness on the part of those who do not find a representative space in the public domain, and they refuse to disappear and instead coexist at the margins of any transformative accounts that exist.

Copyleft, Copyright, and Copy Centers

It will be the argument of this chapter that conventional criticisms of piracy are premised on narrow ideas of creativity, because of their exclusive focus on the question of authorship and content to the exclusion of infrastructure. The Malegaon story has shown us that the creativity that goes into the making of the remakes lies as much in the way that the film is made as in the content of the film. There is also a tendency within these critiques to look at the copy as an uncomplicated object, but fetishized for its illegal status. This is not very different from the ways in which the entertainment industries also fetishize the object (held up in press conferences as evidence, mass destruction by steamrollers, etc.).

Historically, for instance, there is an entire realm inhabited by figures such as the trickster, the copier, the thief, the pirate who inhabit a marginal site of production and circulation. How does the recovery of various histories assist us in unpacking the idea of creativity and later the terms of the linear progressive account that is often provided of the public domain? If we move away from the normative account of the creator citizen and engage with an entire set of practices that renders any straightforward representation impossible or difficult, what are the intellectual horizons that open up? We would also ask for patience from public domain scholars and ask of them the same careful attention that they pay to understanding the larger political and cultural politics of copyright when they look at the phenomenon of piracy.

One of the ways, then, of moving beyond the impasse is to reformulate our object of enquiry. Let us take for granted the illegal status of piracy, but let us not stop there. Instead it might be more useful for us to ask the question of not what piracy is but what piracy does. The shift in focus from the discursive and moral representation of the illegal deed to the wider social world in which the deed is located allows us to bring into light the very nature of the law that names a particular act as an illegal one. Does the naming of the deed as an illegal one prevent us from reflecting on the nature of the act?

The shift away from what piracy is to what piracy does enables us to consider on the same plane its linkages to the normative considerations that public domain advocates argue for and are often unable ever to achieve. The best example is in the domain of cheap books, wherein public domain advocates try to reform copyright law to enable more educational exceptions, pirated books, and unauthorized photocopies. Rather than looking at the neat spaces of legal/illegal it might be more advantageous to consider the spaces in which piracy plays itself out, the transforming urban landscapes, the specific histories of the nooks and crannies that render this space an illegal one, the accumulated histories of regulation, tacticity and negotiation that renders this topography intelligible.

One way of looking at what piracy does, rather than at what piracy is, is offered by the following. In a comparative study on the price of books in South Africa, India, and the United States, we had an opportunity to examine the sharp inequality in purchasing power, as well as what seems to be the difference between two countries where access is clearly a problem (Liang and Prabhala, 2006).

We begin by taking the per capita income (PCI) for different countries (the United States, India, and South Africa), as well as the absolute cost of one particular good/commodity in major bookstores in these three countries. We then calculated the percentage/ratio that the price of this commodity would be in relation to the per capita income of the country—for example, if GDP per capita of India is $750 and the price of a book is $10, then the cost of purchasing the book would be 1.33 percent of the GDP per capita income of the country; if the PCI of the United States is $37,500, then the cost of purchasing the book would be 0.026 percent of the per capita income of the United States.

TABLE 4.1. *Absolute Cost of Three Book Titles in South Africa/ India/ USA*

Country	The God of Small Things, Arundhati Roy (US$)	Long Walk to Freedom, Nelson Mandela (US$)	Oxford English Dictionary (US$)
South Africa	16.23	24.30	47.00
India	6.60	15.40	14.10
USA	10.50	12.10	21.50

TABLE 4.2. *Cost of Three Book Titles as a Percentage of Average Income in South Africa/ India/ USA*

Country	The God of Small Things	Long Walk to Freedom	Oxford English Dictionary
South Africa	0.0046%	0.0069%	0.0134%
India	0.0117%	0.0273%	0.025%
USA	0.0002%	0.0003%	0.0005%

TABLE 4.3. *Cost of Three Book Titles in USA at Proportions of Income Paid in India and South Africa*

Book	Projected cost in USA at South Africa proportions (US$)	Projected cost in USA at India proportions (US$)
The God of Small Things	173.00	440.50
Long Walk to Freedom	259.77	1027.80
Oxford English Dictionary	504.50	941.20

This exercise provides several layers of insight. One: Absolute prices of books can be higher in the South than in the North, as the South African figures indicate. Two: Consumers in the South have to commit significantly higher proportions of their income to consume these books. If consumers in the United States had to pay the same proportion of their income for these books as their counterparts in South Africa and India, the results would be ludicrous: $1,027.50 for Nelson Mandela's *Long Walk to Freedom* and $941.20 for the *Oxford English Dictionary*. It is instructive, then, that the prospect of paying $440.50 for Arundhati Roy's *God of Small Things* in the United States is assumably alarming. Yet, the notion of paying $6.60 for the book in India (which in Indian terms is exactly the same value as $440.50 in the United States) is not treated with similar alarm.

The interesting difference between India and South Africa is that while both countries are majorly affected by the high costs, all the books mentioned are easily available in pirated form at a fraction of the costs in India. The pirated versions of *The God of Small Things* and *The Long Walk to Freedom* are available on most Indian streets for approximately two dollars. And if one were to photocopy either of the books, they would cost around a dollar. The difference, then, on questions of access between India and South Africa seems to be around the infrastructure of distribution (both organized print piracy as well as the innumerable number of copy centers). And the problem of access in South Africa is precisely the absence of a strong pirate market that makes the books available to a much wider population.

In a study on copyright piracy in India, the Ministry of Human Resources and Development had the following to say:

Book piracy, in India, primarily depends on two factors, namely, the price of the book and its popularity. These two factors positively contribute to piracy. Piracy is generally confined to foreign and good indigenous books. Because these books are demanded in large quantities and are also priced high. The types of books pirated mostly are medical, engineering and other professional books, encyclopaedia and popular fictions. The piracy is also wide spread with respect to books published by National Council of Educational Research & Training (NCERT), National Open School and Board(s) of Secondary Education. These books even if priced low are having large demand.

Besides the above, piracy in the form of mass photocopying of books is largely prevalent in India, especially in and around educational institutions. Students borrow books from libraries and then get these photocopied from the photocopier kept at the institution where from the books are borrowed. While copyright law permits photocopying of literary works for limited private uses such as research, review or criticism what happens, many a time is that the entire book is photocopied including the cover pages. In the process student community and the photocopy operators gain, but the publishers lose a huge revenue. Unfortunately, the institutions turn a blind eye to this.

While the report is supposed to be critical of piracy, if one were to see it in light of the situation in South Africa, which does not have a vibrant pirated books market, it seems to me that the problem of access in India is partially addressed by the infrastructure of piracy that exists, and if a similar infrastructure existed in South Africa, we would be addressing many of the problems.

But the question that remains is this: How do pirate infrastructures get built? The very idea of pirate infrastructures suggests to us a certain derivative nature of these infrastructure. Infrastructure has tradition-ally been the domain of the state or of private business. It seems to me that pirate infrastructures lies somewhere between the two. Just as slums have been described as shadow cities, and just the copy is seen in terms of the shadow of the original, the world of pirate infrastructure emerges through organic forms that are not immediately obvious to us, if we focus only on their visible form.

At the heart of pirate infrastructures and at the core of conflict mark-ing the battles over copyright is the copy, whether it is the ubiquitous DVD or the fake Adidas shoe. The world of the copy is an intriguing site from which we can look at the larger question. Marx famously remarked that the commodity was the place from which we could understand the larger dynamics of global capitalism, and it seems to me that in the era of immaterial value, it might well be the copy, the thing itself, which is the point of origin.

Rethinking the Creativity of the Copy

If this world of everyday media experience transforms our contemporary experience and yet paradoxically does not make a claim to creativity, does it invite us to revisit our ideas of creativity's relation to the copy? Ravi Sundaram suggests that it might be fruitful for us to revisit the histories of the copy, from early print culture to the forger in art history through the crisis in aesthetic experience precipitated by the "age of mechanical reproduction" as a way of understanding the current transitions and conflicts. It is also a useful way in which we can understand the general anxiety around the consumption and circulation of cheaply reproduced media commodities. The reproducible work that brings into play a network of circulation also inaugurates a series of cultural possibilities and readings.

We have seen that one objection to piracy is the fact that it operates within the domain of slavish reproduction, without any transformative act of creativity allowing for its redemption from its status as an illegal object. We are therefore forced to reflect on the nature of the copy in contemporary culture: What is the precise cultural status of the duplicate CD or DVD in relation to the world of creativity and innovation? In a brilliant story, Borges narrates of the efforts of an eclectic scholar, Pierre Mernard (author of a range of scholarly and taxonomic works), who decides to rewrite Cervantes's *Don Quixote*. It is certainly not a version that he wants to rewrite, but to rewrite in whole, and reproduce the Cervantes classic. Mernard proceeds to copy the book verbatim, but when he completes it and compares the two books, he finds that they are different.

In a typically Borgesian fashion, he lays out the entire complex history of the interaction between the original and the copy. After Borges, is there anything such as the untransformed copy at all? Roland Barthes and Michel Foucault have already enabled us to shift the locus of originality and creativity from the text and look for it instead at the process of consumption. What would happen if we also extended the search into the domain of circulation, for instance?

Consider, for instance, the ubiquitous pirated DVD, that prized commodity of pirate aesthetics. Does this new product of digital reproduction still allow for differences to be produced? After all, it is the machine, instead of human hands, that does the copying. Laikwan Pang examines a very interesting aspect of the pirated DVD to raise a set of interesting questions and concerns about political economy and cultural politics around our contemporary culture of the digital copy. One of the strange things that people who have watched films on pirated DVDs will find is the phenomenon of the subtitles' being different from the actual words

that are being spoken onscreen. The reason for this is that the pirates usually get an early copy of the film, usually a screening copy, that does not
yet have all the frills and extras that the actual DVD will eventually have.
So a number of features, including the dubbing or the subtitling, will
have to be done by the pirates themselves.

Laikwan Pang uses an example of a pirated DVD of *Kill Bill* in which
the politics of translation results in very interesting results. The scene is of
the conversation in kitchen of Vernita Green (Copper Head), when the
two fighting women are taking a break after Green's daughter comes back
home from school. The dialogue between the two is as follows:

> GREEN: "You bitch, I need to know if you will gonna starting more shit
> around my baby girl."
> THE BRIDE: "You can relax for now, I'm not going to murder you in front
> of your child, ok?"
> GREEN: "I guess you are more rational than Bill led me to believe you are
> capable of."
> THE BRIDE: "It's mercy, compassion, and forgiveness that I lack, not ratio-
> nality."

But the subtitles of the pirated version translate them as:

> GREEN: "You bitch, never want to hurt my daughter."
> THE BRIDE: "Can we have a chat? I won't hurt your child."
> GREEN: "I can't believe you have such a temper."
> THE BRIDE: "That's my way, passion; not nationality."

One can imagine a modern-day Pierre Mernard struggling to reproduce *Kill Bill* in its exact form, wanting to reproduce the digital aura and
authenticity that subsist in the original and yet submitting to destiny
something else altogether. *Kill Bill*, of course, positioned itself not as an
original film but an assemblage of movie quotations.

Brian Larkin's work on piracy in Nigeria similarly forces us not merely
to look at and listen to the onscreen content but also to consider the conditions under which texts are pirated and circulated. Larkin demonstrates
the critical importance of paying attention to infrastructures of produc-

tion in developing countries where the very process of cultural production is also tied to the relative lack of infrastructure and also becomes the basis for the transformation of the conditions of production by generating a parallel economy of low-cost infrastructure.

He says:

> My interest in technological collapse is somewhat different. It is not in extravagant spectacles like collapsing bridges or exploding space shuttles but in the small, ubiquitous experience of breakdown as a condition of technological existence. In Nigeria, cars, televisions, VCRs, buses, and motorbikes are often out of service. Even when they work, electricity supplies are unreliable and beset by power surges that damage consumer equipment. NEPA, the Nigerian Electric Power Authority, is famously known by the epithet "Never Expect Power Always," and phone lines are expensive and difficult to obtain. Poverty and the disorganization of the Nigerian economy mean that consumer technologies such as scooters and cars arrive already used and worn out. After their useful life in Belgium or Holland, cars are exported to Nigeria as "new" second-hand vehicles. After these vehicles arrive in Nigeria, worn parts are repaired, dents are banged out, and paint is resprayed to remake and "tropicalize" them. This is, of course, a temporary state of affairs. Other parts expire, second-hand parts break down, while local "innovations" and adjustments designed to make cars, televisions, and VCRs work fail. A cycle of breakdown, repair, and breakdown again is the condition of existence for many technologies in Nigeria. As a consequence, Nigeria employs a vast army of people who specialize in repairing and reconditioning broken technological goods, since the need for repair is frequent and the cost of it cheap.

This economy of recycling, which Ravi Sundaram also describes as the "pirate modern,"[10] becomes the arena for all sorts of technological innovation to begin with and extends further to experiments with cultural forms such as parodies, remixes, cover versions, and the like. In a sense, Larkin's invocation of the importance of infrastructure contrasts with the obsessive fixation with content that one sees in most Western accounts of creativity. In this case the content also has to be filtered through the regime of its own production.

Piracy imposes particular conditions on the recording, transmission, and retrieval of data. Constant copying erodes data storage, degrading image and sound, overwhelming the signal of media content with the noise produced by the means of reproduction. Larkin says that because pirated videos often have blurred images and distorted sound, they create a kind of material space "that filters audiences' engagement with media technologies and their senses of time, speed, space, and contemporaneity. In this way, piracy creates an aesthetic, a set of formal qualities that generates a particular sensorial experience of media marked by poor transmission, interference, and noise." Larkin uses the question of pirate infrastructure to open up the debate on intellectual property and foreground the importance of addressing the question of content while looking at a legal aspect of culture. If infrastructures represent attempts to order, regulate, and rationalize society, then breakdowns in their operation, or the rise of provisional and informal infrastructures, highlight the failure of that ordering and the recoding that takes its place. By subjecting the material operation of piracy and its social consequences to scrutiny, it becomes clear that pirate infrastructure is a powerful mediating force that produces new modes of organizing sensory perception, time, space, and economic networks.

One of the significant approaches used by public domain scholars is their emphasis on the ability to create new content by building on existing works. They in fact use metaphors of infrastructure ("bridging the knowledge divide," "information highway") to understand the public domain of ideas. But it often ignores the material linkages between content and infrastructure. The overemphasis on the creation of new content of course raises the question of who uses the new content, and what is the relationship between such content and the question of democratization of infrastructure.

In most cases the reason for the fall in price of electronic goods and computers, great access to material, and an increase in photocopiers (the infrastructure of information flows) is not through any radical revolution such as free software or open content but really through the easier availability of standard mainstream commodities like Microsoft and Hollywood. When Stallman and others castigate people for pirating Hollywood, it is only from a position of being able to disavow the global. But in many countries, the very question of what it means to be modern has always been defined in relation to an idea of the global; thus the culture industries of the United States have always created economies of desire and access to the latest films and music has also been a part of the subjectivity of "being in with the latest." While these aspirations are complexly configured and sustained through political economies of monopoly and control, they are also experienced by most people precisely as a "lack." So even as a person working in a sweatshop in Thailand produces a pair of Nike shoes, s/he is unable to buy one. For Stallman and other copyleft-ers coming from a position of privilege, opportunity abounds to engage through alternatives. But for many people at the world's peripheries, the idea of finding their place within the global demands engaging with a world of counterfeit commodities, replicating the global directly.

We can either play the higher moral ground game and lecture consumers on their real information needs or provide crude theories of how they are trapped by false consciousness. Or we can move away from these judgmental perspectives and look at other aspects such as the impact of the expansion of the market for these gray market goods has on the general pricing of these goods, the spread of computer/IT culture, the fall in price of consumables such as blank CDs, DVDs, the growing popularity of CD writers. I find it a little strange and dogmatic that people who preach access also preach the kind of access that should be given.

I would like to end this segment by quoting an interesting conversation. There is currently a lot of excitement about the contemporary art scene in China, and indeed it seems to be the flavor of the month in the global art circles. Thousands of people are lining up to join art schools, and one of the Chinese curators had this to say: "When you can buy a Tarkovsky film for a dollar, you will obviously produce many more artists."

The existence of contemporary art and other forms of cultural production is always predicated on the material conditions of the life of its practitioners. The myriad daily acts of practicing, reading, inscribing, interpreting, and repurposing the substance of culture, across cultures, constitute these conditions of life. The availability of texts, of machines and of spaces, in which these ideas can be accessed, debated, and discarded, are all interwoven, and to understand a complete picture of the transformative possibilities of new technologies, we need to pay closer attention to how these forces interact. When we subject the material operation of piracy and its social consequences to scrutiny, it becomes clear that pirate infrastructure is a powerful mediating force that produces new modes of organizing sensory perception, time, space, and economic networks.

The Waiting Room of Culture

The idea of access has generally been centered on the question of cost and availability. But I think another crucial element to consider while thinking about access is its relation to temporality. We are aware that the global licensing regime in copyright attempts to maintain the ordered flow of commodities—in time and in space. But if the information and communication technology that erases time and space facilitates the global flow of commodities and services, it also leaks out through unofficial channels to create alternative journeys that resists official maps.

Copyright uses the logic of windowing and licenses to control the temporal and spatial dimensions of film circulation. This temporality is, however, tied to its status as a commodity, but film as a cultural object exceeds its status as commodity, and in fact the commodity phase of the life history of an object can never exhaust its social biography.

Thus, cinema—that great eraser of time—can never be limited to a one-sided temporal logic. The circulation of the DVD traverses diverse worlds, from that of monetary exchange to barter to gift to ubiquitous reproduction, and acts of circulation always exceed the monetary idea of exchange value. The movement of the DVD from monetary economies to psychic economies has to be thought of as a transaction between imaginary capital confronting the world of imagination and desire. We therefore need to shift our attention to the temporal life of cinema in psychic economies.

The temporal nature of distribution is tied not just to an economic logic but also to an economy of anticipation. The buildup to the latest film, the trailers, the posters, the release of the soundtrack, the first-day/first-show phenomenon all work within an economy of waiting. At the heart of the temporal logic of film is also a culture of aspiration, fulfillment of desire or deferred pleasure. The windowing system of distribution unequally distributes the share of waiting, with the wait getting longer as you move away from the northern hemisphere and toward different parts of the global south, or from the metropolises to small towns and villages.

In films like *Main Madhuri Dixit Banna Chahti Hoon* (2003), *Haasil* (2003), and Pankaj Kumar's documentary *Kumar Talkies* (1999), we get a glimpse into this—waiting-room world of cinema—as a field of differently distributed sensibilities. The newness of the films, the high quality of their reproduction, and the experience of moviegoing come to stand for temporal and cultural difference, between the north and the south, between the town and the city, and between global modernity and those who are "not quite modern." In a delightful scene in *Main Madhuri Dixit*, the protagonist goes to watch Devdas, but after a few reels the film stops and they have to wait for the arrival of the other reels from the neighboring village. The audience complains that the last time they had to wait for over two hours since the cycle in which the reels were being brought broke down, because of a flat tire, caused by the bad roads. The big city, not surprisingly, becomes the place where this fracture can be repaired, where films are shown in their entirety, and where audiences do not have to confront their physical and cultural marginality every time they attend the cinema (Larkin, 2004), and the social life of piracy occurs at the intersection of the economy of anticipation and the culture of aspiration. Cinema history involves the reinvention not merely of technological formats but also that of social selves (Vasudevan, 2003).

Waiting for the latest Hollywood or Bollywood release then becomes an apt metaphor for those placed differently within the circuit of "technological time." A useful way of connecting piracy to the temporal experience of cinema might then be to look at the infrastructure and technology that enable the circulation of films. Brian Larkin and Ravi Sundaram, who both study the conditions of the "pirate modern," argue that in contrast to the dizzying, real-time global integration of the information era, a large number of people experience time not through the trope of speed but through the experience of interruptions and breakdowns; breakdowns create a temporal experience that has less to do with velocity and more to do with the process of waiting.

From waiting for e-mail messages to open, machines to be repaired, or electricity to be restored, the experience of technology is subject to a constant cycle of breakdown and repair. In most countries the promise of technological prosthesis is thwarted by the common experience of technological collapse. Each repair enforces another waiting period, an often frustrating experience of duration brought about by the technology of speed itself. The temporal experience of slowness comes as a consequence of speed-producing technologies, so that speed and acceleration, deceleration and stasis are relative, continually shifting states. The experience of technological modernity in most countries is premised on waiting for it to trickle down, often through pirate indigenizing (Larkin, 2004).

An interesting instance of this in film technology is the history of VCDs and DVDs. Sony and Philips jointly introduced the VCD technology in 1993 to record video on optical discs the size of CDs. It was cheap, digital, and convenient and seemed to be setting the standard. At the time of the introduction of the new format, however, the development of the technologically far superior digital videodisc (DVD) was already underway. Even from the beginning, Philips was well aware of the pending arrival of the high-density DVD and the threat it would bring to VCD. Philips decided then not to further develop or produce VCD but rather to wait for DVD. Seeing the new format facing a more or less doomed future, Philips and Sony decided to launch VCD in China instead because it was "a technology that was fit for a poor cousin in laggard developing countries instead of cutting edge economies" (Wang, 2004). The introduction of VCDs into China proved to be the biggest boom to cheap reproduction technologies. Ironically, the industry at that time believed that CDs would help fight video piracy (Wang, 2003, 2004; Pang, 2006).

A large number of Asian markets adopted the format enthusiastically, bypassing global distribution networks in order to "steal" enjoyment. Darrell Davis calls VCD a form of cockroach capitalism because of its proliferation. Within a short period of time, VCD became the major movie carrier in many developing countries. If you take China's VCD player production and household presence it is startling: In 1998 there were 16 VCD players per 100 households and by 2000, there were 36.4 VCD players per 100 households; in 2000, there were 14.5 million units manufactured, but by 2001 this number fell to 1.2 million units since the manufacturing move into DVDs.

VCD technology spread rapidly from east Asia to other parts of Asia, and within a few years of their introduction, VCDs replaced VHS as the standard format in most parts of Asia. In India, for instance, while the price of the VCR never fell below Rs. 10,000, a VCD player was available for as low as Rs. 1,000. VCD culture also spread from Asia into other parts of the world very rapidly. In Nigeria, which incidentally has the largest film industry in the world (producing more than 1,200 films a year), most of the films are available only on VCDs and DVDs. But given its complete absence in the Western market, there seems something distinctly "Asian" about VCD technology (Hu, 2007).

The VCD story for me is one in which the temporal questions of copyright encounter an indigenous modernity that feeds of and yet creates its own sense of the relationship between time, technology, and commodity culture.

Rethinking Access beyond Developmentalism

Finally, I would like to look at what these self-organized forms of infrastructure development mean for our understanding of access. There are two ways in which we can think of access. We can think of access either as paternal access or defiant access.

Paternal access implies a recognition of a "lack" that is sought to be corrected with benign intervention. Sometimes the language of paternal access dovetails into the language of rights (communication rights, information rights, etc.), but underlying the idea of paternal access are assumptions that are driven either by piety or by a pedagogic motivation. We advocate for access to the things that people *should* enjoy access to; learning materials but not popular films, rice and Dal but not McDonald's. This is often the mode taken by scholars of access to knowledge.

The other way that one can think of access—one seen more commonly in the logic of consumers themselves—is in terms of a defiant access by virtue of which people attempt to access things that they are not meant to (whether by virtue of class, age, social status, or caste) have. This can range from pornography to academic textbooks. It would, however, be a mistake to assume that the instinct of defiant access stands only from an anticensorial instinct. Defiant access is also a form of self-making that refuses to follow any preordained rule of social status and is best exemplified in the figure of the autodidact (from whom we shall have much to learn further). A large number of initiatives that seek to promote greater access in fact consciously or unconsciously recycle the idea of paternal access.

While concerns about inequitable access begin with statements about the "knowledge divide," we must also recognize that in a country like India, it is just one of the many other divides and there is no guarantee that greater access to knowledge necessarily builds a more equitable country. Irrigation projects, dams, green revolution—there have been a host of technological fixes proposed in the past, each of which has ended up creating as many problems as solving them. A number of initiatives to promote digital access (ICT4D projects in particular) are marked by a political naïveté that would be touching if it were not so disastrous.

There is, however, another kind of critique I wish to propose regarding the conceptual field suggested by the notion of knowledge divide, viz. that issues of difference in the knowledge economy require us to think beyond the question of access and look instead at the simultaneity of desire and anxiety; of access and conflict; of knowledge and representation.

The point I am making is this: The rhetoric of inclusiveness is also always accompanied by the prospect of violence; the claims of the poor are always a matter of contests and negotiations rather than the benevolence of the state and the corporate world. There are anxieties that often translate into violence, lest the poor who are the objects of development take a path that cannot be justified in terms of liberal theory.

Let me then move to the next part—what happens when you do get access. What about thinking and creativity? Or are the non-elite merely destined to be the objects of the discourse of digital access and can never be the authors of digital imaginaries? For us to imagine other ways of inhabiting the digital world, we will have to do better than recycle the framework of the knowledge divide.

Earlier I mentioned that one of the problems of piracy seems to lie in the fact that it is associated more with the world of pleasure and desire than that of "pure needs." In this segment, I will attempt to examine the intersection between the world of desire, subjectivity, and the experience of piracy.

Let me begin with an interesting story, which is a typical example of interventions in the field of the digital divide. An NGO in Bangalore that works in the field of Information and Communication Technologies for Development (ICT4D) was conducting a workshop on accessing the Internet for the information needs of rural women trainers. The facilitator guided the women through the basics of the Internet, on accessing information relevant to their work ranging from rural credit to women's health. The training was highly appreciated, and all the women volunteers seemed to be enjoying themselves fiddling with the computers and exploring the Internet. At the end of the training, when the NGO started cleaning up the computers including the history and the cached copies, they were a little aghast to find that most of the women volunteers had been surfing pornography, and a range of pornography at that. So while the trainers were holding forth eloquently about the real information needs of the poor, the poor were quite happy to access their real information needs.

The link between pleasure, desire, aspiration, and trespass has always been a complicated one, and the closer that the transgressive act is to the domain of pleasure, the more difficult it seems for it to be redeemed socially. Thus while one finds easier justifications for transgression that deal with questions of livelihood and survival, and in the case of intellectual property to free speech and access to information, when the matter involved is about new subjectivities and pleasurable transgressions, it gets very differently framed.

The uncomfortable relationship between public domain scholarship and pirates also partially stems from the fact that we are entering a terrain in which the pirated commodity is a tainted one. While the question of medicine and textbooks is far easier to deal with, movies, music, and software get characterized as being outside of the moral economy of development. The demand for low-cost entertainment commodities is seen to be one that is normatively more difficult to sustain. Yet at the same time, the sheer proliferation of these practices, both within the elite and also by the traditional "subaltern" classes, forces us to question our own assumptions about the terms through which people engage with the global economy of information, and about finding their place in the global. What, then, are the critical conceptual resources that we can draw on to be able to address this question of pleasurable transgressions and subjectivities that resist easy framing?

As noted earlier, the way in which the IP debate panned itself out in countries like India was that it was almost immediately linked to questions of development, and it was taken up by various civil society groups working on issues of development, especially in relation to agriculture and seeds. This also extended to the question of access to affordable medicines, and the linking of the IP debate to the development sector also brings with it the inherited language that frames the "subaltern subject of development." But what happens when we move toward the realm of nonlegal media practices where all of a sudden the transgression is highly pleasurable, but not in any way connected to the essential character of the "subaltern subject"? In other words, how do we work through the fact that the terms set up by existing public domain scholarship end up excluding the ability to engage with practices guided not as much by necessity as by curiosity? The rhetoric of inclusiveness that is implicit in public domain discourse is necessarily accompanied by the prospect of exclusion, an exclusion that relies on either on piety or pedagogy.

Jacques Rancière in his brilliant rethinking of labor history paves the way for us to start thinking seriously about the hidden domain of aspiration and desire of the subaltern subject as autodidact, while at the same time thinking about the politics of our own aspirations and desires. Rancière goes into an unexplored aspect of the labor archive of nineteenth-century France, where he starts looking at small, obscure, and short-lived journals brought out by workers, in which they were writing about their own lives. But they were not necessarily writing about their work, and if they were, they were not writing about it in glorified terms but with immense dissatisfaction. Instead, they were interested in writing poetry, about philosophy and the other pleasures to which nonworkers or intellectuals were entitled. At the same time, of course, intellectuals have been fascinated with the world of work and the romance of working-class identity. Rancière says, "What new forms of misreading will affect this contradiction when the discourse of labourers in love with the intellectual nights of the intellectuals encounters the discourse of intellectuals in love with the toilsome and glorious days of the labouring people?"

Rancière's motley cast of characters includes Jerome Gillard, an ironsmith tired of hammering iron, and Pierre Vincard, a metalworker who aspires to be a painter. In other words, a series of sketches of people who refused to obey the role sketched out of for them by history and wanted to step across the line and perform the truly radical act of breaking down the time-honored barrier separating those who carried out useful labor from those who pondered aesthetics. He says,

> A worker who has never learned how to write and yet tried to compose verses to suit the taste of his times was perhaps more of a danger to the prevailing ideological order than a worker who performed revolutionary songs. . . . Perhaps the truly dangerous classes are not so much the uncivilized ones thought to undermine society from below, but rather the migrants who move at the borders between classes, individuals and groups who develop capabilities within themselves which are useless for the improvement of their material lives and which in fact are liable to make them despise material concerns.

Thus, the moral dictates that govern the lives of the poor are not merely from the state ("Don't steal," "Don't beg") but equally from those who theorize the lives of the poor ("Be aware of your class," "Don't get trapped by false consciousness"), but when people start moving out of the frame of representation that has been so carefully and almost lovingly crafted for them, then they either have to be shown their true essence or their transgression has to be brought within the terms of their representative class. Thus when Hugo was shown a poem written by a worker, his embarrassed and patronizing response was, "In your fine verse there is something more than fine verse. There is a strong soul, a lofty heart, a noble and robust spirit. Carry on. Always be what you are: poet and worker. That is to say, thinker and worker." This was a classic instance of what Rancière would term an "exclusion by homage." Just as the aspiration and desires of the poor have to be "something more than fine verse," the information needs of the poor have to be more than wanting to watch a film or even dreaming of becoming a filmmaker.

These injunctions certainly tell us more about the fantasies of the state, of the intellectuals, than they do about people engaging in the practice. We may do well to start rethinking the terms on which intellectual property scholars engage with the language of access.

Notes

1. Researcher, Alternative Law Forum. This chapter arose out of discussions with my colleagues Ravi Sundaram and Jeebesh Bagchi at Sarai. We first presented it collectively in the Contested Commons conference, New Delhi; and shorter versions of the paper and argument will appear in anthologies to be edited by Peter Jaszi and Amy Kapczynski respectively. I thank Lea Shaver for her insightful comments and her incredible patience.

2. An equivalent discussion in fair use law would be to distinguish between a case like *Campbell v. Acuff Rose*, which looks at whether parody falls within the ambit of fair use. This could be said to be addressing a content concern. In contrast, a case like *Sega v. Accolade* concerns itself with issues of monopolies and the value of competition and plurality in software development. This could be said to be a concern with an infrastructure of knowledge production. There are a number of equivalent examples in Indian Fair dealing law. Sec. 52(1)(j) of the Act allows for version recordings to be made. This is with a view to promote competition within the music industry.

3. See, Contested Commons Public Report: A Public Record (New Delhi: Sarai: CSDS, 2005), vi.

4. See David Lange, Recognizing the Public Domain, 44 Law & Contemp. Probs. 147, 147, 150 (Autumn 1981); Jessica Litman, The Exclusive Right to Read, 13 Cardozo Arts & Ent. L.J. 29, 32–33 (1994); James Boyle, The Second Enclosure Movement and the Construction of the Public Domain, 66 Law & Contemp. Probs. 33, 33–74 (Winter/Spring 2003); James Boyle, Foreword: The Opposite of Property?, 66 Law & Contemp. Probs. 1 (2003); James Boyle, Shamans, Software, and Spleens: Law and the Construction of the Information Society, at x–xiii (1996); Yochai Benkler, Free as the Air to Common Use: First Amendment Constraints on Enclosure of the Public Domain, 74 N.Y.U. L. REV. 354, 364–86 (1999); Keith Aoki, (Intellectual) Property and Sovereignty: Notes Toward a Cultural Geography of Authorship, 48 Stan. L. Rev. 1293, 1333–38 (1996); Lawrence Lessig, Free Culture: How Big Media Uses Technology and the Law to Lock Down Culture and Control Creativity (New York: Penguin, 2004). But for a critique of the public domain arguments, see Anupam Chander and Madhavi Sunder, The Romance of the Public Domain, 1332 CALIFORNIA LAW REVIEW [Vol. 92:1331].

5. See Peter Drahos and John Braithwaite, Information Feudalism, (London: Norton, 2003); Susan Sell, Private Power, Public Law: The Globalization of Intellectual Property Rights (Cambridge University Press, 2003); Power and Ideas: North-South Politics of Intellectual Property and Antitrust (State University of New York Press, 1998).

6. Martha Woodmansee, The Author, Art, and the Market: Rereading the History of Aesthetics (New York: Columbia University Press, 1994); Martha Woodma-

nsee and Peter Jaszi, eds., The Construction of Authorship: Textual Appropriation in Law and Literature (Durham, N.C.: Duke University Press, 1994), 15–28; Mark Rose, Authors and Owners: The Invention of Copyright (Cambridge, Mass.: Harvard University Press, 1993).

7. Christine McLeod, Inventing the Industrial Revolution: The English Patent System, 1660–1800 (Cambridge: Cambridge University Press, 2002); "The Paradoxes of Patenting: Invention and Its Diffusion in 18th and 19th Century Britain, France, and North America," Technology and Culture, 32 (1991), 885–910; "Concepts of Invention and the Patent Controversy in Victorian Britain," in Robert Fox (ed.), Technological Change (Harwood Press, 1996), 137–53; Doron Ben Atar, Trade Secrets: Intellectual Piracy and the Origins of American Industrial Power (New Haven, Conn.: Yale University Press, 2004), http://www.cptech.org/, www.eff.org. See also www.twnside.org.sg/trade.htm.

8. Vandana Shiva, Patent, Myths and Reality (New Delhi: Penguin, 2001). For more writings by Vandana Shiva, see http://www.vshiva.net/. See also Nagesh Kumar, IPR, Technology and Economic Development: Experiences of Asian Countries, EPW Jan. 18, 2003, 209.

9. Tejaswini Niranjana (1993) "Introduction to careers of modernity," Journal of Arts and Ideas 25/26 (December): 115–126.

10. See Ravi Sundaram (1996) "Beyond the Nationalist Panopticon: The Experience of Cyberpublics in India," available at http://amsterdam.nettime.org/Lists-Archives/nettime-l-9611/msg00018.html; "Recycling Modernity: Pirate Electronic Cultures in India," *Sarai Reader* 01 93–99; "Uncanny Networks: Pirate, Urban and new Globalization," *Economic and Political Weekly* 39(1).

5

Prospects for a Global
Networked Cultural Heritage

Law versus Technology?

Stanley N. Katz

MY SUBTITLE is of course misleading. Law in itself is not against anything, and certainly it is not necessarily against the full and fair development of technology. But domestic law is an expression of national culture,
and culture is sometimes clearly against the development of technology
as a matter of national policy. The history of the United States has been a
long dialogue between culture and technology—the quickest and broad-
est development of technology has been a national cultural and legislative
priority since the early nineteenth century. The most important restraint
on such development has been the law of intellectual property, protecting
rightsholder monopoly in the name of creativity. For two hundred years
Americans learned how to subsidize technological and economic development within the constraints of trademark, patent, and copyright law, favoring creator and producer interests over those of consumers, who were presumed to benefit from the gains in creativity. This, arguably, was as true in
the knowledge industries as it was elsewhere in the economy.

But the twin revolutions in telecommunications and information
technology over the last third of the twentieth century have vastly

expanded the scope and have transformed the nature of the production, manipulation, and transmission of information. The digital universe is larger, more flexible, and more universal than the Gutenberg universe it is supplanting. One development in particular, the Internet, has swiftly created a more genuinely global environment than exists in any other sector. The concept of "information flow" is as new as the process is old—something both qualitatively and quantitatively new is taking place in the knowledge world.

Nowhere has the information and telecommunications revolution been more apparent than in issues of international security. On the one hand, we have experienced the sad spectacle of New York police officers and firefighters unable to communicate with their own forces, much less those of the other department, as a result of the failure of telephone repeaters in the World Trade Center towers on September 11, 2001, leading to a tragedy for humanity and a triumph for Al-Qaeda.

On the other hand, four years later the *Washington Post* reported that "*al Qaeda* has become the first guerilla movement in history to migrate from physical space to cyberspace":

> With laptops and DVDs, in secret hideouts and at neighborhood Internet cafes, young code-writing jihadists have sought to replicate the training, communication, planning and preaching facilities they lost in Afghanistan with countless new locations on the Internet. (*Washington Post*, 7 August 2005)

The *Post* reported that Al-Qaeda is building "a massive and dynamic online library of training materials—some supported by experts who answer questions on message boards or in chat rooms—covering such varied subjects as how to mix ricin poison, [and] how to make a bomb from commercial chemicals . . ." These sites address the younger generation in the Arab world and constitute "one big *madrassa* on the Internet." A follow-up article on the insurrectionist Abu Musab al-Zarqawi pointed out that he distributed videos and other data through an "information wing" that supports a "specially designed Web page, with dozens of links [to his videos] so users could choose which version to download."

There were large-file editions that consumed 150 megabytes for viewers with high-speed Internet and a scaled-down four-megabyte version for those limited to dial-up access. Viewers could choose Windows Media or RealPlayer. They could even download "All Religion Will Be for Allah" to play on a cell phone. Never before has a guerilla organization so successfully intertwined its real-time war on the ground with its electronic jihad.

"The technology of the Internet facilitated everything," said an al-Zarqawi site on the Internet, the Global Islamic Media Front. "Today's Web sites are 'the way for everybody in the whole world to listen to the mujaheddin.'" The *Post* quoted a security expert as saying, "Iraq is an urban combat zone. Technology is a big part of that. I don't know how to distinguish the Internet now from the military campaign in Iraq" (*Washington Post*, 9 August 2005). And both sides use the same technology. A few days later the *Post* ran a piece about the use of Web logs by U.S. soldiers in Baghdad. When Sgt. Elizabeth LeBel's Humvee was hit by a roadside bomb, she posted 1,000 words on her "little war story" at http://www.sgtlizzie.blogspot.com. Her site has received 45,000 hits in the past year. Not surprisingly, U.S. army commanders have now "required that all blogs maintained by service members be registered [and] . . . also barred bloggers from publishing classified information" (*Washington Post*, 12 August 2005).

The war in Iraq is simply one example of the failure of law to keep up with technology, but within the United States law creates the environment within which technology must exist. Many different forms of law have structured the development of communications technology and the media over the course of American history. The two most important have been the various regulatory schemes (state and federal) governing communications systems, and the laws protecting copyrighted material. The question for us now, however, is how has the role of law in the stimulation and regulation of information technology changed as a result of the twin revolutions?

In principle, there is no reason why the technologies of telecommunications and information should have changed the long-term American pattern of norms and behaviors in the law of intellectual property. We are, after all, still working from the same constitutional text, in Article I,

Section 8 of the Constitution of the United States, which gives the federal legislature authority "To promote the Progress of Science and the
useful Arts, by securing for limited Times to Authors and Inventors the
exclusive Right to their respective Writings and Discoveries." A series of
statutes and court decisions have settled the general parameters of this
limited monopoly intended to stimulate artistic and intellectual creativity, and in so doing to set the policies under which creators could profit
from this right. Should it matter that, increasingly, modes of publication
are digital rather than analog? The explicit policy of the late-twentieth-
century revision of the U.S. federal law of intellectual property (the Digital Millennium Copyright Act of 1998) was that the law of intellectual
property should apply without respect to changes in technology—and
indeed this was also the theory of our legislative revision of IP law in
1976. A strong body of opinion, especially in the commercial sector, vehemently supports this position, contending that the issue is still (and simply) the protection of creativity, though simultaneously contending that
"minor" accommodations to the old system (anticircumvention rules, for
instance) are necessary, and consistent with the traditional IP system.

But others, largely in the consumer community (and note that an
increasing number of consumers are also creators), argue that "intellectual
property" is no longer an adequate metaphor to describe the realities of
the era of digital information. Their view is that the new mechanisms in
the DMCA, along with other changes in the marketing of digital cultural
objects, constitute an essentially new IP system, one in which rightsholder
prerogatives have been strengthened at the expense of the interests of the
consumers of culture. Perhaps the best example of a parallel change consumers find threatening is the transition from sales to licensing in the marketing of digital culture. Purchasers have stronger rights and greater protection for their interests than licensees, and the practical implications for
users are profound, and not only in increased costs.

The nonprofit cultural sector has almost universally taken such a position with respect to the DCMA. The for-profit cultural sector, which has
now nominally reinvented itself as the "creative industries," is firmly in the
rightsholder intellectual property camp. But of course there are many creators in the nonprofit cultural camp, and there are also many creators in the
for-profit sector who feel that they do not sufficiently benefit from the legal

position of the firms that produce and distribute their products. The cultural property world is as messy as any other. But the politics of the debate over networked digital culture are generally polarized bilaterally and asymmetrically, with user nonprofits set against producer/distributor for-profits.

At least this is how it seems to someone who has spent the past twenty years struggling to help create a national and international networked cultural heritage system. When I became president of the American Council of Learned Society (ACLS), our national humanities organization, in 1986, I felt that my initial duty was to identify the national and international policy issues on which the U.S. humanities community had to focus. Although I was and am a techno-nerd, I quickly came to the opinion that we faced one overwhelmingly opportunity and challenge—the information technology/telecommunications revolution on the creation and communication of arts and humanities knowledge. It seemed clear that nearly everything was changing—libraries, publishing, the conditions for scholarly creativity, the possibilities of scholarly communication generally, the accessibility of sound and image, and cultural preservation.

While my humanities Learned Society constituents did not yet agree with me in the mid-1980s, it was not hard to find allies in the library, computer science, and early-adopter humanities worlds. We soon formed a coalition (initiated by the Coalition for Networked Information, ACLS, and the Getty Art History Information Project) that we called the National Initiative for a Networked Cultural Heritage (NINCH). Our idea was to create a space for the digital arts and humanities communities, to better understand the implications of the digisphere for the development of our fields and institutions, and to explore the ways in which our emerging interconnectedness could be expanded and exploited. The original coalition was based heavily on the academic research library community (represented by the Association of Research Libraries), parts of the arts world (the Getty and the Association of American Museums), some of the larger humanities associations (especially the College Art Association and the American Historical Association), a few federal agencies (especially the Smithsonian Institution and the Library of Congress), and a significant number of smaller institutions. While we called NINCH a "national" initiative, the organization was in fact fairly successful in networking, especially to Europe.

We did not have at the outset a clear view of either strategic objectives or short-term tactics. Our sense was that we were related communities that had not collaborated fully in the past, communities for whom the digital environment created both the opportunity and necessity for working together. But it did not take us long to realize that an external agenda was being set for us, because NINCH was starting up just as the Geneva WIPO negotiations were heating up. ACLS, like the Association of Research Libraries, was then represented in the CONFU (U.S. Department of Commerce, Conference on Fair Use) discussions. The question of fair use seemed a proxy for the sorts of IP issues that were basic to humanities involvement in digital cultural heritage, but what we learned at CONFU was that even collectively we did not have the clout to get a hearing for our concerns, much less the power to stand up to the large commercial entities in the communications, software, and entertainment industries that dominated the discussion (and later the framing of the DMCA). Interestingly, up to that point in time neither the universities nor the cultural nonprofits had been much interested in IP policy. We had allowed the library community to carry our IP water, and the ARL in particular had traditionally done well by us. But by the early 1990s our concerns ranged far beyond "fair use," "first sale," and the other longtime library issues. And yet the universities, which had long since recognized their financial interest in patent law developments, did not see the emerging relevance of copyright law to their core concerns. The AAU took several years before taking the issue seriously. And by then the DMCA was a *fait accompli*, the Sonny Bono Act (properly known as the U.S. Copyright Term Extension Act of 1998) had come and gone, and our task was to accommodate ourselves to the New World IP Order. Meanwhile, by about 2002 or 2003, even though we had successfully expanded to include the art museum community, it had become clear that the cultural heritage community could not sustain even the modest overhead expenses of NINCH, which set into the digital sunset.

Which is where the nonprofit networked cultural heritage community is now. In many ways, of course, a global networked cultural heritage is thriving. More and more cultural information of all kinds is either being digitized or created in digital form; networks are wider, faster, and more dense; there is greater access to the Internet worldwide; and there is a heightened understanding of the significance of the cultural digisphere. Most cultural institutions now have a presence on the Internet, and some of them are creative and interactive in the kinds of information they display, although too many (especially museums) view their Web sites as little more than marketing tools. Culture is expressed in an increasing number of languages, though English is still dominant. Improved searching technologies enable us to find relevant information, and some of it is even being archived (though this remains a huge cultural challenge). Image and, increasingly, sound are moving to the fore. When I think back a decade, I realize that all of this far exceeds the expectations of the founders of NINCH.

Are we having fun? No. Why is it that I do not feel good about the current state of global information flows? Mainly because I believe that we have not been able to get a handle on the sorts of legal constraints that preoccupied NINCH from the start. It is fascinating to think that although the organization was not built in contemplation of participating in the intellectual property wars, IP almost immediately became the principal factor defining our agenda. The simple fact of the matter is that the U.S. legal regime imposes severe constraints on the development of a vigorous and extensive networked cultural heritage domain. I do not argue, and am not arguing here, for an entirely open access/public domain world. I believe that rights of creators should be respected, and that creativity should be rewarded economically. But I do hold with those who believe that the laws of IP currently reflect a hardening of rightsholder dominance in a manner that is not based on the original constitutional principle of offering limited protection to creators. The examples are too numerous and obvious for me to mention, but suffice it to say that I think that rightsholders, unreasonably afraid of giving up more than they realize they are conceding, are restricting access to cultural objects that are crucial to the digital cultural heritage—recent works of literature and music, artistic images, and much more. We will see, for instance, whether the current discussion with the U.S. Copyright Office about "orphaned works" leads to a thoughtful resolution of an important cultural access question. Permit me to doubt that it will.

The refusal to sell digital information and the unwillingness to archive it reliably constitute another important range of problems. The funding necessary to digitize, archive, and transmit the cultural heritage is an increasing problem for the nonprofit sector. The much-heralded space for nonprofit–commercial joint enterprises is being oversold, because it will work for only a narrow range of cultural objects. As Americans, I suppose we should not be surprised that law reflects the dominant economic interests in the society, but I do not think we have yet come to terms with the ways in which the current law of intellectual property stands athwart the development of local digital culture—and, by extension, global digital culture.

Not that there are not additional problems in the global information environment. We are surrounded by them. Let me briefly mention two. The first is the Google Books project. This is a vastly ambitious commercial project by the leading U.S. search engine site. Or at least Google used to be no more than the world's best digital indexer of material already on the Web. But now Google has decided to convert analog content to digital form by entering into agreement with five of the largest international libraries. The basic idea is to digitize and index everything, and to display for free anything in the public domain, while displaying such "snippets" of copyright-protected materials as "fair use" will permit. The company asserts that its mission is "to organize the world's information," nothing less. It admits that "much of that information isn't yet online. Google Books aims to get it there by putting book content where you can find it most easily—right in your Google search results" (www.print.google. com/googleprint/about.html).

So who could be against such a public-spirited effort to stimulate the global flow of information? Rightsholders, which is to say publishers. The first group of publishers to respond was the academics, the Association of American University Presses, which in May 2005 called the Google effort "a broad-sweeping violation of the Copyright Act."

The fact is Google Books Library Project appears to be built on a gigantic fair use claim, which we think is questionable at best. If the fair use is not valid, it could be a gigantic copyright violation. There are fundamental questions about copyright that need to be answered.

Could the Association of American Publishers be far behind? Hardly. A month after the AAUP letter of protest to Google, President Pat Schroeder of AAP weighed in with a letter to Google asking for a six-month moratorium on digitization until the fair use issue could be settled. Two months later, in early August, Google announced that it would not scan (i.e., digitize) any copyrighted books until November to allow for time for discussion with the publishers. Here we have two corporate behemoths (Google is the most successful IPO in many years, after all) going against each other, with the larger entity apparently displaying contempt for assertions of rightsholder prerogatives. The AAP was reduced to alleging that the Google "procedure places the responsibility for preventing infringement on the copyright owner rather than the user, and turns every [sic] principle of copyright on its ear" (*New York Times*, 12 August 2005).

Think about what is involved here. Google is attempting to digitize large quantities of copyrighted material and is offering publishers the opportunity to withhold consent for "snippets" to be displayed (along with links to publishers' online sales portals); publishers say that permission must be granted before display. Rights before efficiency. Whatever one's view of the legal niceties (or of economics, for admittedly a lot of money is potentially at stake here), this is a dispute that simply could not have occurred at any earlier point in U.S. history. What is new is that a leading telecommunications corporation thinks that it can profit hugely by making information available without cost. The publishers are simply contending that the cost is being shifted to the "rightsholders." Who's on first?

And it is not only the property owners who are complaining. The Europeans are now telling us that Google is fomenting an international culture war. The head of the Bibliothèque nationale de France, M. Neanneney, is opposing the creation of the Google Library: "It is not a question of despising Anglo-Saxon views. . . . It is just that in the simple act of making a choice, you impose a certain view of things. . . . I favor a multipolar view of the world in the 21st century. I don't want the French Revolution retold just by books chosen by the United States." He also didn't want the story told in the English language, I assume. But, more positively, he is undertaking a project to make twenty-two French periodicals and newspapers dating back to the nineteenth century available in digital form on the Internet. Later, the European Union jumped into the war on the side of the French and announced a European text digitization project, which should remind us that cultural and linguistic nationalism have not been abolished by the Internet. To the contrary, they have simply found new sites for expression. And we know that national attempts to regulate speech on the Internet have the potential to disrupt cultural communication much more generally.

But a much more important concern is signaled by the current debate over the UNESCO Draft Convention on the Protection of the Diversity of Cultural Contents and Artistic Expressions. This came out of the 2003 UNESCO General Conference, and it is currently being debated by the member states. The Preamble of the Draft Convention affirms the "fundamental right of all individuals and societies to share in the benefits of diversity and dialogue as primary features of culture, as the defining characteristics of humanity." It ups the ante of the discussion by analogizing cultural diversity to biological diversity, as the "mainspring of sustainable development." The Preamble recognizes that "cultural diversity is nurtured by constant exchanges between cultures, and that it has always been a result of the free flow of ideas by word and image." It reaffirms that:

... freedom of thought, expression and information, and its corollary, pluralism of the media, ensure that cultural expressions may flourish within societies, and that the greatest possible number of individuals may have access thereto.

And it recognizes the "fundamental right of social groups and societies, in particular of members of minorities and indigenous peoples, to create, disseminate and distribute their cultural goods . . . to have access thereto, and to benefit there from for their own development." It emphasizes the "vital role of the creative act" and the role of creators, "whose work needs to be endowed with appropriate intellectual property rights."

So far so good, but the drafters are convinced that although "cultural goods and services are of both an economic and a cultural nature," "they must not be treated as ordinary merchandise or consumer goods." And now we get to the moment of truth: "while the processes of globalization, which have been facilitated by the rapid development of information and communication technologies, afford unprecedented conditions for enhanced interaction between cultures, these same processes also constitute a threat to diversity and carry with them a risk of impoverishing expressions" (Preamble, Preliminary draft of a convention on the protection of the diversity of cultural contents and artistic expression, Paris, July 2004).

Why such concern about cultural diversity? There seem to be two separate reasons. The first is the fear of major countries that their national cultures (including national languages) under globalization will be swamped by either particular foreign cultures (for which here read: the American entertainment industry, especially films and TV) or by the homogenizing force of market-driven global culture. France is the poster child for this response, though Canada is not far behind, and it is embodied in the famous *exception culturelle*. The second reason is the desire of many countries, especially those in the developing world, to protect the cultures of indigenous peoples from being commodified and appropriated by corporate interests. The underlying theory of free trade (and neo-liberalism) is, after all, that of international capitalism, and in principle protectionism of any kind threatens the free exchange of property. Should cultural protectionism be an exception?

As an article in the 2 March 2005 *International Herald Tribune* put it, France and Canada seek protection beyond that gained in the last round of global trade liberalization:

> By enshrining cultural diversity in a legally binding UNESCO convention, they hope to shield culture from the free trade rules of the Geneva-based World Trade Organization. Why France and Canada? Both countries view cultural independence as an essential part of their political identity. . . . In contrast, as the world's largest exporter of movies, television programs and other audiovisual products, the United States can only lose from any restriction on cultural exchange. . . . While supporting the principle of cultural diversity, [the U.S.] warned that "controlling cultural or artistic expres-

sions is not consistent with respect for human rights or the free flow of information." It further noted: "Mounting trade barriers, including efforts to prevent the free flow of investment and knowledge, is not a valid way to promote cultural liberty or diversity since such measures reduce choices."

Well, here we have globalization and culture caught in a web of contradictions. What does this mean in terms of legal public policy for culture? The "principle of balance, openness and proportionality" of the Draft Convention (Art. 2, sec. 8) says that nations adopting measures to support national cultural diversity must also commit themselves to guaranteeing "openness to the other cultures of the world." But member states have the right to adopt financial and regulatory measures to protect and promote diversity of local cultural expression, and, to that end, they may subsidize local culture through public financial aid.

One does not have to think long about the Draft Convention in order to perceive conflicts of law, economy, and culture inherent in its framework. How does one reconcile WTO standard of free trade with the suggested norms of cultural protection in the Draft Convention? It contains explicit solicitude for minorities and indigenous peoples within nations, and implicit support for cultural nationalism. Is one man's (one nation's) information flow another man's (nation's) Sword of Damocles? Should a combination of intellectual property and free trade law be permitted to ensure the rule of the wealthiest national cultures in a networked cultural heritage infrastructure? Perhaps international law should protect and nurture local cultures? If so, should cultural rights trump (intellectual) property rights? Should international law protect national cultures?

I have been asked to raise the question of the role of cultural heritage in the context of global information flows. This little essay intends to do no more than to moot the question, and to suggest that it is ripe for fuller investigation. My intention here is simply to challenge us to think locally and to ask what the role of the cultural sector might be in shaping the legal environment for the global flow of information. I remind you that everything that is global happens somewhere at some time. My suggestion is that the sector has not been effective in pressing its case within the United States, and to argue that we also need to consider how what we do nationally relates to what needs to be done internationally. The underlying dilemma is the near-total domination of the global information environment by commercial interests, and the definition of information rights as property rights. Those of us who are enormously optimistic about the role of information and communications technology for cultural development believe that the sun is appearing on a great era of global cultural networking. But as Benjamin Franklin remarked at the Philadelphia Constitutional Convention, we cannot be sure whether that sun is rising or setting.

6

The Cultural Exception to Trade Laws

C. Edwin Baker

Preliminary Comments

Organizers of the discussion to which this chapter contributes asked whether "'flow' [is] the right metaphor to analyze digital information." Although "flow" might suggest to some a natural physical rather than a human interactive process and although scientists rightfully must consider the former, the more important democratic and social concern and the concern that should provide direction even to the scientists is the quality and nature of the latter. Another term in the conference title, "information," however, is more problematic and biased. A focus on "information" encourages fetishistic notions such as the view I hear occasionally that "information is power," a view no better than the notion ridiculed by Arendt that "power grows out of the barrel of gun."[1] It is a view that frequently misguides positivist social science which does not see that the serious matters are the questions and values that provide the basis for any interest in information.[2] Information, like a commodity, is something that in itself is inert but that can be transferred from one person to another. It is not the key element, however, when the Internet is considered from the perspective of either democratic or communications theory. When I e-mail a friend asking, "Where should we meet for dinner?" I do communicate information—I communicate that I know some English, which she probably already knew, that I believe we are meeting for dinner but at a yet-to-be-determined location, and that I am interested in her view on that issue. But to identify "information" as the important feature of this e-mail is to emphasize the most commodified and, for many purposes, the least important feature of my activity. The activity here is participation in a communicative interaction, in which information and flow are parts, but the important aspect from most value perspectives is the interpersonal activity. To emphasize information would be like describing the law, upheld by the Supreme Court in *Erie v. Pap's AM*,[3] that required dancers to wear at least pasties and G-strings, as being about textiles and not about the expressive activity of nude dancing. Both digital formats and Internet-type communications are used in many activities that are ill described by the term "information." Much better for describing the interaction, but still sometimes unedifying, might be the more inclusive term "communication," which includes the more politically or sociologically important activities of choosing, sending, and receiving.

Of course, the new digital technologies change and enlarge opportunities in social life. As the ease and expense of activities change—here, for the most part, go down—their occurrence will change. The social and normative significance of these changes can be variable. Consider two examples. These new technologies have at times facilitated politics, allowing easier delivery of salient motivational and organizing communications (of which factual information is often an important but seldom the sole element) that sometimes have led to expressive street activities that have in turn even played central roles in bringing down governments. In general, taking my cue from Brandeis's admonition that "the greatest menace to freedom is an inert people,"[4] I count this development mostly as a plus. In contrast, my experience tentatively suggests that one consequence of student use of the Internet has been student papers containing increased amounts of trivial information that to some degree displaces references to, and consideration of, better-quality writing and, even more important, shows less careful and original thought about the meaning or significance of information in the paper. Of course, this need not happen—the paper could have better information with no reduction in other qualities. Still, the change in the "cost" of one element that goes into a paper could predictably lead to this unwanted change.

More relevant for what follows, the normative and evaluative significance of changes in the difficulty and expense of a particular activity is likely to vary with context. Cultural contexts, for example, vary in whether isolation from a broader world or colonization by outside interests presents the greater threat to the welfare of members of the given culture. The relevant economic observation is that the first threat is potentially reduced and the second potentially increased because of the increased ease of transmission of cultural materials or participation in cultural activities. With this thought I will turn to making several observations, and drawing several distinctions, in reference to four topics relevant to trade in cultural or communication products: culture, economics, protectionism, and legal policy.

Culture: Two Comments and Two Distinctions

Culture's importance for human life merits some brief comment. First, following observations well developed by Will Kymlicka, for many persons, engagement in an effective, operative, living culture in which they learn of human practices may be essential for a healthy identity, autonomy, and the experience of life having meaning.[5] Experiences of cultural loss or major disruptions to a person's culture can not only be impoverishing but can lead literally to suicide—or more generally to a loss of confidence and sense of value and meaning. Any liberal must recognize that a cultural "home" is often a central element of the context that makes autonomy or meaningful individual choice possible.[6] Second, although possibly somewhat more controversially, cultural diversity is a significant public good. It can add resilience and resources to human civilization almost as, biologists report, genetic variety can for nonhuman animal species. Likewise, many find that cultural diversity can add to the quality of human experience—as illustrated by the delight many people have long taken in cultural tourism or sampling.

Kymlicka stresses a distinction between orientations toward culture. First is what may be described as a fundamentalist valuation—something American critics often accuse, usually unfairly, the French of promoting. The fundamentalist ideal is "preservation"—a closed culture that restricts as much as possible outside, and often inside, forces of change. I describe this as the "museum" view of culture because, in effect, it would make the inhabitants museum specimens for whom change is, to the extent possible, forbidden. Second is a liberal conception that emphasizes culture's openness to change. This liberal conception affirms community members' individual as well as collective right to change their culture and their cultural commitments but recognizes that the very possibility of exercising this freedom often can depend on a secure cultural grounding.

The other significant distinction here is between activities and commodities—or between doing and consuming culture. Neither should be disdained. Still, for many purposes, "doing" may be most significant. Like education, involvement in cultural creation and cultural practices produces meaningful personal experiences and increases not only personal but also collective capacities that are beneficial to members of the community beyond the individual actor.[7] Moreover, those benefits accrue whether or not the activity produces commodities that sell in markets. It would be a crabbed and uninformative economics that valued these cultural activities solely on the basis of the market value of its output. George Gerbner, communications scholar, activist, and former dean of the Annenberg School for Communication, captured the distinction's importance when he argued that the quality of society declines sharply when children hear stories primarily from people with something to sell rather than people—usually parents, teachers, or friends—with something to tell.

Economics

Probably the economically most significant feature of intellectual products, including many cultural products, is a high creation (first copy) cost as compared with low (or nonexistent) costs for subsequent copies. The consequences of this feature most relevant here are, first, a tendency toward competitive dominance of larger-audience products. Generally an average consumer would prefer to receive at a given price a creation on which more attention or resources have been lavished. At a given cost in terms of price or time, audience members will tend to prefer an expensive product to a cheaply produced product. The first typically attracts the larger audience. In this scenario, the large audience pays for the high-cost, presumably high-quality, first copy. Second, as long as price discrimination is not costless and complete, the market will not produce some of these products that, collectively, people do or would value (as measured by their willingness and ability to pay) more than they cost. Third, competition from the large products first described can cause additional products to fall in the second described category. Competition from the expensively produced products can reduce the demand for other products, newly making products unprofitable even though they still would be valued at more than their cost. That is, introducing a blockbuster (expensive) product can cause a downward shift in the demand for alternative products, and this shift can make some of those alternative products unprofitable (without perfect price discrimination) even if the products are still valued more than they cost. In fact, this impact of competition sometimes will occur even though the successful product generates less surplus (value over resources used) than the products that it competitively displaced would produce. In these circumstances competition would directly cause increased economic inefficiency.

Fourth is an issue suggested by Gerbner and brilliantly developed in a legal context by Yochai Benkler in his discussion of copyright.[8] As long as the only significant economic effect of a legal or technical change is to reduce costs, the change might seem at first unambiguously beneficial. But reflection shows that this is not so clear. Commercial production of cultural products often competes with noncommercial production. Both commercial and noncommercial forms are valuable and inevitable. Thus, a change that reduced costs even if it advantaged one more than the other would seem unambiguously good—and would be largely irrelevant for policy purposes—except for two facts. Cost reductions or increased ease of production that differentially benefit either commercialized or noncommercialized production affects their respective competitive position—the share of people's attention, often described in the commodified term of market share, of the form most benefited would predictably increase. Moreover, as is likely, commercial and noncommercial production systematically may have different degrees of positive and negative externalities. If the competitively disadvantaged form of production generally generated either higher surplus value or greater net positive externalities, competition could cause a change that allows for cost reduction or greater ease in production to actually lead to a net social loss. If alternative legal or technical changes (or legal responses to technological changes) are possible, the choice between them raises the policy issue of which is most valuable. Troublingly, the market provides no basis to make the comparison. Even if the market gives some evidence of the changes' value in respect to commercial production, it offers no measure of the value of the actual or potential benefit or harm to noncommodified production. Similar points might be made about how legal or technological changes can affect competition between more individually or locationally specific production and collective and diffused noncommercial production.[9]

Economists' tendency to equate profits with welfare efficiency merely clouds the issue.[10] Given inevitable competition between forms of production and consumption combined with the potential of competition to cause the failure of the most valuable creative activities, a technological innovation that decreases the cost or increases the ease of one form of cultural production, by advantaging that form, could have a net effect of reducing social welfare. Certainly, there is no guarantee that the new result of competition is the best available. Particularly to be feared, I suggest (but have not demonstrated), are changes that lead to less participation by people in a community in cultural production and to an increase in the relative extent of commercialized production. Moreover, these observations are exacerbated if the technological or legal change—copyright was Benkler's example—that reduces costs for or increases benefits of one form of production increases costs of another form.

Expanded use of digital technologies and the Internet has affected many market and nonmarket activities—such as the activity of political discussion and organizing mentioned earlier. However, for the present discussion probably the most important economic consequence is that they make *distribution* of (or, from the consumer perspective, access to) cultural products easier and cheaper. Reduced distribution costs will tend to have two somewhat conflicting effects on the type of cultural product produced and consumed. First, the decrease in *this* cost should increase the economic role of high first copy/low subsequent copy effect. The reduced distribution cost should encourage mega-products and greater audience concentration.[11] Second, this reduced cost should encourage production of new products that previously were not profitable (even if earlier they were also valued at more than their cost) and of noncommodified or noncommercial cultural products by those who do not seek an economic return and for whom subsidized production is possible given the elimination or drastic reduction of distribution costs. This second effect provides the ground for many of the romantic visions about new abundances and empowerments flowing from online digital technologies—but the first foretells the possibility of problematically increased concentration of audience attention on relatively few sites in the online world. The net result may be both greater dominance of audiences by a few commercial giants and greater availability of diverse content for those ready to seek it. Academics and visionaries who tend to fall into the second group should not blind themselves to the likelihood of—in fact, the empirical evidence suggesting—the first effect. Still, for both economic and democratic reasons that I do not try to develop here, policy might be well designed to seek to enhance the second effect as compared with the first.

Protectionism: Strong and Weak

Protectionist cultural trade policies take a wide variety of forms. At least in the cultural and media context, a useful, policy-relevant qualitative distinction can be made between strong and weak protectionism. Strong protectionism strives to keep out either all or certain categories of foreign "culturally polluting" material or, when this is not possible, to seriously limit its circulation. Weak or soft protectionism constitutes policies that systematically burden without eliminating or aiming to eliminate foreign access to the domestic market, often with the burden specifically designed to help subside local cultural material. Keeping foreign content out is neither a goal nor a dominant effect of weak protectionism.

The most extreme version of strong protectionism bars imports and adopts other rules and practices, such as limitations on television or radio receivers that can be tuned to foreign broadcasting or jamming electronic transmissions or filtering Internet content, aimed at that exclusionary result. More targeted versions of strong protectionism are also possible. Requiring an import license for each specific video, audio, or written program or publication that involves censorial content judgments is an example. Similarly, the aim of reducing the presence of foreign content, for instance by limiting the number of import licenses given per year, also illustrates strong protectionism. Sufficiently high tariffs may achieve a similar exclusionary goal of allowing elite access without creating mass cultural pollution (or unwanted political ideas).

Weak protectionism, on the other hand, should not be understood as merely a quantitatively watered-down version of strong protectionism. Rather than being merely further down a protectionism continuum, it is a qualitatively different type of policy implemented mostly by different types of rules. As noted, it does not aim to keep foreign culture out but rather to promote local culture. Examples of weak protectionism include taxing sales of imports more than domestic content or even taxing sales of both but using the revenue to subsidize only local content or cultural endeavors. Likewise, screen or play time quotas that impose no limit on presentation of foreign material but require proportionate presentation of local material in effect props up the market for local material. Theaters can always show profitable foreign content as long as they are willing to show, even at a loss, domestic content. The policy thereby uses the former, the foreign, to "subsidize" the latter, the domestic. Soft protectionism can also take the form of legal rules biasing advertising expenditures toward supporting domestic rather than foreign cultural or media materials.[12] These supports for domestic or local culture can receive a variety of justifications. As the discussion of market failures in the media or cultural context suggests, these justifications will be shown below to often be fully consistent with the liberal premise of respect for individual choice.

Liberal and Democracy-Oriented Trade Policies

A closed or museum culture requires keeping out foreign cultural materials just as many authoritarian states often seek to keep out foreign media that show advantages of non-authoritarian (or alternative authoritarian) political regimes. If such a repressive accomplishment is not feasible, the goal is at least to reduce circulation of foreign material as much as possible, especially among the broader public. Thus, cultural preservation from this museum cultural perspective maps onto the policy of strong protectionism almost perfectly. Often critics of cultural protectionism assume that this museum concept of culture provides the only justification—other than the economic goal of advantaging a politically powerful domestic industry or overtly serving authoritarian ends—for any deviation from "free" trade in the media or cultural spheres. These critics then rightly proceed to show both the illiberality and ultimate futility of cultural protectionism so conceived. Nevertheless, most democratic countries that pursue cultural preservation neither have this exclusionary aim nor adopt strong protectionist measures.

Weak protectionists do not deny that its citizens value, benefit from, and should receive outside media content. Such content can provide material vital for cultural and political development. Any bar on its import, as is implicit in strong protectionism, would be a significant violation of international human rights law[13]—and that human rights law provides the arena in which objections to restraints on cultural imports should be debated. However, these international rights should not provide an objection to weak protectionism. A country's use of taxes, tariffs, subsidies, or similar legal policies attempts to structure beneficially an inherently artificial economic realm—a realm that necessarily takes its form on the basis of legal choices implicit in the design of property rights, contractual options, and income distributions. As to this world of commerce, a polity has the responsibility to craft rules that it believes best serve human interests, both consumptive and, hopefully, democratic interests.

My claim is that weak cultural protectionism can be fully consistent with, and in some circumstances arguably required by, a liberal commitment to promotion of individual choice and autonomy. As noted, two economic features of intellectual or media products support this claim. First, the mostly mega-products of international trade will increase competition's tendency to displace smaller market products (and, here, specifically domestic products) despite these smaller products' being valued more than they cost. Competition can do this even when the displaced products produce more surplus value than the imported products. Second, international trade also creates new marketing windows that increase opportunities for comparatively easy price discrimination that exacerbates this effect of displacing products that produce considerable surplus value with goods that produce little if any. That is, a mere desire for a market to ideally serve people's money-backed preferences can justify weak protectionism.

Weak protectionism can also serve a healthy democratic order. In most contexts, local media are more likely than foreign media to provide positive democratic externalities—to serve the media's democratic watchdog function and to participate in and inform domestic political discourse. Likewise, local media can both help teach, and equally relevantly be part of a cultural group's implicit discussion of, self or group identity. For many people, local media support and help provide the secure context from which meaningful choice is possible as well as the understanding necessary for wisely choosing changes. In addition to these market-improving pro-democratic effects, any egalitarian commitment to serve all people's cultural, identity, and political needs should see even a market perfectly responsive to money-backed preferences—with its implicit one-dollar/one-vote weighting—as an improper measure of and inadequate response to individual preferences. The market exacerbates this problem by its inherent tendency to provide more for dominant cultural positions because of their larger or richer set of consumers over which the market firm can spread first copy costs. Weak protectionism can improve responsiveness to the claims of these groups not well served by the market.[14] And as long as the weak protectionism is enacted by a democratically legitimate political order, the presumption must be that it represents responsiveness to a one-person/one-vote measure of people's preferences in place of the less egalitarian (arguably less legitimate) dollar-backed measure.

All these considerations point to the legitimacy of subsidizing some otherwise marginal local cultural content and improving its competitive position relative to materials with larger audiences over whom first copy costs are spread or which are better able to price discriminate. These considerations go to liberal and egalitarian affirmative valuations of a historically grounded but changing culture as a context of individual choice. They go to the economic welfare maximization goals. That is, they provide a reason to support weak protectionism as a trade policy in the media realm and a cultural exception to international trade agreements.

A contextual asymmetry in this argument should be noted. The idea of an open culture as well as democratic needs that sometimes justifies weak protectionist measures can at other times justify virtually the opposite. Weak protectionism does not deny that people in all countries can value and benefit from culturally alien content as well as from foreign informational content. Rather, its premise relates to specific qualities of markets in intellectual or cultural content that can lead to the competitive failure of more valuable—and in the foregoing argument, domestic—cultural material and activities. Nevertheless, whether free trade oversupplies foreign and undermines more valuable domestic content is contextually variable. This damaging consequence of free trade is more likely the smaller and poorer the country. The opposite "inefficiency" is also possible. The market may supply people in some countries less foreign material than they want as measured by the economic standard of willingness and ability to pay. At times, these foreign materials may be more valuable than the domestic content that displaces them. Weak protectionism may further disadvantage already economically disadvantaged foreign content.

Debates surrounding the MacBride Commission and a New World Information Order once emphasized this point about asymmetries—namely, that an imbalance existed in which the developed world received inadequate information about the South.[15] (And because news agencies of the North dominated, especially in cross-national contexts, countries of the South often received inadequate information about and from its neighbors—and sometimes about itself—and instead obtained primarily news filtered through the economic lens and, hence, content interests of the North!) Very roughly, whether too much or too little imported content is the problem will correspond roughly to whether the country is a net cultural product exporter or importer. Reliance on the market would predictably result in the United States especially and maybe some regional powerhouses—potentially Brazil, India, and China—receiving insufficient imports to serve either its democratic needs or its consumer desires. Though unlikely to be politically acceptable within international trade negotiations, the ideal policy might be to allow weak protectionism but only for net cultural importing countries. In fact, except for the real likelihood of political manipulation of many forms of subsidies, people in a country like the United States could benefit from subsidizing imports—as arguably occurs to a limited extent when its public broadcasting stations present foreign (usually British) content. Certainly, both Americans and the world might benefit if the American public were more aware of both cultural and informational content from abroad. More specifically, the economic tendencies described above that sometimes justify both weak protectionism and subsidies of domestic content also suggest that markets may provide consumers in the United States and other cultural exporting countries with less foreign material than their citizens value.

Finally, two further observations might be made about this political-cultural-economic argument. First, though not spelled out, this economic argument as well as justice-based distributive values also supports variation between different states' intellectual property laws. The competing policy issues are complex, but there is no reason to think the same rules are ideal for different contexts and, hence, so-called harmonization will often be an misguided aim. Second, it should be noted that these arguments against a pure free trade regime internationally apply equally to domestic media and cultural policies. Subsidizing and otherwise favoring certain domestic cultural materials and activities, especially noncommercial content and commercial materials aimed at poorer and smaller cultural or identity groups, can lead to welfare and democratic or egalitarian gains in any country.[16] Traditional notions of free trade are warranted neither internationally nor domestically in relation to media content, just as suppression (censorship or strong protectionism) is objectionable in both contexts. Domestically, this difference is partially embodied in U.S. constitutional doctrine that permits virally all structural regulation directed specifically at the media sphere while ruling out censorship.[17] A similarly attractive result would occur in the international context if protectionism were debated in terms of human rights law rather than of trade law.

Postscript: A Global Public Sphere

Globalization presents a possible new, democracy-based argument against protectionism: Multinational corporations currently dominate the world in the interest of profits. Only international legal responses can provide adequate responses serving the interests of people. The situation parallels the American (constitutional) recognition of the necessity of federal, rather than sole reliance on state, regulation of the domestic U.S. economy. *Legitimacy* in this international regulation requires more than transparency. Major democratic deficits exist unless the international regulatory regime, whether by new entities or those such as the World Bank or International Monetary Fund, is itself subject to control by a global democratic public sphere. From these conclusions, the need for a global culture and public sphere, supported by unimpeded international trade in informational products, might be proposed.

Whatever the merits and possibilities of an eventual democratically responsive international political order, democrats might wisely conclude that, in the short to intermediate term, legal or policy power at the international level will be even more dominated by multinational corporate economic interests than it is at the domestic level. Thus, for now, possibly democratic advocates should be most oriented toward increasing the democratic quality as well as the power of more local governments. If so, communications policy should most centrally aim at promoting a more robust and democratically supportive domestic communications order. For many countries, this will include weak protectionism as well as domestic subsidy programs that would be contrary to standard free trade principles.

Even if in the long term the international order develops global democratic governmental institutions, recommendations of free trade and for a unified global cultural order may be misguided. The capacity for groups to participate in a nondominated authentic manner within any broader political or cultural discourse requires that they be grounded in an informed and secure sense of their own values and identity. Purportedly open public spheres are often actually dominated by the most power groups or interests—at least unless more marginal groups are first given the opportunity to have their own "subaltern counterpublic" spheres in which they formulate their own positions.[18] Thus, an inclusive democratic sphere presumes the existence of robust smaller public spheres in which identity groups—and nations—formulate, debate, maintain, and change their own values. This point does not deny that global government requires some form of global public sphere but does problematize its appropriate structure. The inherent economic advantages of the global commercial cultural and information products as contrasted to the value of smaller public spheres suggest that, though both are needed, free trade's tendency to give legal priority to commercial global communications firms would be misguided. In a sense, such a policy represents a misguided conception of how multiple public spheres contribute to democracy. It fails to see the necessity of nurturing smaller public spheres for each cultural (or national) group that an inclusive democratic should hope will be able to participate globally.

Notes

This essay is loosely based on previously published materials, especially C. Edwin Baker, *Media, Markets, and Democracy* Part III (2002).

1. Hannah Arendt, *On Violence* 11,52–53 (1969). She claimed, instead, that "power springs up whenever people get together and act in concert . . . ," an account not far from Jürgen Habermas's view that a public sphere results whenever people come together to speak.

2. See C. Edwin Baker, "Viewpoint Diversity and Media Ownership," 61 *Fed. Comm.L.J. 651* (2009).

3. 529 U.S.277 (2000).

4. Whitney v. California, 274 U.S. 357, 375 (927) (Brandeis and Holmes, concurring).

5. See, e.g., Will Kymlicka, *Liberalism, Community and Culture* (1989). See also Robert Post, "The Social Foundations of Privacy: Community and Self in the Common Law Tort," in Robert Post, *Constitutional Domains* 51 (1995).

6. C. Edwin Baker, "Sandel on Rawls," 133 *U. of Penn. L. Rev.* 895 (1985) (arguing Rawls argument is fully consistent with this point).

7. Cf. Jack M. Balkin, "Digital Speech and the Democratic Theory of Culture: A Theory of Freedom of Expression for the Information Society," 79 *NYU L. Rev.* 1 (2004) (emphasizing a participatory, democratic cultural theory of free speech).

8. Yochai Benkler, "Free as the Air to Common Use: First Amendment Constraints on Enclosure of the Public Domain," 74 *NYU L.Rev.* 354 (1999). The way law differentially favors or disfavors commercial as compared with noncommercial production has been a significant, innovative theme in Benkler's work. See, e.g., Yochai Benkler, "Coase's Penguin." 112 *Yale L. J.* 369 (2002).

9. See generally, Yochai Benkler, *The Wealth of Networks* (2006).

10. C. Edwin Baker, "Media Structure, Ownership Policy, and the First Amendment," 78 *S. Cal. L.Rev.* 733 (2005).

11. Hamilton reports that though online presentation makes local newspapers available anywhere, online readership of the 100 top newspapers is *more* concentrated online than in print. James T. Hamilton, *All the News That's Fit to Print: How the Market Transforms Information into News* 197 (2004). Further empirical data on this concentration effect is summarized in C. Edwin Baker, *Media Concentration and Democracy: Why Ownership Matters* (2007).

12. Canada - Certain Measure Concerning Periodicals, WT/DS31?AB/R; (97-2653); 1997 WTO DS Lexis 4 (June 30, 1997); Ted Magder, *Franchising the Candy Store: Split-Run Magazine and a New International Regime for Trade in Culture* (Canadian-American Center, U. of Maine, 1998).

13. Much international law protects the right to receive, seek, and disseminate information. See, e.g., Universal Declaration of Human Rights, art. 19; International Covenant on Civil and Political Rights, art. 19; European Convention for the Protection of Human Rights and Fundamental Freedoms, art. 10.

14. The point, however, is contextual. To the extent that an economically disfavored group identifies with people outside the country, weak protectionism could work to their disadvantage. One noted effect of the Internet is its capacity to allow some coalescing on international diasporas.

15. International Commission for the Study of Communication Problems, *Many Voices, One World* (1980) (MacBride Commission Report). See also Wolfgang Kleinwatchter, "Three Waves of the Debate," in George Gerbner, Hamid Mowlana, and Kaale Nordenstrong, ed., *The Global Media Debate: Its Rise, Fall, and Renewal* (1993).

16. James Curran, "Mass Media and Democracy: A Reappraisal," in James Curran, ed., *Mass Media and Society 3rd ed.* (2000).

17. After the Court in Turner Broadcasting System v. F.C/C., 512 U.S. 622 (1994), made clear that Miami Herald v. Tornillo, 418 U.S. 241 (19740, basically all Supreme Court (but not all lower court) challenges to structural regulation of print, broadcast, or cable media have been rejected (except, arguably, regulations that closed down a media without any pro-media justification, City of Los Angeles v. Preferred Communications, 4476 U.S. 488 (1986)) have been rejected while censorious regulation is always invalidated. See generally C. Edwin Baker, The Independent Significance of the Press Clause Under Existing Law, 35 *Hofstra L. Rev.* 955 (2007); Turner Broadcasting: Content-Based Regulation of Persons and Presses, 1994 *Sup. Ct. Rev.* 57.

18. Nancy Fraser, "Rethinking the Public Sphere: A Contribution to the Critique of Actually Existing Democracy," in Craig Calhoun (ed.), *Habermas and the Public Sphere* 109, 123, 127(1992).

II

Politics and Law

7

Weighing the Scales

The Internet's Effect on State–Society Relations

Daniel W. Drezner

HOW DOES THE INFORMATION REVOLUTION affect the relationship between governments and global civil society? Does the Internet lead to greater democratization and liberalization? The political science on this question could be best described as ambiguous.[1] This is because two very different narratives can answer this question. The more popular and prominent argument is that the Internet dramatically lowers the costs of networked communication; therefore, civil society groups are better able to mobilize action to influence governments. Countless articles have been written about how the Internet has facilitated social movements to advocate for some international treaties—like the Landmine Convention—and to block movement on other initiatives—such as the Multilateral Agreement on Investment. Decentralized forms of civil society are particularly likely to thrive with the emergence of Web 2.0[2] technologies like Facebook and Twitter; the networked structure of online communities closely mirrors the structure of global civil society. The coordination of worldwide protests that took place in the run-up to the Second Gulf War is but one example of this phenomenon. The growth of the blogosphere as a force in American politics is only the latest manifestation of this trend.

The counterargument is that states are becoming increasingly savvy in their regulation of the information revolution. The code that forms the backbone of the Internet's architecture leaves several critical nodes vulnerable to regulation by governments.[3] Discriminating governments have the capacity to decide which elements of digital information they choose to let in and which elements they can screen out. Beyond information, authoritarian governments have been willing to make life uncomfortable for the citizens who use online activities to threaten the regime in power. Governments ranging from China's to Iran's to that of Belarus have demonstrated a willingness to crack down on civil society activists and bloggers who defy the state.

These contradictory trends highlight the contradictory trends inherent in analyzing how ICT affects the art and science of politics. Does the Internet empower the coercive control of governments at the expense of citizen activists, or vice versa? As someone who has at different times advanced both sides of this argument, I fully recognize and appreciate the complexities of this question.[4] In this chapter I offer a preliminary answer—that while the Internet has probably empowered nonstate actors more than states, the effect of this empowerment is not constant across all types of political environments. In open societies, there is no question that the Internet has enhanced the power of civil society vis-à-vis the state. In dealing with totalitarian governments or international governmental negotiations, the information revolution does not fundamentally affect the state's ability to advance its interests.

There is an internal tension contained in this answer, and it comes to the surface when considering the ability of online activism to trigger an abrupt shift in public attitudes toward authoritarian states. A quiescent public dramatically lowers the costs of repression for a government. However, information technologies have the capacity to dramatically redirect the "information cascades" that promote quiescence. This forces authoritarian governments into a more stark choice than they would otherwise prefer. These governments must crack down on the global flow of information even further if they wish to protect themselves from the threat of "people power" revolts. In the process, however, they deny themselves the opportunity to exploit the vast economic potential of the information society.

This chapter is divided into five sections. The next section reviews in greater depth the contrasting takes within the political science literature regarding the effect of ICT on state–society relations. The third section discusses how the information revolution has affected transaction-cost economics. This discussion serves as a useful metaphor in understanding how ICT affects the ability of civil society to mobilize and the ability of states to repress. The fourth section examines the choice states face when encountering a civil society empowered with information technology. The final section discusses the relative brittleness of authoritarian governments in a world of information cascades.

Here Come the Smart Mobs

Scholars have generated prodigious amounts of theory and evidence to support the contention that the Internet and other communication technologies empower global civil society (GCS). Part of the logic is the compatibility of their organizational structures. Most observers argue that global civil society is organized like a network, "characterized by voluntary, reciprocal, and horizontal patterns of communication and exchange."[5] Different nodes of a network must be able to exchange information in order for this type of organization to be effective. The more dense the network—in terms of the number of nodes, connections, and diversity of participants—the more effective nonstate actors can be. One undeniable trigger for the emergence of GCS has been the persistent decline in costs of transportation and communication. The development of the Internet, the proliferation of cellular phone networks, and the deregulation of air travel enhance the networking power of global civil society.

Researchers have argued that global civil society played a crucial role in a variety of international negotiations, ranging from human rights advocacy to the Landmine Convention. Perhaps the first exemplar case is the role that transnational activist networks played in the failure of the Multilateral Agreement on Investment (MAI). The MAI was an OECD initiative launched in 1995 that would have standardized how governments could regulate foreign direct investment. A broad array of activist groups opposed the aims of the MAI and took active steps to sabotage the negotiations. Anti-MAI organizations posted draft versions of the treaty on their Web sites. Activists, representing 600 organizations from approximately 70 countries, dogged the negotiators at the OECD headquarters in Paris. In 1998, they also protested the agreement at meetings of the WTO and UNCTAD. French officials acknowledged civil society opposition as a factor in the breakdown of negotiations.[6] Stephen Kobrin concludes: "The story of the MAI is a cautionary tale about the impact of an electronically networked global civil society."[7] Other scholars studying global civil society share this assessment, though it is not without its detractors.[8]

At the domestic level, it has been commonly predicted that the information revolution empowers civil society at the expense of the state. Internet enthusiasts have long dismissed the ability of states to block specific kinds of Internet content. In 1993 John Gilmore, a co-founder of the Electronic Frontier Foundation, famously concluded: "The Net interprets censorship as damage and routes around it." Civil society activists and bloggers have played a prominent role in agitating for greater openness in repressive societies. Weblogs provided crucial information for protesters during the Ukraine's "Orange Revolution" in November and December 2004. They also provided an accessible window to global media outlets through which reporters could interpret and report on breaking news. For the protesters themselves, some blogs functioned as message boards—otherwise known as "focal points"—for coordinating street actions.

The advent of Web 2.0 technologies such as Facebook, YouTube, and Twitter has provided civil society activists with additional mechanisms for coordinating social action. In 2009, Facebook's vice president for global communications and public policy observed, "Some of the most interesting uses of Facebook have been for the purpose of social action, which is essentially political action" (quoted in Tselik 2009).[9] Twitter became a means of rapidly mobilizing flashmobs in Moldova; Facebook became an important forum for Pakistanis to discuss the future of their society.[10] In the aftermath of the June 2009 disputed presidential election in Iran, the U.S. State Department's Policy Planning Staff requested that Twitter delay its scheduled maintenance—to allow protesters to communicate with one another and the outside world. Graphic videos of Neda

Agha-Soltani being shot to death in Tehran were uploaded to YouTube, acting as a focal point for protesters in Iran. With the Iranian government imposing severe restrictions on the activities of Western media outlets, journalists began relying on Web 2.0 sources of information to supplement their news accounts. Prominent bloggers such as Andrew Sullivan and Nico Pitney acted as information aggregators of various Twitter feeds emanating from Iran.[11]

These anecdotes suggest that, under certain circumstances, online activists can affect politics in regimes where there is no thriving independent media sector. For starters, activist Web sites can become an alternative source of news and commentary in countries where traditional media are under state control. Blogs and social networking technologies are more difficult to control than television or newspapers, especially under regimes that are tolerant of some degree of free expression. Faced with various domestic obstacles, online activists based inside these countries, connected to diaspora communities based outside these countries, can try to influence foreign media, with knock-on effects at home. Margaret Keck and Kathryn Sikkink note in *Activists Beyond Borders* that activists who are unable to change conditions in their own countries can leverage their power by taking their case to transnational activists, who in turn publicize abuses and lobby their governments. Keck and Sikkink call this a "boomerang effect," because repression at home can lead to international pressure against the regime from abroad. Indeed, the advent of Web 2.0 technologies allows many online activists to make direct appeals to the global public sphere, bypassing editorial gatekeepers in traditional media outlets.

The State Strikes Back

Despite the apparent symbiosis between the growth of the information society and global civil society, other scholars have pointed out that repressive states have been able to control information technologies more effectively than previously thought. Technological measures to regulate the Internet include the creation of firewalls and proxy servers, routers, and software filters to block content deemed undesirable. Non-technological measures include the imprisonment of relevant individuals, active policing, high taxation, and pressuring Internet service providers (ISPs).[12] Even if these measures are not 100 percent effective, their enactment affects the cost/benefit analysis of activists seeking to use the Internet as a means of acquiring officially frowned-upon content. As Jack Goldsmith and Timothy Wu have observed, "if governments can raise the cost of Internet transactions, they can regulate Internet transactions, even if the regulation is imperfect."[13] Combined, these steps can block undesired content as well as retard Internet use.

The result has been effective government regulation of Internet content across countries. For totalitarian states, the modes of regulation have been historically crude but effective. Cuba simply outlaws the sale of personal computers to individuals; until 2002, Myanmar outlawed the personal ownership of modems.[14] The Syrian government has arrested numerous citizens for using the Internet to send information about government demonstrations.[15] Saudi Arabia censors the Internet by requiring all Web access to be routed through a proxy server that the government edits for content, blocking access to pornographic, religious, and politically sensitive material.[16] An assessment of the Saudi filtering system concluded that substantial amounts of Web content are effectively inaccessible from Saudi Arabia. Similarly successful Internet restrictions have been imposed in countries as diverse as Tunisia and Vietnam.[17]

Cross-national studies provide strong support for the argument that authoritarian and totalitarian regimes have been successful in mitigating the spread of the Internet. One 2001 study found that the combined Internet bandwidth used by eight Arab countries was roughly equal to that used by 500 cable modem subscribers in the United States. Richard Beilock and Daniela Dimitrova found that countries with lower Freedom House scores for civil liberties had significantly lower Internet usage—even after controlling for economic development. Helen Milner's research into Internet diffusion yields similar results. Using multiple measures of regime type, time series cross-sectional regressions demonstrate that, *ceteris paribus*, democracies permit much greater online access, both in terms of Internet users per capita and Internet hosts per capita.[18]

State control over the Internet goes beyond crude repression techniques, however. Authoritarian states with a greater interest in maximizing economic growth have—to date—succeeded in restricting political content on the Internet without sacrificing its commercial possibilities. Singapore would be the exemplar for this sort of regulatory framework; its government has been eager to attract foreign investment in information technologies. At the same time, a 1996 law required all political parties, religious organizations, and any individuals with Web pages discussing either religion or politics to register with the Singapore Broadcasting Authority.[19] Singapore's approach has been the model for many East Asian governments, including China's.[20] Starting in 2000, China passed a series of laws criminalizing the production or consumption of "unauthorized" political content.[21] In July 2002, China was able to persuade more than 300 Internet service providers and Web portals, including Yahoo!, to sign a voluntary pledge refraining from "producing, posting, or disseminating pernicious information that may jeopardize state security and disrupt social stability."[22] The central government also rerouted attempts to access search engines like Google to search engines owned or regulated by the government.[23]

State efforts at censorship have also succeeded in disrupting Web 2.0 technologies when it serves government interests. Governments can stymie their citizens' access to a large fraction of the blogosphere by filtering out standardized blog domains such as Blogger and Typepad. In 2005, China required all bloggers with independent Web sites to register with the government. Microsoft, acceding to the Chinese regime's request, also blocked blog entries that contained words like "freedom," "democracy," "human rights," and "demonstration."[24] Google and Yahoo! took similar steps.

Increasingly, however, coercive governments are learning how to turn Web 2.0 technologies to their advantage. By monitoring social networking sites like LiveJournal, Belarusian authorities were able to end the use of "smart mob" tactics in 2006; as Evgeny Morozov observes, "social media created a digital panopticon that thwarted the revolution; its networks, transmitting public fear, were infiltrated and hopelessly outgunned by the power of the state. . . . The emergence of new digital spaces for dissent also [led] to new ways of tracking it."[25] Similarly, the Iranian government struck back at Green Revolution protesters by identifying their leadership through their use of Facebook and Twitter. Expatriates who criticized the regime discovered that their relatives still in Iran faced persecution.[26] Nor is this activity limited to authoritarian states—the Israeli military has formed a unit to combat anti-Israeli rhetoric on Web 2.0 platforms.[27]

A Transaction Costs Metaphor

As the previous section suggests, parsing out how ICT affects the tug-of-war between states and civil society activists is exceedingly difficult. Metaphorically, the problem is akin to the one economists face when predicting how the communications revolution would affect the optimal size of the firm. Beginning with Ronald Coase, economists have argued that individuals face transaction costs when they use the market, and that these costs determine the optimal size of firms.[28] Transaction costs can range from the time spent searching for more information about prices, costs, and the reputations of other buyers and sellers. If these costs of market exchange exceed those of more hierarchical governance structures—that is, firms—then hierarchy is the optimal choice.

As communication costs have fallen over the past years and decades, the obvious prediction from transaction costs economics would have been a concomitant decline in the optimal size of the firm.[29] There were lots of predictions about how the communications revolution would lead to an explosion in independent entrepreneurship.[30] Empirically, however, there has been minimal change. Corporate size remains relatively unchanged in the aggregate. To be sure, the Internet has encouraged firms to engage in various forms of outsourcing, offshoring, and subcontracting as a form of experimentation in management.[31] This has not affected aggregate firm size, however.

Part of the reason for this lack of change has been that the information revolution has lowered the organization costs of hierarchy as well. Better data management has enabled large firms in the retail sector to rationalize their inventory management, dramatically boosting their productivity.[32] Better data mining techniques have improved the efficiency of online advertising and marketing. While individuals encounter fewer costs in contracting with the market, firms experience fewer costs in managing their internal hierarchies. Indeed, for some sectors—retail finance and professional services, for example—the information revolution has increased the optimal size of the firm.

The implications of this discussion for the Internet's effect on states and civil society should be apparent. There is a tendency among pundits to pay attention to how the Internet lowers the costs of organization among citizen activists. However, what must be acknowledged is that the Internet lowers the costs of government monitoring as well. Even if a government chooses not to censor online political activity, the enhanced monitoring capabilities make it easier for the state to anticipate and regulate civic protests.

Whom Does the Internet Empower?

Political scientists and international relations scholars think of power as a zero-sum commodity. The more power that one actor acquires, the less relative power there is for others. This begs two questions. First, even if ICT facilitates the coordination capabilities of both states and civil society groups, which actors are more empowered? Second, does the change in the distribution of power fundamentally affect politics at the domestic and global levels?

The answer to the first question is relatively clear—civil society groups benefit more from the information revolution. This is mostly due to the paucity of pre-Internet tools these groups had at their disposal. The nongovernmental organizations (NGOs) that form the backbone of global civil society lack significant amounts of the hard power resources that governments possess. NGOs are characterized by limited budgets and small staffs and have a limited ability to compel state action. Long before the information revolution, governments were already able to rely on a welter of coercive instruments. The information revolution has allowed NGOs to better utilize their political tools. It has allowed previously nonexistent actors, such as bloggers, to make their political presence felt. Although the net shift in the distribution of power is less than cyberenthusiasts believe, the size of preexisting coercive resources means that the marginal benefit from the Internet is lower for governments than for nongovernmental actors.

Is this shift in the distribution of power an important one, however? The answer to this question has less to do with the power of information technology and more to do with the power of norms. Even if the Internet empowers global civil society, the question is whether governments are willing to tolerate more vocal citizen activists or not. In democratic governments, the stable rule of law automatically stacks the normative deck in favor of nonstate actors. Unless governments are willing to deploy their coercive capabilities, then obviously civil society elements will gain from the information revolution.

However, there are arenas of political contestation where existing norms—or the lack thereof—permit the regulation or control of civil society groups. In international negotiations, for example, global civil society advocates deride the "green room" process, in which key decisions are made by powerful states behind closed doors. However, because doing so would dilute their influence, great powers are decidedly unwilling to open up the green room. Analysis of the various UN conferences reveals that over time, states have become more adept at excluding various NGOs from key bargaining sessions and preparatory committee meetings.[33] Even in the case of content regulation of the Internet itself, global civil society and human rights activists have been thwarted in their efforts to establish a norm of online press freedom. At Tunis in 2005, for example, the first World Summit for the Information Society's official Plan of Action encouraged governments to "combat illegal and harmful content in media content," a stark reminder of the limits of civil society influence upon multilateral negotiations.[34] Because the power of liberal norms remains constrained at the global stage, it is unlikely that this state of affairs will change anytime soon.

Similarly, governments determined to cement their grip on power will also be willing to flout norms of open expression. These governments will be able to mitigate the ability of civil society groups to exploit the Internet. In February 2005 a spokesman for Amnesty International told the BBC that the organization "has recorded a growing number of cases of people detained or imprisoned for disseminating their beliefs or information through the internet, in countries such as China, Syria, Vietnam, the Maldives, Cuba, Iran and Zimbabwe. . . . It is also shocking to realize that in the communications age just expressing support for an internet activist is enough to land people in jail."[35] Following the most recent wave of democratic transitions, authoritarian governments in Belarus and Uzbekistan stepped up their crackdowns on Internet activists in response to rising internal dissent.[36]

It would seem, therefore, that the Internet merely reinforces the pre-existing dynamics between states and nonstate actors. In societies that value liberal norms—democracies—the Internet clearly empowers non-state actors to influence the government. In arenas where liberal norms are not widely accepted—interstate negotiations and totalitarian governments—the Internet has no appreciable effect.

However, there is one category where the Internet could prove to have a pivotal effect on state–society relations: the large group of authoritarian and semi-authoritarian states that wish to exploit the economic possibilities of the information society. There is increasing evidence that greater access to global information flows increases growth opportunities for states.[37] However, any state that permits Internet or cellular phone use for commercial possibilities will face difficulties in perfectly censoring undesirable communication or halting all attempts at political coordination.

Information Cascades and Illiberal Civil Societies

Given the other coercive tools of government, imperfect censoring would appear at first glance to be a minor inconvenience. However, the wave of revolutions and uprisings in Serbia, Georgia, the Ukraine, Lebanon, Kyrgyzstan, Belarus, Moldova, Myanmar, and Iran suggests one area where information and communication technologies can have a dramatic effect—correcting information cascades.

An *informational cascade* takes place when individuals acting in conditions of uncertainty strongly condition their choices on what others have done. More formally, an information cascade is a situation in which every actor, based on the observations of others, makes the same choice independent of his/her private information signal.[38] Less formally, an information cascade demonstrates the power of peer pressure—many individuals will choose actions based on what they observe others doing.

Information cascades can often lead to suboptimal outcomes when compared with decentralized and independent decision making.[39] In repressive societies, information cascades often lead citizens to acquiesce to government coercion, even if a broad swath of the public would prefer coordinated action. Citizen coordination and mobilization is highly unlikely among risk-averse actors unless there is some assurance that others will behave similarly. At the same time, however, a shock to the system—a scheduled election, natural disaster, sporting event, or unrest in a neighboring country—can trigger spontaneous acts of protest and trigger a reverse in the cascade. This explains why repressive societies often appear stable for years and yet without warning can face a massive scaling up of protests and civic action.[40] A little bit of public information can reverse a longstanding *informational cascade that contributed to citizen quiescence.* Even if people may have previously chosen one action, seemingly little information can induce the same people to choose the exact opposite action in response to a slight increase in information.[41]

The spread of information technology increases the fragility of information cascades that sustain the appearance of authoritarian control. This effect creates windows of opportunity for civil society groups. While governments may be able to censor Internet content and repress activists during periods of "normal" levels of unrest, that ability may not remain constant over time. This is particularly true as more and more Web 2.0 technologies are created that bypass the state's ability to control the flow of information.

At moments when a critical mass of citizens recognizes their mutual dissatisfaction with their government, the ability of the state to repress can evaporate. In some cases of "people power" mobilization, government-controlled media outlets have often switched sides and supported activists against repressive governments.[42] Such moments dramatically increase the state's price of using coercion to reassert political control. The role of new media—be it Twitter or text messaging—has the potential to be even more significant.

If repressive governments were previously unaware of the information revolution's effect on political coordination, the most recent wave of democratization has undoubtedly made them aware. Recent events in Moldova and Iran demonstrate that repressive governments can still coexist with the information revolution. If civil society movements fail to dislodge a repressive government during the first set of large-scale protests, those governments will be more likely to keep information cascades working in their favor. And yet, while these governments can choose to crack down even harder on civil society groups that exploit the Internet, the long-term opportunity costs of such a crackdown are also on the increase. Over time, authoritarian governments will be faced with a difficult choice—accept a greater risk of popular revolt, or engage in costly acts of repression.

This does *not* mean that if repressive societies become more open, they automatically become more liberal. The term "networked civil society" conjures an image of law-abiding, civic-minded activists committed to Western notions of liberal democracy. The reality is quite different. In the United States, the Internet has fueled extremist groups dedicated to the proposition that the George W. Bush administration caused the 9/11 attacks, or that Barack Obama is actually a radical Muslim not born in the United States. As Cass Sunstein has observed, online networking allows for information to be filtered through rigid ideological lenses, contributing to more extreme political beliefs.[43]

These effects are equally likely to be at play in the rest of the world. The 1979 revolution in Iran and 1994 genocide in Rwanda showed that information technologies are conduits for any kind of information transmission—not just "desirable" forms. Extremists, criminals, terrorists, and hypernationalists have embraced the information society just as eagerly as classical liberals. Insurgents have used text messaging from cell phones to recruit, track, and intimidate other Iraqis—as well as set off improvised explosive devices. One of the most robust forms of online activism in China has been nationalist outrage over Chinese investments in the United States. In Lebanon, the political actor that has adapted to Web 2.0 technologies the quickest has been Hezbollah. YouTube is popular among Mexican criminal gangs because they can upload assassination videos as a form of intimidation. Russian nationalists contributed to cyberattacks against Georgian Web sites and have targeted ethnic minorities via Google Maps.[44]

The U.S. State Department has begun to invest serious resources in the use of online technologies to promote civic activism. In November 2009, Secretary of State Hillary Rodham Clinton announced the Civil Society 2.0 Initiative to build the capacity of grassroots organizations though the use of blogs, social networks, and other Web 2.0 technologies. In her announcement, she pledged that the United States would "send experts in digital technology and communications to help build capacity" for civil society groups worldwide.[45] This initiative might yield the desired results, but it suffers from the misperception that these technologies aid only "good" groups. It is also possible that the initiative could fail because of the coercive apparatus of a repressive government—or succeed in empowering illiberal forces worldwide.

Notes

A previous version of this paper was presented at the April 2005 Conference on the Global Flow of Information, Yale University, New Haven, CT. I am grateful to Charli Carpenter, Patrick Meier, Jacob T. Levy, Henry Farrell, Emily Meierding, Marvin Ammori, Michael Froomkin, and especially Jack Balkin for their feedback and encouragement. The usual caveat applies.

1. Howard Rheingold, *Smart Mobs: The Next Social Revolution* (New York: Basic Books, 2003); Bruce Bueno de Mesquita and George Downs, "Development and Democracy," *Foreign Affairs* 84 (September/October 2005): 77–86; Yochai Benkler, *The Wealth of Networks: How Social Production Transforms Markets and Freedom* (New Haven: Yale University Press, 2006); Clay Shirky, *Here Comes Everybody* (New York: Penguin Press, 2008); Patrick Philippe Meier, "The Impact of the Information Revolution on Protest Frequency in Repressive Contexts," presented at the International Studies Association annual meeting, New York, NY, March 2009; Jacob Groshek, "The Democratic Effects of the Internet, 1994–2003," *International Communications Gazette* 71 (April 2009): 115–136; Evgeny Morozov, "How Dictators Watch Us on the Web," *Prospect*, November 18, 2009.

2. For a fuller discussion of Web 2.0, see Charli Carpenter and Daniel W. Drezner, "IR 2.0: The Implications of New Media for an Old Profession," *International Studies Perspectives* 11 (August 2010): forthcoming.

3. Lawrence Lessig, *Code and Other Laws of Cyberspace* (New York: Basic Books, 1999). See also Rajiv Shah and Kay Kesan, "Manipulating the Governance Characteristics of Code," *Info* 4 (September/October 2003): 3–9.

4. Daniel W. Drezner, "The Global Governance of the Internet: Bringing the State Back In." *Political Science Quarterly* 119 (Fall 2004): 477–498; Daniel W. Drezner and Henry Farrell, "Web of Influence," *Foreign Policy* 145 (November/December 2004): 32–40.

5. Margaret Keck and Kathryn Sikkink, *Activists Beyond Borders* (Ithaca: Cornell University Press, 1998), p. 8. See also Emilie Hafner-Burton, Miles Kahler, and Alex Montgomery, "Network Analysis in International Relations," *International Organization* 63 (Summer 2009): 559–592.

6. Government of France, "Rapport sur l'Accord Multilateral sur l'invetissement (AMI)," September 1998. http://www.finances.gouv.fr/pole_ecofin/international/amio998/amio998.htm, accessed July 18, 2002.

7. Stephen Kobrin, "The MAI and the Clash of Globalizations," *Foreign Policy* 112 (Fall 1998), p. 98. Kobrin elaborates on these arguments in "Economic Governance in an Electronically Networked Society," in Rodney Bruce Hall and Thomas J. Biersteker, eds., *The Emergence of Private Authority in Global Governance* (Cambridge: Cambridge University Press, 2002). See also Ronald Deibert, "International Plug 'n Play? Citizen Activism, the Internet, and Global Public Policy," *International Studies Perspectives* 1 (July 2000): 255–272.

8. Craig Warkentin and Karen Mingst, "International Institutions, The State, and Global Civil Society in the Age of the World Wide Web," *Global Governance* 6 (June 2000). For contrary takes on the GCS effect on the MAI, see Edward M. Graham, *Fighting the Wrong Enemy* (Washington: Institute for International Economics, 2000), and Daniel W. Drezner, *All Politics Is Global: Explaining International Regulatory Regimes* (Princeton: Princeton University Press, 2007), chapter one.

9. Quoted in Lee Hudson Tselik, "New Media Tools and Public Diplomacy," http://www.cfr.org/publication/19300/, May 11, 2009.

10. On Moldova, see Evgeny Morozov, "Moldova's Twitter Revolution," http://neteffect.foreignpolicy.com/posts/2009/04/07/moldovas_twitter_revolution, April 7, 2009; on Pakistan, see Sanjeev Berry, "Pakistanis Debate their Future on Facebook," *Huffington Post*, May 18. http://www.huffingtonpost.com/sanjeev-bery/pakistani-debate-their-fu_b_204272.html.

11. On Iran, see Mark Landler and Brian Stelter, "Washington Taps into a Potent New Force in Diplomacy," *New York Times*, June 17, 2009, and Robin Wright, "In Iran, One Woman's Death May Have Many Consequences," *Time*, June 21, 2009.

12. Jesse Scanlon, "7 Ways to Squelch the Net," *Wired*, August 2003.

13. Jack Goldsmith and Timothy Wu, *Who Controls the Internet?* (New York: Oxford University Press, 2006).

14. Robert Lebowitz, "Cuba Prohibits Computer Sales," Digital Freedom Network, March 26, 2002; Associated Press, "Internet Remains Prohibited in Myanmar," May 3, 2000; Myanmar's subsequent expansion of Internet access was strictly regulated to screen out any politically sensitive material. See Amy Kazmin, "Burmese Get Glimpse of Superhighway," *Financial Times*, April 25, 2002.

15. *BBC News*, "Iran's President Defends Web Control," December 12, 2003; Nazila Fathi, "Iran Jails More Journalists and Blocks Web Sites," *New York Times*, November 8, 2004; *BBC News*, "Syrian Jailed for Internet Usage," June 21, 2004.

16. Khalid Al-Tawil, "The Internet in Saudi Arabia." *Telecommunications Policy* 25 (September 2001): 625–632.

17. Ronald Deibert, John Palfrey, Rafal Rohozinski, and Jonathan Zittrain. *Access Denied: The Practice and Policy of Global Internet Filtering* (Cambridge: MIT Press, 2008).

18. Richard Beilock and Daniela Dimitrova, "An Exploratory Model of Inter-country Internet Diffusion," *Telecommunications Policy* 27 (April/May 2003): 237–252; Helen Milner, "The Digital Divide: The Role of Political Institutions in Technology Diffusion," *Comparative Political Studies* 39 (March 2006): 176–199. See also Shanthi Kalathil and Taylor C. Boas, *Open Networks, Closed Regimes: The Impact of the Internet on Authoritarian Rule* (Washington: Carnegie Endowment for International Peace, 2003).

19. Garry Rodan, "The Internet and Political Control in Singapore." *Political Science Quarterly* 113 (Spring 1998): 63–89.

20. Ibid.; Georgette Wang, "Regulating Network Communication in Asia," *Telecommunications Policy* 23 (April 1999): 277–287; Shanthi Kalathil, "China's Dot-Communism," *Foreign Policy* 122 (January/February 2001): 74–75.

21. Ethan Gutmann, "Who Lost China's Internet?" *The Weekly Standard*, February 25, 2002.

22. Christopher Bodeen, "Web Portals Sign China Content Pact," Associated Press, 15 July 2002.

23. Joseph Kahn, "China Toughens Obstacles to Internet Searches," *New York Times*, 12 September 2002.

24. BBC, "Microsoft Censors Chinese Blogs," June 14, 2005. If a Chinese blog-ger uses these terms, the user receives a pop-up warning that states: "This message contains a banned expression, please delete this expression."

25. Morozov, "How Dictators Watch Us on the Web."

26. Farnaz Fassini, "Iranian Crackdown Goes Global," *Wall Street Journal*, December 4, 2009.

27. Anshel Pfeffer and Gili Izikovich, "New IDF unit to fight enemies on Facebook, Twitter," *Ha'aretz*, December 1, 2009.

28. Ronald Coase, "The Nature of the Firm," *Economica* 4 (November 1937): 386–405; Armian Alchian and Harold Demsetz, "Production, Information Costs, and the Economic Organization," *American Economic Review* 62 (December 1972): 777–795; Benjamin Klein, Robert Crawford, and Armian Alchian, "Vertical Integration, Appropriable Rents, and the Competitive Contracting Process," *Journal of Law and Economics* 21 (October 1978): 297–326.

29. A decade ago, the *Economist* concluded, "Most previous technological breakthroughs have increased the optimal size of firms either by reducing production costs and increasing economies of scale, as with electricity and steam, or by reducing transport costs, as with railways, thus favouring concentration. By contrast, outside the digitisable sectors such as software the Internet reduces

economies of scale in most of the economy by increasing the opportunities for outsourcing and by lowering fixed costs." *Economist*, "Knowledge Is Power," September 21, 2000.

30. Chris Anderson, *The Long Tail* (New York: Hyperion, 2006); Benkler, *The Wealth of Networks*.

31. Suzanne Berger et al., *How We Compete* (New York: Currency Books, 2005).

32. See Carl Shapiro and Hal Varian, *Information Rules* (Boston: Harvard Business School Press, 1999); Eric Brynjolfsson and Loren Hitt, "Beyond Computation: Information Technology, Organizational Performance, and Business Performance," *Journal of Economic Perspectives* 14 (Fall 2000): 23–49; William W. Lewis, *The Power of Productivity* (Chicago: University of Chicago Press, 2004), chapter four.

33. Ann Marie Clark, Elizabeth Friedman, and Kathryn Hochstetler, "The Sovereign Limits of Global Society," *World Politics* 51 (October 1998): 1–35.

34. Quoted in David Souter, "The View from the Summit: A Report on the Outcomes of the World Summit on the Information Society," *Info* 6 (January/February 2004): 6–11.

35. Quoted in Jo Twist, "Global Blogger Action Day Called," BBC News, February 22, 2005.

36. Internet Censorship Explorer, "Belarus . . . A Bit of the Old and New," http://ice.citizenlab.org/?p=89, March 19, 2005; Daniil Kislov, "Ferghana.Ru's open letter to sponsors of the Uzbek provider UzSciNet in the UN Central Asian Development Program," http://enews.ferghana.ru/detail.php?id=74725274725.291,1752,17888839, April 13, 2005.

37. Leonard Waverman, Meloria Meschi, and Melvyn Fuss, "The Impact of Telecoms on Economic Growth in Developing Countries." Centre for Economic Policy Research, March 2005; *Economist*, "Calling Across the Divide," March 12, 2005.

38. Sushil Bikhchandani, David Hirshleifer, and Ivo Welch, "Informational Cascades and Rational Herding: An Annotated Bibliography." Working paper, *UCLA/Anderson and Ohio State University and Yale/SOM*.

39. James Surowiecki, *The Wisdom of Crowds* (New York: Random House, 2004).

40. See, for example, Susanne Lohmann, "The Dynamics of Informational Cascades: The Monday Demonstrations in Leipzig East Germany, 1989–91." *World Politics* 47 (October 1994): 42–101.

41. Bikhchandani, Hirshleifer, and Welch, "Informational Cascades and Rational Herding."

42. See, for example, Roman Olearchyk, "Regime's Control over TV Media Crumbling," *Kyiv Post*, November 25, 2004; Sebastian Usher, "Ukraine State TV in Revolt," BBC News, November 26, 2004.

43. Cass Sunstein, *Republic.com 2.0* (Princeton: Princeton University Press, 2007).

44. Data in this paragraph comes from Morozov, "How Dictators Watch Us on the Web," and Peter Singer, *Wired for War* (New York: Penguin Press, 2009).

45. Hillary Clinton, "Remarks at Forum for the Future," Marrakech, Morocco, November 3, 2009. Accessed at http://www.state.gov/secretary/rm/2009a/11/131236.htm.

8

Local Nets on a Global Network

Filtering and the Internet Governance Problem

John G. Palfrey Jr.

MORE THAN THREE DOZEN STATES around the world take part in censoring what their citizens can see and do on the Internet. This practice is increasingly widespread, with extensive filtering regimes in place in China, Iran, Burma (Myanmar), Syria, and Uzbekistan. Censorship using technological filters is often coupled with restrictive laws related to what the press can publish, opaque surveillance practices, and severe penalties for people who break the state's rules of using the Internet. This trend has been emerging since at least 2002.

As Internet use overall and the practice of online censorship grow, heads of state and their representatives have been gathering to discuss the broad topic of "Internet governance" at a series of high-profile, global meetings. These meetings have taken the form of periodic World Summits on the Information Society and, more recently, meetings of the Internet Governance Forum. The widespread practice of blocking citizens from accessing certain information on the Internet from within a given state offers a point of engagement for the Internet governance debate that takes place at these summits and forums. Those who have participated in and lead these global efforts—the World Summit on Information Society's planners, the members of the United Nations

ICT Task Force, the members of the United Nations' Working Group on Internet Governance, the Internet Governance Forum's leaders—have by and large avoided this matter of Internet filtering. These influential meetings could profitably be focused on this issue in order, at a minimum, to establish a set of principles and best practices related to Internet filtering.

The reason the Internet filtering issue is not at the top of the agenda for these global discussions may seem obvious. On a superficial level, this topic is an unattractive candidate for the Internet governance decision makers to take up. Diplomatic niceties make hard conversations about divisive issues unpleasant. A serious discussion of Internet filtering would dredge up thorny topics like free expression, privacy, national security, international enforcement, and state sovereignty—issues on which states are likely to disagree vehemently.

But as a result, the Internet governance debate might take on new life and importance. It might, in the process, engage more stakeholders in the conversation in meaningful ways. It could focus discussion on the core problems related to the divergence of views among states as to what a "good" Internet looks like. It would put in relief the jurisdictional issues related to every country in the world sharing a single, unitary public network of networks, far more powerful than any such network that has come before, with the power to bring people together and to divide them—while also acknowledging the fact that states can and do exert power over what their citizens do on this network. It could help situate local conversations about issues like network neutrality into a global context. It would prompt an examination of whether any single set of rules might serve to address concerns related to content on the Internet. And, in the process, it would encourage states to come clean about the lengths to which they are willing to go to block their citizens from accessing information online. At best, such a discussion would bring the issue of state-based Internet censorship into the spotlight and might, in the process, lead some states to reform their Internet filtering practices so as to become more open and transparent.

The Internet Governance Debate

No one is quite sure what the Internet governance debate is all about, exactly. Since the round of preparatory conferences leading up to the first meeting of the World Summit on Information Society (WSIS) in December 2003, the net has buzzed with a mixture of fear, mistrust, conspiracy theories, posturing, and horse-trading. Most people who have involved themselves in the law and policy in this area are certain that Internet governance is quite important. And, surely, it is. But points of orientation—handholds—in the debate are elusive, beyond the set of abstract principles set forth at the end of the first WSIS gathering. Consider that the initial efforts of the United Nations' Working Group on Internet Governance, ably chaired by veteran Swiss diplomat Markus Kummer, were oriented toward coming up with a *definition* of Internet governance—a year and a half after the first WSIS meeting. Since that time, a useful conversation has ensued, but the topics on the agenda have largely revolved around perennial issues, without substantial resolution. The Internet Governance Forum surely plays an important role in the global discussion of this topic, but it alone is not sufficient to resolve important differences in how the Internet is, in fact, governed, locally and globally.

The problem is *not* that there is a shortage of candidates worthy of the attention of the many capable minds focused on Internet governance.[1] The primary lightning rod for Internet governance discussions continues to be issues related to the management of Internet resources, including the domain name system and related policy issues. Discussion of the beleaguered Internet Corporation for Assigned Names and Numbers (ICANN) continues to play a central role. While deeply flawed from a structural perspective and still much in need of overhaul, ICANN occupies an arcane bit of turf—essentially, the port allocation business—that matters very little to most users of the Internet, particularly in a world in which most people find Internet resources through search engines and, increasingly, mobile devices and applications.[2] Within the context of the Internet Governance Forum of 2009, meeting in Egypt, the first substantive panel of the event was devoted to traditional ICANN-related matters such as the transition from IPv4 to IPv6 and the addition of new top-level domains (TLDs). Possibilities for consideration other than ICANN reform and these highly specific technical issues, each more important to the end users of the Internet and their sovereigns, have included a fund for developing countries to build Internet infrastructure, the quandary of what to do about spam, and a cluster of problems ordinarily considered intellectual property concerns.

Internet filtering is a better candidate for consideration and focus by the world's heads of state and their designees than these traditional Internet governance topics. While it raises a wide array of issues, a discussion of Internet filtering would hone in on whether states actually want their citizens to have full access to the Internet. It would help guide a public conversation about what is truly most important about having access to the Internet and the extent to which states place a premium, if at all, on the global flow of information. Without collective action, the Internet will likely continue to become balkanized into a series of local networks, each governed by local laws, technologies, markets, and norms. As Jonathan Zittrain has noted, we may be headed toward a localized version of the Internet, governed in each instance by local laws.[3] If such a version of the Internet is inevitably part of our future, perhaps there is a way to embrace it that can preserve elements of the network that are the most important. And if the free and open, truly "world wide" Web is what we are after, intervention may be needed to preserve it.

The Internet Filtering Problem

The fact that extensive Internet filtering occurs around the world is well documented. Through a collaborative research effort called the Open-Net Initiative,[4] the Citizen Lab at the University of Toronto, the Berkman Center for Internet and Society at Harvard University, and the SecDev Group (formerly the Advanced Network Research Group at the University of Cambridge and the Oxford Internet Institute) are together comparing the Internet filtering practices of a series of states in a systematic, methodologically rigorous fashion. A primary goal of our research is to reach useful, substantive conclusions about the nature and extent of Internet filtering in roughly seventy states and to compare practices across regions of the world. The OpenNet Initiative has released extensive reports that document and provide context for Internet filtering, previously reported anecdotally, in each of the states we have studied closely. Our reports released to date have focused on states in the Middle East and North Africa, Southeast Asia, and Central Asia, where the world's most extensive filtering takes place, though research also covers states in every region of the world, including North America and Western Europe.

Filtering implementations (and their respective scopes and levels of effectiveness) vary widely among the countries we have studied. China, as documented in a number of studies and supported by the OpenNet Initiative's findings, institutes by far the most intricate filtering regime in the world, with blocking occurring at multiple levels of the network and covering content that spans a wide range of topic areas. Though its filtering program is widely discussed, Singapore, by contrast, blocks access to only a handful of sites, each pornographic in nature. Most other states we are studying implement filtering regimes that fall between the poles of China and Singapore, each with significant variation from one to the next. These filtering regimes can be understood only in the political, legal, religious, and social contexts in which they arise.

Internet filtering occurs in different ways in different parts of the world. Some states implement a software application developed by one of a small handful of U.S.-based technology providers. Burma, in the first incarnation of its filtering regime, has used an open source product called DansGuardian. Others rely less on technology solutions and more on "soft controls." Sometimes the filtering regime is supported explicitly by the state's legal code; in other cases, the filtering regime is carried out through a national security authority, or just presumed to be permissible. The content blocked spans a wide range of social, religious, and political information. Our studies have combined a review of whether individual citizens could access sites in a "global basket" of bellwether sites to test in every jurisdiction across a variety of sensitive areas—akin to a stock index sorted by sector—as well as a list of Web sites likely to be sensitive in some categories only in some countries.

Extent, Character, and Locus of Filtering

More than three dozen states around the world practice technical Internet filtering of various sorts.[5] The number is growing over time. Those states that do filter have established a network of laws and technical measures to carry out substantial amounts of filtering that could allow the practice to become further embedded in their political and cultural environments. Web content is constantly changing, of course, and no state we have yet studied, even China, seems able to carry out its Web filtering in a comprehensive manner—that is, consistently blocking access to a range of sites meeting specified criteria. China appears to be the most nimble at responding to the shifting Web, likely reflecting a devotion of the most resources to the filtering enterprise.

A state wishing to filter its citizens' access to the Internet has several initial options: DNS filtering, IP filtering, and URL filtering.[6] Most states with advanced filtering regimes implement URL filtering, as it can avoid even more drastic overfiltering or underfiltering situations presented by the other choices and discussed below ("Filtering and Overbreadth").[7] To implement URL filtering, a state must first identify where to place the filters; if the state directly controls the ISP(s), the answer is clear. Otherwise, the state may require private or semi-private ISPs to implement the blocking as part of their service. The technical complexities presented by URL filtering become nontrivial as the number of users grows to millions rather than tens of thousands. Some states appear to have limited overall access to the Internet in order to keep URL filtering manageable. The government of Saudi Arabia, for example, made the ability to filter a prerequisite of public Internet access, delaying any such access for a period of several years until the resources to filter were fully in place.

Citizens with technical knowledge can generally circumvent filters that a state has put in place. Some states acknowledge as much: The overseer of Saudi Arabia's filtering program, via the state-run Internet Services Unit, admits that technically savvy users simply cannot be stopped from accessing blocked content. Expatriates in China, as well as those citizens who resist the state's control, frequently find up-to-date proxy servers through which to connect to the Internet and through which they can evade filters in the process. While no state will ultimately win a game of cat-and-mouse with those citizens who are resourceful and dedicated enough to employ circumvention measures, many users will never do so—rendering filtering regimes at least partially effective despite the obvious workarounds.

Pause here. Some of the earliest theorizing about control in the online environment suggested that such state-run control of Internet activity would not work. It's important to note that states such as China have proven that an ambitious state can, by devoting substantial technical, financial, and human resources, exert a large measure of control over what their citizens do online. States, if they want, can erect certain forms of gates at their borders, even in cyberspace, and can render them effective through a wide variety of modes of control.[8]

That does not mean that the issue is simple. For starters, states ordinarily need a great deal of help in carrying out filtering and surveillance regimes. Enter Internet service providers, many of whom require a license from the government in order to provide Internet access to citizens lawfully. Much Internet filtering is effected by these private ISPs under respective states' jurisdictions, though some governments partially centralize the filtering operation at private Internet Exchange Points—topological crossroads for network traffic—or through explicit state-run clearing points established to serve as gatekeepers for Internet traffic. Some governments implement filtering at public Internet access points such as the computers found within cybercafés. Such filtering can take the form of software used in many American libraries and schools for filtering purposes, or "normative" filtering—government-encouraged interventions by shop owners and others as citizens surf the Internet in a public place.

Sometimes the technical control is not enough. The exercise of more traditional state powers can have a meaningful impact on Internet usage that does not require the complete technical inaccessibility of particular categories of content. China, Vietnam, Syria, and Iran have each jailed "cyber-dissidents."[9] Against this backdrop, the blocking of Web pages may be intended to deliver a message to users that state officials monitor Internet usage—in other words, making it clear to citizens that "someone is watching what you do online." This message is reinforced by methods allowing information to be gathered about what sites a particular user has visited after the fact, such as the requirement of passports to set up accounts with ISPs and tighter controls of users at cybercafés.

As we learn more and more about how Internet filtering takes place, the problems of "governing" the Internet come more sharply into relief—about how control is exerted, about how citizens in one state can or cannot connect to others in another state, about the relationship between each state and its citizens, and about the relationships between states.

Types of Content Filtered

Around the world, states are blocking access to information online based upon its content—or what applications hosted at certain sites can do—for political, religious, and social reasons. Sensitivities within these categories vary greatly from country to country. Not surprisingly, these sensitivities track, to large extent, local conflicts. The Internet content blocked for social reasons—commonly pornography, information about gay and lesbian issues, and sex education information—is more likely to be the same across countries than the political and religious information to which access is blocked.

Several states carry out extensive filtering on certain topics, where our OpenNet Initiative testing has shown that 50 percent or more of the sites we tested on a given topic—say, sex education; or in terms of applications, anonymization tools—are inaccessible. Very rarely does any state manage to achieve complete filtering on any topic. The only areas in which 100 percent filtering is approached are pornography and anonymizers (sites that if themselves unfiltered would defeat filtering of other sites by allowing a user to access any Internet destination through the anonymizers' gateways). States like Burma, which reportedly monitor e-mail traffic, also block a high percentage of free e-mail service providers. Such complete, or near-complete, filtering is additionally found only in countries that have outsourced the task of identifying pornographic sites to one of several for-profit American companies and is inevitably accompanied by overblocking. Outside of these three areas, OpenNet Initiative testers are consistently able to access some material of a similar nature to that found on the sites that were being blocked.

Filtering and Overbreadth

Wholly apart from the propriety of extensive government censorship as a threshold matter, Internet filtering is almost impossible to accomplish with any degree of precision. There is no way to stem the global flow of information in a consistently accurate fashion. A country that has decided to filter the Internet must make an "overbroad" or "underbroad" decision at the outset. The filtering regime will either block access to too much or too little Internet content. Very often, this decision is tied to whether to use a home-grown system or whether to adopt a commercial software product, such as SmartFilter, WebSense, or an offering from security provider Fortinet, each of which are products made in the United States and are believed to be licensed to countries that filter the Internet. Bahrain, for instance, has opted for an "underbroad" solution for pornography; its ISPs appear to block access to a small and essentially fixed number of "blacklisted" sites. Bahrain may seek to indicate disapproval of access to pornographic material online, while actually blocking only token access to such material. The United Arab Emirates, by contrast, seems to have made the opposite decision by attempting to block much more extensively in similar categories, thereby sweeping into its filtering basket a number of sites that appear by any metric to have innocuous content. And Yemen was rebuked by WebSense for allegedly using the company's filtering system to block access to material that was not pornographic in nature, contrary to the company's policies.[10]

Most of the time, states make blocking determinations to cover a range of Web content, commonly grouped around a second-level domain name or the IP address of a Web service (such as http://www.twitter.com or 66.102.15.100), rather than based on the precise URL of a given Web page (such as http://www.twitter.com/*username*), or a subset of content found on that page (such as a particular image or string of text). Iran, for instance, has used such an approach to block a cluster of weblogs that the state prefers not to have reach its citizens. This approach means that the filtering process will often not distinguish between permissible and impermissible content so long as any impermissible content is deemed "nearby" from a network standpoint.

Because of this wholesale acceptance or rejection of a particular speaker or site, it is difficult to know exactly what speech was deemed unacceptable for citizens to access. It's even harder to ascertain why, exactly, the speech has been blocked. Bahrain, a country in which we found only a handful of blocked sites at the outset of our first round of testing, blocked access to a discussion board at http://www.bahrain-online.org. The message board likely contains a combination of messages that would be tolerated independently as well as some that would appear to meet the state's criteria for filtering. Likewise, we found minimal blocking for internal political purposes in the UAE, but the state did block a site that essentially acted as a catalog of criticism of the state. Our tests cannot determine whether it was the material covering human rights abuses or discussion of historical border disputes with Iran, but inasmuch as the discussion of these topics is taking place within a broad dissension-based site, the calculation we project onto the censor in UAE looks significantly different from that for a site with a different ratio of "offensive" to approved content.

For those states using commercial filtering software and update services to try to maintain a current list of blocked sites matching particular criteria, we have noted multiple instances where such software has mistaken sites containing gay and lesbian content for pornography. For instance, the site for the Log Cabin Republicans of Texas was blocked by the U.S.-based SmartFilter as pornography, apparently the basis for its blocking by the United Arab Emirates. (Our research shows that gay and lesbian content is itself often targeted for filtering, and even when it is not explicitly targeted, states may not be overly concerned with its unavailability.)

As content changes increasingly quickly on the Web and generalizations become more difficult to make by URL or domain—thanks in part to the rise of simpler, faster, and aggregated publishing tools, like those found on weblog sites—accurate filtering is likely to get trickier for filtering regimes to address over time unless they want to take the step of banning nearly everything.

For example, free Web hosting domains tend to group an enormous array of changing content and thus provoke very different responses from state governments. In 2004, Saudi Arabia blocked every page we tested on http://freespace.virgin.net and www.erols.com.[11] However, our research indicated that the www.erols.com sites had been only minimally blocked in 2002, and the http://freespace.virgin.net sites had been blocked in 2002, but accessible in 2003 before being re-blocked in 2004. In all three tests, Saudi Arabia practiced by-URL blocking on www.geocities.com (possibly through SmartFilter categorization), blocking only 3 percent of more than a thousand sites tested in 2004. Vietnam blocked all sites we tested on the www.geocities.com and members.tripod.org domains. In our recent testing, we have found that Turkey and Syria have been blocking all of Blogspot's hosted blogging service.[12]

China's response to the same problem provides an instructive contrast. When China became worried about bloggers, it shut down the main blogging domains for a period of weeks in the summer of 2004. When the domains came back online, the blogging systems contained filters that would reject posts containing particular keywords.[13] Even Microsoft's MSN Spaces blogs software blocked writers from publishing terms like "democracy" from China. In effect, China moved to a content-based filtering system but determined that the best place for such content evaluation was not the point of Web page access but the point of publication, and it possessed the authority to force these filters on the downstream application provider. This approach is similar to that taken with Google to respond to the accessibility of disfavored content via Google's caching function. Google was blocked in China until a mechanism was put in place to prevent cache access.[14] These examples make clear the length to which regimes can go to preserve "good" access instead of simply blocking an entire service.

These examples also demonstrate the increasing reliance by states on "just-in-time" filtering, rather than filtering that occurs in the same, constant way over time. While the paradigmatic case of Internet filtering was initially the state that wished to block its citizens from viewing any pornography online at any time (for instance, Saudi Arabia), the phenomenon of a state's blocking particular speech or types of speech at a sensitive moment has become commonplace. For instance, the Chinese state blocked sites such as Twitter and YouTube at the time of the twentieth anniversary of the Tiananmen Square demonstrations in June 2009. A few weeks later, the Iranian state blocked similar sites, including Facebook, at the time of demonstrations in the streets of Tehran. These blocks are often lifted once the "trouble" has passed. One means of tracking these changes in the availability of applications and Web sites is a project called Herdict.org, which enables people from around the world to submit reports on what they can and cannot access in real-time.[15]

Alternate approaches that demand a finer-grained means of filtering, such as the use of automated keywords to identify and expunge sensitive information on the fly, or greater manual involvement in choosing individual Web pages to be filtered, are possible so long as a state is willing to invest in them. China in particular appears to be prepared to make such

an investment, one mirrored by choices demonstrated about more traditional media. For example, China allows CNN to be broadcast within the
country with a form of time delay, so the feed can be temporarily turned
off when, in one case, stories about the death of Zhao Ziyang were broadcast.[16] The global flow of information is tempered by the ingenuity of the
censors, expressed through technical controls at many layers.

Law and Soft Controls

Just as dozens of states use technical means to block citizens from accessing content on the Internet, most also employ legal and other "soft"
means of control. Many states that filter use a combination of media, telecommunications, national security, and Internet-specific laws and regulatory schemes to restrict the publication of and access to information
on the Internet. States often require Internet service providers to obtain
licenses before providing Internet access to citizens. Some states—China
and Turkey, for instance, which have each enacted special regulations to
this effect—apply pressure on cybercafés and Internet service providers to monitor Internet usage by their customers. With the exceptions of
Saudi Arabia and Qatar, no country seems explicitly to communicate to
the public about its process for blocking and unblocking content on the
Internet. Most countries, instead, have a series of broad laws that cover
content issues online, both empowering states that need it to carry out
filtering regimes and putting citizens on general notice not to publish or
to access content online that violates certain norms.

Often these "soft" controls are exercised through social norms or
through control at the far edges of the network. Sometimes the state
requires nongovernmental organizations and religious leaders to register before using the Internet to communicate about the topics they work
on. In China and in parts of Central Asia, very often the most fearsome
enforcer of the state's will is the old woman on one's block, who may or
may not be on the state's payroll. The control might be exercised, as in
Singapore, largely through family dynamics. The call by a local police
force to the Malaysian blogger to come and talk about his publishing to
the Web might have as much of an effect on expression as any law on the
books or technical blocking system.

Whether through advanced information technology, legal mechanisms, or "soft" controls, a growing number of states around the world are seeking to control the global flow of information. Ordinarily, this control takes the form of blocking, through technical means, that state's citizens from accessing certain information online. In other instances, the blocking stops the state's citizens from publishing information online, in effect disallowing people outside the state from hearing the voices of the state's citizens. Most filtering regimes cause a chilling effect on the use of information technologies as a means of free expression, whether for political, religious, or cultural purposes.

Transparency in Filtering as the Focus of the Internet Governance Debate

The Internet governance debate could profitably take up the issue of filtering on the net. The practice of filtering is now a widely known fact, but the hard problems that stem from this practice are infrequently discussed as a matter of public policy. The blocking and surveillance of citizens' activity on the Internet—by virtue of the network's architecture, an issue of international dimensions—calls for discussion at a multilateral level. Rather than fret over the finer points of the domain name system, time would be better spent in Internet governance discussions considering rules that relate, for instance, to specific issues like transparency in Internet filtering or to broad issues of interconnection of the global network. The Internet filtering problem offers much more to be gained—even through frank discussion, if not action—and provides an exercise worthy of an extraordinary gathering of world leaders who want to talk about the global "Information Society."

There is certainly an argument to be made that Internet filtering is a private matter between a state and its citizens as to what information citizens may access online.[17] States that censor the Internet assert the right to sovereignty. From the state's perspective, the public interest, as defined in one state, say Saudi Arabia, is different from the public interest as defined by the state in Uzbekistan, or in China, or in the United Kingdom. States can, and do, exercise their sovereignty through control of the information environment.

Even if true, that argument should not end the conversation about Internet filtering. A global discussion about the relationship between these filtering and surveillance practices and human rights could be extremely fruitful. Specifically, states might consider rules that relate to common standards for transparency in Internet filtering and surveillance practices as they relate to individuals and those corporations drawn into the process. On a broader level, the issue raised here is about interconnection between states and the citizens of those states—and ultimately about what sort of an Internet we want to be building and whether the global flow of information is a sustainable vision.

For instance, we have yet to join the ethical interests at play in filtering. States vary greatly in terms of how explicitly the filtering regime is discussed and the amount that citizens can come to know about it. No state that we studied makes its block list generally available.[18] The world leaders who gather periodically at United Nations–sponsored meetings and at the Internet Governance Forums could make the most of their leadership by taking up the mantle of seeking to establish a set of principles and best practices related to Internet filtering and the transparency related to filtering regimes. They might also focus profitably on the difficult problems facing those multinational companies which do business in regimes that require them to filter and support surveillance of the network in ways that would not be legally permissible in the company's home jurisdiction.

This broader vision of Internet filtering—about what sort of a future we seek for the Internet—is just the sort of topic on which the Internet governance debate ought to focus. Even though Internet filtering is hard to talk about as part of a global conversation, it is important that we do so. The net is becoming each day larger and more fractured. Trends in favor of more speech from more people in more places around the globe— using Web 2.0 technologies generally, such as blogs, wikis, Twitter, SMS, podcasting, and so forth—are countered by the increasing sophistication and reach of Internet filtering and surveillance practices. A richer understanding of the complexities at play in Internet filtering would help develop a foundation that does not yet exist for building a sustainable, and truly global, network.

Notes

This chapter is based in large part on work by the OpenNet Initiative, which is a collaborative research effort between the Citizen Lab at the Munk Centre, University of Toronto (Professor Ron Deibert, principal investigator), the SecDev Group (formerly the University of Cambridge) (where Rafal Rohozinski is principal investigator), and the Berkman Center for Internet & Society at Harvard University (where the author and Jonathan Zittrain are co-principal investigators). The author is especially grateful to ONI coordinator Jill York for helpful comments and updates to this chapter.

1. The International Telecommunication Union, the official host of WSIS in Geneva, has held several events designed to refine the debate further. Through these events, the ITU has convinced dozens of observers to publish what comprises an extensive body of work on this topic on the ITU Web site. In addition, longtime experts in this field, such as Professor Milton Mueller of Syracuse and others, have constructed helpful models to structure the conversation. For pointers to further information of this general nature, please see http://www.netdialogue.org, a joint project of Harvard Law School and Stanford Law School.

2. Witness the abysmal turnout for ICANN's election of 2000, in which a free and open election for five ICANN directors attracted fewer than 100,000 votes globally.

3. Jonathan Zittrain, *Be Careful What You Ask For*, in Who Rules the Net? Internet Governance and Jurisdiction, 13–30 (Adam Thierer, et al., eds., 2003).

4. http://www.opennetinitiative.net/; see also Ronald Deibert, John Palfrey, Rafal Rohozinski, and Jonathan Zittrain, eds., Access Denied: The Practice and Policy of Global Internet Filtering (MIT Press, 2008).

5. *See* Deibert et al., Access Denied, *supra* note 4.

6. http://ice.citizenlab.org/index.php?p=78.

7. For instance, IP filtering forces the choice of blocking all sites sharing an IP address. A recent ONI bulletin found more than 3,000 Web sites blocked in an attempt to prevent access to only 31 (see http://www.opennetinitiative.net/bulletins/009/). DNS blocking requires an entire domain and all subdomains to be either wholly blocked or wholly unblocked (http://ice.citizenlab.org/index.php?p=78).

8. *See* Jack L. Goldsmith and Tim Wu, Who Controls the Internet: Illusions of a Borderless World (Oxford University Press, 2006), 65–86.

9. Iran: Reporters Sans Frontières, "Appeals court confirms prison for cyber-dissident while blogger is re-imprisoned," available at http://www.rsf.org/article.php3?id_article=12564 (Feb. 15, 2005). ("Javad Tavaf, a student leader and the editor of the popular news website Rangin Kaman, which for a year had been criticising

the Guide of the Islamic Revolution, was arrested at his home on 16 January 2003 by people who said they were from the military judiciary, which later denied it had arrested him.") China: Reporters Sans Frontières, Internet - China, available at http://www.rsf.org/article.php3?id_article=10749. Vietnam: Reporters Sans Frontières, Internet - Vietnam, available at http://www.rsf.org/article.php3?id_article=10778.

10. See http://opennet.net/blog/2009/08/websense-bars-yemens-government-further-software-updates (last accessed November 6, 2009).

11. Saudi Arabia blocked every page on www.erols.com except for the root page at www.erols.com itself, potentially indicating a desire to manage perceptions as to the extent of the blocking.

12. All data from OpenNet Initiative testing can be found in the country-by-country summaries at http://www.opennet.net/.

13. http://www.opennetinitiative.net/bulletins/008/.

14. This mechanism turned out to be extremely rudimentary, as outlined in a previous ONI bulletin (http://www.opennetinitiative.net/bulletins/006/).

15. See http://www.herdict.org, the brainchild of Harvard's Jonathan Zittrain. The histories of reports of these just-in-time blocking patterns can be viewed from this Web site.

16. See http://cyber.law.harvard.edu/blogs/gems/tka/EPriestReactionPaper2.pdf.

17. Some states make an effort to suggest that their citizens (in Saudi Arabia and the UAE specifically) are largely in support of the filtering regime, particularly when it comes to blocking access to pornographic material. For instance, the agency responsible for both Internet access and filtering in Saudi Arabia conducted a user study in 1999 and reported that 45 percent of respondents thought "too much" was blocked, 41 percent thought it "reasonable," and 14 percent found it "not enough." These studies stand for the proposition, in the context of our report, that some states that filter seek to make the case that their filtering regime enjoys popular support, not that such support necessarily exists.

18. Saudi Arabia publishes its rationale and its blocking practices on an easily accessible Web site, at http://www.isu.net.sa/saudi-internet/contenet-filtring/filtring.htm ("The Internet Services Unit oversees and implements the filtration of web pages in order to block those pages of an offensive or harmful nature to the society, and which violate the tenants of the Islamic religion or societal norms. This service is offered in fulfillment of the directions of the government of Saudi Arabia and under the direction of the Permanent Security Committee chaired by the Ministry of the Interior"). In Saudi Arabia, citizens may suggest sites for blocking or for unblocking, in either Arabic or English, via a public Web site. Most sites include a block-page, indicating to those seeking to access a Web site that they have reached

a disallowed site. Most states have enacted laws that support the filtering regime and provide citizens with some context for why and how it is occurring, though rarely with any degree of precision. As among the states we have studied, China seems to obscure the nature and extent of its filtering regime to the greatest extent.

9

Law as a Network Standard

Dan L. Burk

GLOBAL INFORMATION FLOWS are reshaping the international information landscape, channeled from nation to nation through the new outlets provided by global computer networks. Such movement of information between jurisdictions invites conflicting applications of local regulations over advertising, intellectual property, hate speech, personal data, and other communicative content. Understanding the role of the Internet in this context is crucial to understanding the phenomenon of transborder information exchanges, as the Internet both forms an active conduit for much of this information flow and provides a case study for understanding information flows outside the network.

To a greater extent than any previous communications medium, the Internet facilitates the interconnection of potentially incompatible law regimes. The natural response to such incompatibility is to seek harmonization or centralization of legal standards at a supranational level. The case for harmonization or centralization of regulation at the international level is in many instances compelling; however, enthusiasm for an international regulatory approach must be tempered by caution over the potential costs and drawbacks of centralized hierarchical control. Improperly applied, international Internet regulation threatens to mitigate the very benefits that make the network most valuable and could in fact negate the very benefits that the regulation is intended to preserve.

The cure may therefore be as bad as the disease; at a minimum, it carries with it a variety of troublesome results. In this chapter, I briefly discuss two related cautionary models implicated in the argument for international regulation. I argue that Internet regulation at an international level may be conceived as a standards-setting problem, presenting at a multinational level the same dangers and benefits of uniformity, competition, and strategic behavior familiar from analyses of technical standards-setting. This approach arises in turn from the conceptualization of law as a product, and from the potential for interchanging law and technology as regulatory methods.

I begin by reviewing the literature analyzing law as a product; I then extend the basic concepts of that model to discuss implications of international regulation in light of network effects in the market for law. I conclude that these models point to only a limited and particularized case for international regulation in order to preserve the benefits of decentralized innovation in law. Consequently, in any given instance, the case for harmonized international regulation must be evaluated according to its potential for curtailing the competitive benefits of localized regulatory innovation.

Law as a Product

The problem of transborder data regulation implicates economic models previously developed to analyze interjurisdictional competition. In 1956 Charles Tiebout published his now-classic paper modeling local provision of public services on a theory of interjurisdictional competition that closely resembles market competition for provision of private goods.[1] Tiebout theorized that if citizens are free to migrate between jurisdictions, competition for desirable citizen immigrants will arise. Local communities will offer to potential immigrants the most attractive packages of goods and services at the lowest tax rate possible. Similarly, migrants will relocate to jurisdictions offering the maximum package of public goods at the tax rate that the migrant is willing to pay. Local communities may even tailor their offerings to appeal to particular types of immigrants, and immigrants would be expected to sort themselves out into groups of similar means and tastes by jurisdiction.

Under Tiebout's approach, the production of local public goods and services might resemble the production of private goods in a competitive market: Competitive pressure from other jurisdictions will prevent any given jurisdiction from offering too much or too little in the way of public services.[2] Jurisdictions that offer too much will experience an influx of immigrants from less generous jurisdictions; jurisdictions that offer too little will experience an exodus to more generous jurisdictions. Migration in or out of the jurisdiction will continue until parity with competing jurisdictions is reached.[3] These forces therefore act as a check on overproduction or underproduction of local public goods. By "voting with their feet," or exiting, citizens force efficiency in allocation of resources to such goods.

Tiebout's insight was quickly expanded to encompass strategic preferences of local governments regarding business firms. Just as in the consumer/citizen model, businesses too may "vote with their feet," locating their operations in jurisdictions that offer the most attractive set of local public goods. This in turn implies that jurisdictions may tailor their offerings to attract businesses, or to attract certain kinds of desirable businesses, or even to repel undesirable businesses.[4] In this "market" for business migration, the "price" of migration may take a variety of forms: Jurisdictions may offer anything from tax incentives, land grants, and liability waivers to museums, sports arenas, and public transportation systems.[5] Some jurisdictions will have raw materials or other natural competitive advantages to attract business; others will create attractive public infrastructures that give them an advantage.

Local law constitutes an important component of each jurisdiction's competitive package. Regulation with economic effects may be tailored to foster and to attract certain industries. For example, environmental regulations may be eased in order to lower the operating costs of favored industries. Patent and copyright laws may be strengthened in order to maximize the economic return to industries that generate new innovation. Corporate and partnership laws may be designed to accommodate investment and control structures amenable to certain industries. Indeed, development of desirable law "products" may be even more important to attract and retain high-value businesses than it is to attract and retain high-value individuals.

This model therefore implies that competition for business and for desirable immigrants will prompt jurisdictions to compete with one another to offer the most attractive law "products"—in effect, creating a market for law. Optimally, such competition will tend not only toward the production of law that is differentiated to suit certain business profiles but also to produce better and more efficient regulation; the threat of losing businesses to another jurisdiction will tend to weed out the inefficient legal regimes—a "race to the top," to the optimal package of law. However, it is also possible for this "race to the top" to become a "race to the bottom." The Tiebout model assumes that jurisdictions are tightly compartmentalized so that no external costs or benefits accrue from the local provision of public services.[6] If jurisdictions are "leaky," then individuals could perhaps enjoy the positive benefits of a neighboring jurisdiction's policy without actually incurring the cost of migrating to it. More significantly, in a world of "leaky" borders, jurisdictions could lower the costs to local firms by imposing all or part of those costs on neighboring jurisdictions, for example by relaxing environmental regulation to allow effluent dumping into a river that flows into a neighboring country. This would serve to attract firms, but not necessarily by generating a net gain in efficiency.

Consequently, in a world of "leaky" borders, the race to the bottom might best be characterized as a race to externalize—for jurisdictions to seek ways to gain at the expense of their neighbors. Because the externalized costs of such local regulation are imposed upon others, jurisdictions will tend to overspend on law "products," offering immigration incentives for which they themselves need not pay. The Internet, of course, is a source of transborder leakiness, at least for digitized products and for data migration. This raises the concern that that the Internet may trigger such races to externalize costs, providing a conduit for local costs to be imposed upon other jurisdictions.

Thus, to take an example that has been hotly debated in the jurisprudence of the Internet, one possible characterization of the peer-to-peer music file-sharing phenomenon—whereby digitized music, software, and sometimes movies are shared via the Napster, Kazaa, or other online services—is one that suggests a race to the bottom. Much of the supply of such files comes out of jurisdictions with lax copyright law or lax copy-

right enforcement. Indeed, businesses supplying software for such file sharing have taken advantage of the attractive incorporation of law and legal immunity provided by small and somewhat obscure jurisdictions such as the Pacific island of Vanuatu. Lurking in permissive jurisdictions, these entities free-ride off of the creativity fostered in protective jurisdictions, using the Internet as a conduit to bleed legitimate incentives away from the owners and producers of valuable creative works.

But in branding such a scenario an inefficient "race to the bottom," we must exercise care. Early analyses of incorporation races among jurisdictions in the United States branded this race a "race to the bottom," a race to benefit corporate officers at the expense of shareholders. Later, more careful analyses suggested that it may in fact have been a "race to the top," a competition among jurisdictions to produce the best package of corporate law "products."[7] In the making of such characterizations, the perspective adopted may dictate the conclusion.

Thus, in our peer-to-peer file-sharing example, a rather different story might be told on the same facts: In this version, offshore encouragement of peer-to-peer entrepreneurship becomes a race to the top, forcing a bloated and complacent U.S. entertainment industry to revise its outmoded business models. On this view, consumer adoption of digital technology has outstripped the recording labels' sluggish pace of change, creating a gap between consumer demand and the dated products provided by entertainment firms. Peer-to-peer entrepreneurship filled that gap, providing not only innovative distributional services but also models for traditional entertainment firms to emulate. Without the harsh market discipline of file sharing, the authorized music downloading services that are now beginning to cater to consumer demand might never have been launched.

Law Cartels

Where borders leak, undesirable transborder migrations might be curtailed by equalizing the benefits on each side of the border. Jurisdictions might agree to set a uniform standard for their law products, removing the incentive to race to the top or to the bottom. Then, much like a classic private-sector economic cartel, governments that participate in an international agreement may be able to avoid "ruinous competition" in the market for law as a good. By standardizing the law product, they may succeed in effectively fixing the "price" for business migration.

Taking copyright as an example in the Internet context, enforcement of high protectionist standards would prevent cartel nations from lowering their "price" to attract information distributors—that is, so-called pirates. Fixing the price for information distributor migration would in turn allow domestic producers to avoid foreign information competition and engage in monopoly overcharge for information products. On an international scale, this type of monopoly overcharge effectively taxes nonproducing nations—particularly developing nations—to support the information producers of the developed world.

Such collusive international activity may be highly advantageous to politicians at the national level. First, through collusion with foreign politicians, domestic politicians can protect themselves against superior foreign law products. Exodus of firms to more attractive regulatory regimes may place domestic politicians under pressure to streamline local regulation, perhaps at the expense of favored but inefficient rent-seeking constituents. Such streamlining may, however, be avoided by agreement with foreign counterparts to cooperate in suppressing formulation of more efficient regulation in their respective jurisdictions.

At the same time, local politicians may use an international agreement to deflect domestic voter dissatisfaction over domestic special interest legislation, by characterizing the local protectionist measures as a necessary part of international cooperation. This in essence facilitates *intrajurisdictional* externalization of regulatory costs: Rather than shifting costs to other jurisdictions, costs are shifted to a different constituency within the jurisdiction. Thus, international collusion may not only prevent "exit" from correcting political improvidence but may also suppress the "voice" of internal constituents from prompting correction.

Returning to our example of peer-to-peer technology, we might query whether the active campaign for increased intellectual property protection in the face of widespread file sharing fits this model. Indeed, this characterization suggests that the fierce lobbying and advocacy campaigns waged by the entertainment industries have merely been rent-seeking attempts to preserve their current business positions by legislative fiat, which often may be had for a small investment in lobbying activity—cheaper than making the sizeable investment necessary to restructure their outmoded business models. If this characterization is correct, elevating the results of such lobbying efforts to the international level only encourages socially inefficient behavior by removing the possibility of more efficient extraterritorial competition.

However, the success of national protectionists, or any other group of price-fixers, requires a stable cartel, and cartels of any sort are notoriously unstable.[8] Such instability results in part from a sort of "Prisoner's Dilemma" version of the "race to the bottom" effect. Cartels extract monopoly profits by agreeing to restrain output so as to push prices to levels that would be impossible to maintain if the members engaged in production at competitive levels. Cartel members therefore have a strong incentive to cheat: If a cartel member engages at competitive-level production while competitors restrain output, the cheater can reap enormous profits. But because all members of the cartel are tempted by this same possibility, one member is unlikely to be able to cheat without triggering cheating by all the other members, leading back to competitive pricing and loss of the profits that prompted the cheating.

In the case of private economic cartels, a collusive organization is believed to be most feasible and stable where the quality of the product is homogeneous, the price elasticity of demand for the product is low, barriers to entry are high, all suppliers of the product have similar cost functions, and there is a dominant supplier who can act as price-leader. In the case of international collusion over Internet law "products," several of these requirements may be met by the configuration of participation in law production.

First, it would appear that the universe of law producers on an international scale is largely closed, forming something of a barrier to entry. Price-leadership or "dominant firm" effects may also be seen in the market for law products. The number of sovereign states is relatively large, but certain nations, particularly the United States, are able to exert considerable diplomatic and economic pressure toward conformity.[9] By promulgating its copyright and patent law products as a proposed standard for inclusion within the Berne treaty revisions, or TRIPs trade agreements, the United States has rather successfully attempted to coordinate the international market for such law products. The European Union has taken much the same approach in promulgating its standards for data privacy protection and proprietary database protection.

If the conditions for a stable intergovernmental cartel can be attained, the expected damage to innovation and competition will follow naturally from the principles outlined in the literature on law as a product. First, by homogenizing information law, an international agreement forces international businesses to operate in a world in which "one size fits all." Opportunities for jurisdictional experimentation and innovation are curtailed. New information industries that might have arisen under innovative schemes may be stifled. Established information industries will be confined to an international norm, rather than offered the opportunity to select, from a diversity of systems, that which is best suited to their operation. As a corollary effect, information firms will be exposed to greater business risk because they will be less able to diversify their operations across jurisdictions with differing legal systems. Thus, one reason to approach centralization with caution is that the international inefficiencies resulting from an international intellectual property cartel may be no less serious than the inefficiencies resulting from lack of coordination.

Law as a Standard

Conceptualizing the centralization of Internet law as international cartel activity in the market for law implicates another set of economic models related to the issue of standards-setting for technical compatibility. "Standards" in this context may be defined as a set of technical specifications that provides common design features for a product or process.[10] The potential benefits of uniform technical standards, and the problems attending incompatible standards, are common knowledge.[11] As any traveler carrying an electrical appliance has discovered, the costs of non-uniform technical standards can be profound: Voltage, current, and even physical plug configuration vary enormously among different regions, requiring either expensive duplication of locally compatible appliances or a panoply of adapters and transformers allowing a noncompatible appliance to function locally. Coordination of technical design, even among competitors, is often necessary to avoid the costs and inconvenience associated with such technical incompatibility. This design coordination is known as standards-setting.

This standards-setting problem occurs as a consequence of what economists term "network effects." Such network effects typically arise in situations where the value of a system increases as users are added.[12] Purchasers of such "network" goods find the good increasingly valuable as others also purchase the good. Typically, the increased value accrues to subsequent adopters and accrues as a positive externality. For example, a telephone system is of relatively little value if it has only two subscribers; each subscriber can call only one other person. The system is of greater value if it has more subscribers, because each subscriber can then communicate with many others. Those who subscribe to the system after it has accrued a large number of subscribers may obtain a more valuable service than those who subscribed early, when there were few other subscribers. At the same time, the value of the service to the early subscribers grows as additional users sign on to the network.

This insight can be generalized to other types of human artifacts with shared compatibility: Languages, for example, may be thought of as goods having network effects. The ability to "interoperate" internationally with a wide diversity of individuals is illustrated by the benefits of speaking Greek in the ancient Western world, Latin in the medieval Western world, French or Spanish in the European colonial era, or English in the current global era. As another common example, many commentators have noted that computer operating systems tend toward a uniform standard because of the natural benefits of a uniform standard: Users need invest in learning the characteristics of the system only once, technical support for a single standard is simple to provide, and producers of compatible software applications need develop products to function with only a single platform.

The Internet itself, not surprisingly, is a prime candidate for display of such network externalities: Network access becomes more valuable as it becomes ubiquitous.[13] Much of the success of the Internet itself is due to the creation of a new type of physical network: The internetworking protocols on which the Internet operates allow disparate types of computer hardware, running many different software systems, to interact on a single network. This is the so-called "end-to-end" principle, under which the network is designed to constitute a simple and unspecialized common technological denominator. Thus, users with previously incompatible equipment can now join the same system and interoperate.[14] Additionally, any given application run on the network may show a different kind of network effect from usage: E-mail, for example, is a more valuable service if it can be used more widely. Similarly, the World Wide Web becomes more valuable as it accumulates more reference linkages, allowing more information to be indexed and accessed.

Both types of network activities are simultaneously possible because the Internet exhibits more than one type of network effect, a point that may require some brief explanation. Katz and Shapiro have distinguished between actual and virtual networks.[15] Actual networks may be characterized as those that physically interoperate with one another, virtual networks as those that have common features without direct interoperation. To the extent that the Internet generates benefits to users by having their machines physically connected to the network, allowing interaction between users, it represents an actual network. Simultaneously, the benefits accruing from similarity of software platforms or, for that matter, from the content on the system, constitute a virtual network of shared compatibility. By providing a common technical standard, the Internet generates both types of beneficial effects.

The creation of a common standard is often beneficial, and indeed may be critically important, where network efficiencies can be realized. At the same time, the potential downside of any standards-setting process is profound.[16] Networks may also produce negative effects, as the cost of leaving the network, even when it would be socially desirable to do so, may be prohibitively high. The likelihood of "lock-in" to an inefficient standard remains a disputed but nonetheless serious consideration.[17] The concern in such situations is that once a standard is adopted, network effects may raise the cost of changing to a newer or better alternative, causing the standard to become permanently entrenched. This may possibly occur where the short-term costs of switching away from the old standard are greater than the long-term benefits of the new standard— indeed, it has been argued that development of new standards may be deterred if network effects raise the short-term cost of development and deployment is above the perceived savings of a new standard.

As a consequence, the development of standards carries potential risks to competition, related to the potential negative consequences of network effects. Eventually, the prevailing standards in a networked industry might be displaced by the promulgation of new or better standards, but there is a serious danger of anticompetitive manipulation of the standards-setting process, or of the standard itself, to achieve some form of market dominance.[18] Standards-setting organizations, for example, may sometimes cloak anticompetitive cartel-like activity if their membership is limited and conditions permit them to control adoption of the standard.[19] Either within or without an organizational setting, a dominant industry player may be able to arrange "tipping" of the market toward a desired standard—presumably, toward a proprietary standard that can be controlled or exploited by that producer. Network effects may be manipulated in these situations to "lock" users in to the standard, frustrating new entry or technological improvement.

Legal Standards-Setting

As an international network, the Internet presents issues related not only to the actual compatibility of technical products but also to the virtual compatibility of *legal* products.[20] Like language or interoperable computer systems, law may also be characterized as a system with network effects, displaying the same standardization issues familiar from analysis of technological standards. Legal harmonization facilitates a virtual network of compatible legal standards. Efficiencies may be realized when interjurisdictional legal standards are adopted, just as they may be when interjurisdictional electrical or telecommunications standards are adopted. Such legal compatibility allows individuals and entities to invest once in learning the legal system, then apply that investment across multiple jurisdictions.

Indeed, it might be said that law interoperates with law from other jurisdictions, particularly as capital, goods, and individuals interact or move across borders; such movements or transactions may be simultaneously subject to the legal standards of multiple jurisdictions, creating a potential for incompatible standards to impose conflicting demands on the interjurisdictional actor. Where legal standards differ, or are incompatible, compliance with applicable law becomes expensive and uncertain. These uncertainties have long been a focus of concern for Internet-related activities, although this type of interaction is not unique to Internet activity.[21] Individuals who travel are frequently confronted not only with unusual and incompatible electrical outlet configurations but also with unusual and sometimes incompatible legal requirements. Businesses that operate in more than one country must similarly cope with the legal demands of multiple jurisdictions. Indeed, large bodies of adaptive jurisprudence have grown up around routinely encountered questions of jurisdiction and choice of law conflicts—what to do when a traveler from one country commits a crime in another country's territory, or when an industrial activity in one country causes harm in a different country. Such "meta" legal rules designate which law should govern when multiple, conflicting sets of laws could be applied to an interjurisdictional situation.

The Internet greatly facilitates such interjurisdictional interaction, connecting individuals and institutions from differing legal systems and raising the level of virtual movement between regimes. Perhaps more important, the low costs of accessing the network also make such interactions relatively cheap, placing them within the purview of small businesses and average citizens—no longer are transnational interactions relegated to a relatively few highly capitalized transnational firms. However, this new, cheap access to worldwide communications also means that interjurisdictional conflicts may now become commonplace to those who are least likely to have expertise or skill in negotiating inconsistent legal regimes. Negotiating these complex systems of "meta" legal rules is a daunting task even to those knowledgeable in their intricacies, and a nearly impossible proposition to the average person or business entrepreneur. In such circumstances, the existing framework for conflicts of law may not "scale" well—the byzantine, costly legal rules developed for pre-Internet interactions may be too unwieldy to apply to the ubiquitous interjurisdictional interactions the Internet has created.[22]

The problem of transborder conflicts occasioned by the Internet may therefore be characterized as a difference of scale, rather than of type—conflicts simply happen more frequently because connections to the global computer network have become widespread. But the Internet also reveals an additional dimension of interjurisdictional conflicts analysis that may have gone previously unrecognized.[23] The rise of Internet-based "virtual" interactions dramatically illustrates the interconnection of legal and technical networks and implies that law interoperates with technology. The interconnected technological system of the network may be considered an extension of the legal systems arrayed at the periphery of the net. Essentially, the Internet concatenates the legal regimes it touches into a single, seamless network of social interactions.

Thus, the technological system of the network in essence provides a common standard for interjurisdictional interoperation of diverse legal systems. Yet it must be understood that just as the technical network is agnostic toward the applications, platforms, or devices arrayed at its periphery, so too is it indifferent to the legal networks that it interconnects. The open architecture and "end-to-end" design of the network may connect devices with otherwise incompatible operating systems, or it may connect jurisdictions with otherwise incompatible legal systems: Whether it is Unix-based machines interoperating with Windows-based machines or protectionist-based copyright interoperating with access-based copyright, the network treats them all the same. As a result, the network may bridge legal systems with radically different goals and expectations.

Indeed, most of the legal controversies surrounding the Internet may be characterized as arising out of this interconnection of incompatible legal systems, not unlike the problem faced by a traveler attempting to plug into a foreign electrical grid an appliance not intended for the local voltage or socket configuration.[24] A variety of Internet-related controversies have erupted over online activity ranging from the promulgation of pornographic materials to the sharing of software or music files. The design of the network, lacking the natural impediments intrinsic to traditional media, actually facilitates the distribution of problematic information. In some cases, local reaction has centered on such technological solutions as software filters or technological controls. In other cases, the reaction has been to amend or extend legal sanctions for the offending activity or to implement some combination of legal and technical prohibitions. These responses to electronic dissemination of pornography, or of private information, or of copyrighted works, are essentially attempts to either legally or technically retrofit the network to comply with the local legal regime.

Retrofitting the network to local standards via technological or cultural add-ons therefore attempts to adapt a foreign standard to interoperate with local systems, much as the traveler may attempt to retrofit a nonconforming device to local voltage, current, and plug configuration by means of adapters and transformers. As with electrical adapters and transformers, the cost of such inconvenience could be lowered, and a variety of other efficiencies realized, by establishing a single international standard for international legal interoperation, or at least interoperation facilitated via the Internet. On this view, the "harmonization" process for international Internet law essentially constitutes a standards-setting process, establishing uniform legal standards across multiple jurisdictions.

But while this approach offers the benefits of standardization, it carries with it the same dangers indicated previously: There may be serious long-term costs if Internet law becomes "locked" into a single standard, particularly if dominant nations act strategically in establishing that standard. As in the case of technical standards, standardized law raises a real danger that a dominant standard will suppress competition and entry into the market for law products. Just as firms may behave strategically in the technical standards-setting process, nations may well behave strategically in the legal standards-setting process. There is already some evidence that this is occurring in international harmonization regarding privacy and intellectual property, where the United States and the European Union have, respectively, largely eliminated any competing regulatory systems.[25] While the international information law regime may benefit in the short run from the uniformity engineered by the U.S. and EU dominance in these areas, there is little opportunity for displacement of these regimes by newer, possibly more innovative approaches. In this environment, such dominant law producers may well monopolize the market for Internet law for the foreseeable future.

Conclusion

I have suggested here that the costs and benefits of internationalizing Internet law can be evaluated by adapting models drawn from the economic analysis of cartel theory and standards-setting, as law may be considered not only a product but also a standard. The equation of law with interoperable technical standards should hardly come as a surprise. Students of technological meaning have long held that technology comprises reified norms.[26] At the same time, law is largely the formal statement of those norms.[27] The normative meanings of these two cultural artifacts interact in a complex relationship, both reshaping and reinforcing one another. More recently, legal scholars including Reidenberg and Lessig have suggested and extensively explored the interchangeability of law and of technological constraints in achieving social policy objectives.[28] This conceptualization of law is in some sense the logical endpoint of the economic approach conceiving law as a product: If law is an economic good that competes with similar goods from other producers, so too is law a product that interoperates with similar products from other producers, as well as with other systems of complementary or competing products, even if they take the form of technological standards.

Notes

1. Charles Tiebout, *A Pure Theory of Local Expenditures*, 64 J. POL. ECON. 416 (1954).

2. *See* Joseph Stiglitz, *The Theory of Local Public Goods in* LOCAL PROVISION OF PUBLIC SERVICES: THE TIEBOUT MODEL AFTER TWENTY-FIVE YEARS 17, 18 (George R. Zodrow ed. 1983).

3. *See* George J. Stigler, *Economic Competition and Political Competition*, 13 PUB. CHOICE 91, 93 (1972).

4. Susan Rose-Ackerman, Does Federalism Matter? Political Choice in a Federal Republic, 89 J. POL. ECON. 152, 157 (1981).

5. *See* Albert Breton, *The Existence and Stability of Interjurisdictional Competition in* COMPETITION AMONG STATES AND LOCAL GOVERNMENTS: EFFICIENCY AND EQUITY IN AMERICAN FEDERALISM 37, 42 (Daphne A. Kenyon & John Kincaid eds. 1991).

6. Robert P. Inman and Daniel L. Rubinfeld, *The Political Economy of Federalism in* PERSPECTIVES ON PUBLIC CHOICE: A HANDBOOK 71, 83 (Dennis C. Mueller, ed. 1997).

7. *See* Roberta Romano, THE GENIUS OF AMERICAN CORPORATE LAW 5–6 (1993).

8. *See* George J. Stigler, *A Theory of Oligopoly*, 72 J. POL. ECONOMY 44 (1977).

9. Marci A. Hamilton, *The TRIPS Agreement: Imperialistic, Outdated, and Overprotective*, 29 VAND. J. TRANSNAT'L L. 613, 615–16 (1996).

10. 2 HERBERT HOVENKAMP ET AL., IP AND ANTITRUST: AN ANALYSIS OF ANTITRUST PRINCIPLES APPLIED TO INTELLECTUAL PROPERTY LAW § 35.1 at 35–3 (2002).

11. *See* Carl Shapiro and Hal R. Varian, INFORMATION RULES 229 (1999).

12. *See* Michael L. Katz and Carl Shapiro, *Network Externalities, Competition, and Compatibility*, 75 AM. ECON. REV. 424 (1985).

13. *See* Mark A. Lemley and David McGowan, *Legal Implications of Network Economic Effects*, 86 CAL. L. REV. 479, 551 (1998).

14. *See* Mark A. Lemley and Lawrence Lessig, The End of End-to-End: Preserving the Architecture of the Internet in the Broadband Era, 48 UCLA Law Review 925 (2001).

15. *See* Michael L. Katz and Carl Shapiro, *Systems Competition and Network Effects*, 8 J. ECON PERSP. 93, 95 (1994).

16. *See* Carl Shapiro, *Setting Compatability Standards: Cooperation or Collusion*, in EXPANDING THE BOUNDARIES OF INTELLECTUAL PROPERTY: INNOVATION POLICY FOR THE KNOWLEDGE SOCIETY 81, 88 (Rochelle Cooper Dreyfuss et al. eds., 2001).

17. *See* S. J. Leibowitz and Stephen E. Margolis, *The Fable of the Keys*, 33 J.L. & ECON. 1 (1990).

18. *See* Stanley M. Besen and Joseph Farrell, *Choosing How to Compete: Strategies & Tactics in Standardization*, 8 J. ECON. PERSP. 117 (1994).

19. *See* Mark A. Lemley, Intellectual Property Rights and Standard-Setting Organizations, 90 CAL. L. REV. 1889 (2002).

20. *See* Margaret Jane Radin, Online Standardization and the Integration of Text and Machine, 70 FORDHAM L. REV. 1125 (2002).

21. *See* Jack Goldsmith, *Against Cyberanarchy*, 65 U. CHI. L. REV. 1199 (1998).

22. *See* Dan L. Burk, *Federalism in Cyberspace Revisited* in WHO RULES THE NET? INTERNET GOVERNANCE AND JURISDICTION 119 (Adam Theirer & Wayne Crews, eds. 2003).

23. *Cf.* Lawrence Lessig, *The Law of the Horse: What Cyberlaw Might Teach*, 113 HARV. L. REV. 501 (1999).

24. *See* Dan L. Burk, *Cyberlaw and the Norms of Science*, 1999 B.C. INT. PROP. & TECH. F. (June 4, 1999) http://infoeagle.bc.edu/bc_org/avp/law/st_org/iptf/commentary/content/burk.html.

25. *See* Dan L. Burk, *Privacy and Property in the Global Datasphere: International Dominance of Off-the-shelf Models for Information Control* in PROCEEDINGS OF THE FOURTH INTERNATIONAL CONFERENCE ON CULTURAL ATTITUDES TOWARD TECHNOLOGY AND COMMUNICTION 363 (Fay Sudaweeks & Charles Ess, eds., 2004).

26. Bruno Latour, *Where Are the Missing Masses? The Sociology of a Few Mundane Artifacts*, in SHAPING TECHNOLOGY/BUILDING SOCIETY: STUDIES IN SOCIOTECHNICAL CHANGE 225, 244 (Weibe E. Bijker & John Law, eds., 1992).

27. *See* Eric A. Posner, LAW AND SOCIAL NORMS (2002).

28. Lawrence Lessig, CODE AND OTHER LAWS OF CYBERSPACE (1999); Joel Reidenberg, *Lex Informatica: The Formulation of Information Policy Rules Through Technology*, 76 TEX. L. REV. 553 (1998).

III

Science and Medicine

10

Emerging Market Pharmaceutical Supply

A Prescription for Sharing the

Benefits of Global Information Flow

Frederick M. Abbott

NEW INFORMATION TECHNOLOGIES enable individuals in disparate locations to conduct cutting-edge research, to move that research into the development and testing of new medicines, to manufacture high-quality products, and to move those products to patients around the world. Conceptually, the world pharmaceuticals supply market may become increasingly competitive at all stages: basic research, product development, manufacturing and distribution. The diffusion of technological competence to major developing country actors in the pharmaceutical sector, such as India and China, as well as to more specialized actors such as Bangladesh (manufacturing) and Singapore (research), could result in a significant expansion of the pool of products available to treat disease, as well as more affordable prices to consumers.

Ownership of pharmaceutical technology resources is overwhelmingly concentrated in the OECD countries. These resources are protected by legal rights in intangibles and by regulatory and relational barriers to market access. The emergence of developing and middle-income country (hereinafter "emerging market country") competitors in the "originator" and "generic" product supply markets will erode profits of OECD-based enterprises. To address this threat, the OECD-based Pharma companies (hereinafter "Pharma") are engaged in a multipronged strategic effort to maintain control over the global market. The first part of that strategy involves tightening control over technology assets through laws and regulations governing innovation (i.e., patents) and investment in product development (i.e., data protection). The second part of that strategy involves investment in the emerging market countries to acquire or otherwise exercise control over potential competitors. The third part of that strategy involves maintaining control over national distribution systems so as to provide an embedded source of revenues.

This chapter argues that the emergence of wider competition in the quest for new products, the development of those products, and the improvement of production technologies and distribution to patients/end users are strongly in the welfare interest of the global public. It further argues that emerging market countries are not yet at the stage in which the application of competition law will adequately promote and protect domestic pharmaceutical companies. It recommends that emerging market countries adopt industrial policies designed to promote and protect their infant pharmaceutical supply sectors. It recognizes that the United States, among other OECD countries, significantly subsidizes and otherwise protects its pharmaceutical industry and that emerging market countries cannot realistically compete with the advantages presently held by OECD industries without adopting and implementing their own industrial policy measures.

The Pharma companies are engaged in behavior that they consider to be profit maximizing. Profit maximization is argued to be a response to capital markets that allocate investment to industries in accordance with anticipated returns. Jean-Pierre Garnier, chairman of Glaxo, has made the point that the Pharma companies are not charitable institutions.[1] The interests of wider society in affordable prices and wider access to medicines require that external forces be mobilized to offset Pharma's profit-maximizing conduct, whether those forces are enhanced competition, government regulation, or public pressure from NGOs.

The development of a more competitive global pharmaceutical supply market will not be an immediate panacea for significant parts of the world population who are unable to afford medicines, particularly newer ones. National and international policymakers will remain obligated to establish and implement mechanisms designed to make medicines available to those who cannot afford them.

Proliferation of Knowledge and Capacity

The Internet and other information flow innovations are rapidly transforming the global market for the provision of goods and services. Differentials in technological capacity between the OECD countries and developing countries are rapidly closing. India already has emerged as a significant base for computer software research and development, and the outsourcing by U.S.-based software companies of development work to India is a source of political concern in the United States. China is supplanting Japan as supplier to the world of middle-technology goods. While China's rapid ascendance as a technological power can be attributed to appropriation of OECD technological expertise, as its scientific community further absorbs that expertise it is a certainty that China will itself become a source of innovation.

The development of "new" medicines is complex and time consuming and carries a high level of risk. The costs of new pharmaceutical product development are high in comparison with those of middle-technology products. Pharma companies own the overwhelming percentage of existing pharmaceutical technology patents and data protection–based rights, as well as proprietary know-how protected by trade secrets. This technology asset base provides a very significant advantage in the development of new drugs, which often are based on existing technology. The Pharma companies have access to a large capital base in the form of existing assets, and they enjoy access to well-developed capital markets. In the United States, Europe, and Japan, the Pharma companies are connected to laboratories at well-financed universities and teaching hospitals. In the United States, the National Institutes of Health (NIH) has an annual budget of $30 billion, most of which is devoted to research on new treatments for disease. The fruits of NIH research are made available in the form of patented technologies to U.S.-based Pharma companies at very low cost.

In light of the static advantages working in favor of the Pharma companies, it will be difficult for emerging market enterprises to rapidly become competitive in the research and development of new pharmaceutical products (i.e., "originator" products). India-based pharmaceutical companies have focused on improvements to production technologies and are leaders in this area. The Indian government has increased its attention to public research and development funding, and Indian researchers are obtaining more pharmaceutical patents.[2] There is less publicly available information about the state of China's domestic pharmaceutical research and development, but there are reasons to believe that the Chinese government is increasing its attention to this sector. Chinese researchers have been responsible for the development of important new technologies in the treatment of malaria. China has a long tradition of attention to medicines and health. The University of Hong Kong, among others, has launched a program to identify the scientific basis underlying the curative properties of traditional Chinese medicines. China also acts as a major supplier of pharmaceutical chemicals to the OECD and therefore is already competent in production technology.

At the high end of the technology spectrum, Singapore has made pharmaceutical research and development a top national priority, investing substantially in the Biopolis research complex. Scientists at that complex were responsible for identifying the genetic markers of the SARS virus well ahead of the timeline generally projected for this task, and they licensed the results to Roche. The Israeli pharmaceutical industry, which so far has largely focused on generic production, is turning its attention to the development of new products. At the lower end of the technology spectrum, Bangladesh, a least-developed country, is emerging as a major producer of high-quality generic drugs.

In India there is a growing sub-industry of clinical testing subcontractors. Clinical testing of new drugs is the most expensive component of developing such products. Indian subcontractors hold themselves out as a low-cost alternative to clinical testing in the OECD markets.

While the Pharma companies maintain significant technology and capitalization advantages over the pharmaceutical industries of India, China, and other emerging market countries, there are good reasons to believe that these advantages will erode over the next decade.

Global pharmaceutical sales are in excess of $700 billion a year. The Pharma companies are well aware of the threat to their global market dominance represented by the emerging market pharmaceutical industries. They anticipated and have been acting upon this threat since the early 1980s. As the pace of change accelerates, largely based on development of new information technologies and enhanced global information flows, the Pharma response is growing in scope and intensity.

Strategic Response
Protection of Intangible Assets

OPENING ROUND

In the early 1980s, the Pharma companies initiated efforts to limit competition by tightening worldwide intellectual property standards. A failed effort at the World Intellectual Property Organization (WIPO) resulted in the shifting of the forum of negotiations to the GATT. The GATT Uruguay Round negotiations, which commenced in 1986, yielded the 1995 TRIPS Agreement, which was a qualified success from the Pharma standpoint.

The TRIPS Agreement established an obligation to provide pharmaceutical product patent protection, subject to a ten-year transitional exemption in favor of developing countries. The transition period allowed Indian manufacturers to improve their generic production technologies, although it did not provide access to the high-value OECD pharmaceutical markets when patent protection was in place there.

However, from Pharma's standpoint there were several important limitations to the TRIPS Agreement. First, it did not provide protection against the sale of generic drugs to countries where patents had not been obtained. The major Pharma companies traditionally file patent applications in a relatively small number of countries where substantial sales opportunities are foreseen or where competitive producers might emerge. This leaves a fairly wide range for competition from Indian (and other emerging market–produced) generic drugs in less affluent markets. Second, the TRIPS Agreement did not include any control over the pricing of patented pharmaceuticals. This was largely a developed-country problem. Virtually all of the OECD countries outside the United States impose some form of control on drug prices, significantly constraining the pricing power of the Pharma companies. Third, although the TRIPS Agreement requires pharmaceutical product patent protection and data protection, the rules are not airtight. For example, the patent rules do not require countries to offer protection for *second medical indications*. They also allow significant flexibility in defining *inventive step*. This allows countries to limit the number of patents by requiring a significant level of innovation over the prior art. With respect to data, protection is required only as to "new chemical entities" and with respect to "unfair commercial use."

SECOND-LEVEL INTANGIBLE PROTECTIONS

The limitations of the TRIPS Agreements grew in importance as the pharmaceutical industries of the emerging market countries became more competitive. The best tactic for eliminating these limitations would have been negotiation of a second-generation multilateral agreement at the WTO: a TRIPS II. However, in the multilateral setting, developing countries were not interested in closing the few openings left to them by TRIPS flexibilities.

The second-best tactic was negotiation of bilateral and regional trade agreements that eliminate or restrict the flexibilities of the TRIPS Agreement. For complex reasons (explored elsewhere) developing countries have been willing to concede TRIPS flexibilities in bilateral negotiations that they will not concede multilaterally. Concessions include tightening standards of patentability, imposing data protection standards that make it difficult to register and market generic drugs, limiting compulsory licensing and parallel trade, and allowing the prosecution of nonviolation nullification or impairment claims. In the free trade agreement between the United States and Australia, U.S. Pharma companies have won the right to challenge Australian price control decisions (which are given effect through the determination of which drugs are available for insurance reimbursement).

In the bilateral and regional agreements the data protection hurdle is given effect by the national drug regulatory authority, which is responsible for granting marketing approval and registering medicines. Linking regulatory approval authority to the patent status of medicines enhances the power of the patent holder because an affirmative burden is placed on the generic producer to overcome patent claims before it can market its drug. It also places a burden on national regulatory authorities to determine patent status, a burden that may be very difficult for the typical health regulatory authority to carry.

The effect of the second-best solution is to create additional impediments to the penetration of developing-country markets by Indian, Chinese, and Israeli generic pharmaceutical companies, among others.

Acquisition and Control of Potential Competitors

The greatest threats to OECD dominance of the global pharmaceutical market come from the potential emergence of innovator Indian and Chinese pharmaceutical companies, which will similarly be able to take advantage of IP protections, generating substantial research and development and marketing capital. India and China possess not only significant technological infrastructure but also large and growing domestic markets. Russia, Brazil, South Africa, the Ukraine, and a few other countries possess similar, though somewhat less favorable, characteristics for the development of integrated pharmaceutical sectors.

Although the agenda is just now being implemented, it is clear that the tactical move of Pharma is to employ accumulated capital stock to acquire and/or control companies based in India and other emerging market countries. This will be combined with "green-field" investments (i.e., new investments not involving existing local enterprises) in these countries. This trend is visible in Glaxo's expanding relationship with one of India's leading independent pharmaceutical companies, Ranbaxy, several of whose senior managers are former Glaxo employees. It is very difficult for independent companies in India to resist the amount of capital available to foreign multinational investors. From the standpoint of a Pfizer or a Glaxo, it is preferable to spend several hundred million dollars to acquire control of a potential competitor than to risk the emergence of a strong competitor in the global market. Novartis in 2009 announced a planned $1 billion investment over five years to upgrade its research and development capacity in China. According to Novartis, this will allow it to take advantage of the large pool of talented researchers in that country.[3]

The growing penetration of the OECD-based Pharma companies in India and China will be aided by highly paid consultants, accountants, and lawyers who earn from foreign employers fees that cannot be matched by the domestic industry. The capacity for the Pharma companies to take control of the domestic regulatory infrastructure by paying the private regulatory elite to influence government policy is a phenomenon evident throughout the developing world. The result is a new class of locally based service providers with a strong vested interest in the protection of OECD corporate interests.

Control over Distribution

The pharmaceutical supply market is multilayered. Even if a manufacturer is able to remain independent and overcome patent and data protection barriers, it must still find distributors to place its product on the national market and, in the case of prescription medicines, physicians to prescribe the medicine and pharmacists to dispense it. Although this trend has recently abated, in the United States the major Pharma companies have in some cases controlled large pharmaceutical distributors. More commonly they enter into contracts with prescription pharmaceutical distributors under which a broad range of products are supplied. There are substantial efficiencies from the distributors' standpoint in doing business with a limited group of suppliers. The capacity of the major Pharma companies to supply a broad range of products makes it more difficult for smaller enterprises, including developing-country suppliers, to enter the market. The Pharma companies spend significant amounts of money to promote their products with physicians and on direct-to-consumer advertising. Physicians receive ancillary benefits, such as vacation seminars.

The Pharma companies similarly seek to control domestic distribution systems in developing countries. In many developing countries the local Pharmaceutical Manufacturers Association is dominated by the major international Pharma companies, which play a significant role in lobbying domestic drug and health care policies.

Perhaps of most importance, the Pharma companies spend tremendous amounts of money lobbying governments around the world. In the United States, they contribute to election campaigns and lobby Congress and the federal agencies responsible for regulating health care. The Medicare Prescription Drug Benefit program is one of the most costly government programs ever adopted. It was projected to cost the federal government $1.2 trillion over a ten-year period.[4] The terms of the program prohibit the federal government from negotiating the price of drugs with the pharmaceutical industry on behalf of the private insurance companies that give effect to the program (the so-called "non-interference clause"). This program may be one of the largest government-controlled transfers of wealth from the public to the private sector in human history.

Although there does not appear to be an explicit preference in the program for the purchase of drugs from American-based pharmaceutical companies, because the Pharma companies dominate the originator market and have established contractual relationships for the supply of generic drugs with health care providers, it seems highly likely that American-based Pharma companies will be the greatest beneficiaries of the Medicare Prescription Drug Benefit program.

Generic-substitution laws are an important tool for controlling drug prices. Such laws mandate or authorize the pharmacist to substitute generic versions of patented drugs prescribed by physicians, unless specifically directed otherwise by the physicians. The Pharma companies have argued that such laws interfere with their trademark rights. Even though generic-substitution laws are common in the OECD, including among the states of the United States, a specific challenge was made against the introduction of such a law in South Africa based on alleged trademark rights in the case brought by thirty-nine pharmaceutical companies against the government. That challenge was withdrawn (along with the other ill-founded claims).

The single most important item on the current Pharma agenda is the elimination of pharmaceutical price controls, particularly in the OECD markets, though that is also a goal rather difficult to achieve. The companies argue that because the United States does not control pharmaceutical prices while other OECD countries do control such prices, the United States is effectively subsidizing the research and development interests of other OECD countries. They argue that removal of price controls would eliminate the apparent failure of research and development burden sharing. Implicit in that argument is that prices for pharmaceuticals in the United States would be lower if they were higher in other OECD countries. Because Pharma companies control the OECD market for new products, the net effect of eliminating price controls would be to increase Pharma profitability disproportionately as compared with that for emerging market producers, thereby reinforcing Pharma advantages. Fortunately, European governments that control prices do not appear likely to be persuaded of the benefits of increasing further Pharma profitability through the elimination of price controls.

Implications for Consumer Welfare

As India, China, Israel, South Korea, Singapore, and other emerging pharmaceutical research and development centers increase their capacity for bringing innovative products to market, it seems likely that the pace of innovation on a global scale will increase and the public as a whole will benefit from the introduction of new therapeutic treatments. If the diffusion of technology to emerging pharmaceutical research and development centers is sufficiently powerful, we could enter a new era of technology-based competition in the pharmaceutical sector based on a significant increase in the number of products available for treatment in a particular therapeutic class. If there are a number of competing products in a therapeutic class, even if those products are patented, an increase in price-based competition would be expected, leading to lower prices. The possibility for competition within therapeutic classes provides a good reason for preferring that enterprises in emerging markets remain independent of the Pharma companies.

To the extent that emerging market enterprises survive as independent entities, they will seek patent protection for their inventions and attempt to preserve supra-competitive rates of return for as long as possible. They will charge the price the market will bear, with particular aim at the high-value markets of the OECD. In this respect, there is no reason to assume that enterprises in emerging markets such as India and China will behave differently from OECD-based Pharma companies. Problems of access to newer medicines among poorer segments of the global population may depend not upon which country is the source of that medicine, but rather upon whether governments are willing to take steps to promote access.

The preservation of independent pharmaceutical enterprises in emerging markets is more likely to affect pricing and availability in the generic than in the originator products sector. That is, it is critical that a significant number of well-financed generic producers participate in the global supply market because this is what constrains prices and enhances availability. Because high profits from the originator products sector are used to finance the establishment of distribution arrangements in the generic sector, it is important that the emerging market independents be active in both segments of the market.[5] Independent Indian pharmaceutical companies, today mainly active in producing generic products, are deeply concerned that by acquiring significant stakes in the local market, better-financed OECD-based Pharma companies will be able to drive them out of business. If this happens, the resulting decline in generic competition will push prices up worldwide.

The greatest potential threat to global consumers of pharmaceutical products is that the OECD-based Pharma companies will succeed in foreclosing competition in the market for generic products. They may accomplish this using the threefold strategy discussed previously, namely by preserving static technological leads through strengthened intellectual property protection, acquiring and/or controlling potential competitors and dominating distribution systems.

Preserving the Fruits of Global Information Flows

The problem faced by emerging market pharmaceutical industries in competing with the Pharma companies may broadly be described as a competitive markets problem, but not in the sense that the problem may be redressed solely by the application of traditional competition law principles. There are two reasons for this. First, and perhaps most important, the Pharma companies possess very significant advantages in the form of ownership of technology and access to capital markets and government subsidies that create a playing field which is not level. It is difficult to place the problems facing emerging market pharmaceutical industries squarely within the boundaries of traditional competition law. Second, even if the problems might be redressable as traditional problems of anticompetitive conduct, there would still be considerable difficulty with redressing them.

Regarding redress of anticompetitive conduct, most developing-country governments, including those of the major emerging pharmaceutical supply enterprises such as India and China, have only rudimentary competition law infrastructures. There is very little political impetus at the international level for the development of a multilateral competition law infrastructure that might overcome weakness at the individual nation-state level. In addition, the OECD countries have adopted policies that encourage their enterprises to engage in anticompetitive conduct in developing-country markets.[6] U.S. and EU competition laws each exempt anticompetitive conduct with solely foreign effect from their scope of application.

In an ideal world, developing-country antitrust authorities would play an essential role in protecting against consolidation of power in the pharmaceutical sector. At the moment, this can be viewed as only a long-term solution that is unlikely to influence the shape of the global market during the next decade, at least.

The larger solution for the emerging market countries lies in providing infant industry protection and support that will allow their pharmaceutical companies to compete on a level playing field with those of the OECD. Such protection may combine a variety of elements of industrial policy, including but not limited to:

- Placing legal limits on the level of foreign investment penetration of the national pharmaceutical sector. This could be accomplished either by limiting the percentage of ownership or control over individual enterprises or by limiting the overall level of ownership within the domestic market.
- Establishing a framework for public investment in research and development on new pharmaceutical technologies. The U.S. NIH framework principally involves contract projects with universities and private researchers, the results of which are made available for licensing to the local private sector.
- Using the public health budget to bolster domestic production by contracting with locally owned enterprises to provide medicines.
- Limiting the use of public funds for the purchase of new foreign-developed pharmaceuticals absent a clear demonstration of improved efficacy so as to reduce public health expenditure outflows.
- Controlling the prices of originator medicines.

- Using tax policy to bolster the domestic pharmaceutical sector. The United States, for example, recently allowed a tax holiday on the repatriation of foreign-generated profits that resulted in very significant contributions to the balance sheets of domestic pharmaceutical companies.
- Selectively using compulsory licensing to enhance public access to pharmaceuticals by creating competition from locally produced generic drugs, thereby bolstering generic producer capacity.
- Gradually building up the capacity of competition regulatory authorities.

Limitations on foreign equity participation will to some extent lower capital investment in the pharmaceutical sector, at least for the short term. For countries such as India and China, the possibility for foreign investors to take minority equity stakes in domestic pharmaceutical companies should be sufficient to attract a reasonable level of investment. In any case, there is no other viable mechanism for preserving independent enterprises when confronted with foreign investors holding enormous stocks of capital. However, the possibility for underinvestment by foreign enterprises makes it important to combine limitations on foreign equity participation with positive government policies in favor of locally owned enterprises, such as research and development subsidies and tax incentives.

There are important recent examples of infant industry promotion used to establish strong domestic industries. These include the European civilian aircraft sector, the Korean steel sector, and the Japanese supercomputer sector. Because the United States provides such heavy subsidies and incentives to its pharmaceutical industry, emerging market countries will not be able to establish and maintain competitive industries in the absence of comparable countermeasures. Such countermeasures could well be viewed as transitional arrangements until the playing field becomes more level and the means for regulating and preserving competitive markets emerges.

The Role of Governments in Protecting the Poor

As noted at the beginning of this chapter, it is unlikely that developments in the global pharmaceutical market over the next decade will provide substantially enhanced access to pharmaceutical products for the poorest segments of the world's population. That part of the world's population is not a functioning "market" in the sense that financial demand will induce adequate supply. There are a variety of tools that government policymakers can use to correct this market failure. This includes transfer payments such as underlay operation of the Global Fund, compulsory licensing of patents to allow lower-cost production for newer products, and bulk procurement arrangements to take advantage of economies of scale. Differential pricing may play a role, although care must be taken that it not be used as a means to allow dominant-market actors to foreclose the emergence of competitors. Funding for public development partnerships (PDPs) that focus research and development on "neglected diseases" must be placed on a sustainable footing.

Over the next decades a wider geographic distribution of research and development activities will, one hopes, result in an increased pace of discovery and the emergence of a more competitive global pharmaceutical supply market. Competition should bring prices down, improving access across all parts of the world's population. This chapter argues that vigilance and affirmative action are necessary for that new global environment to evolve.

Notes

1. "The furor surrounding Glaxo Smithkline chief executive Jean-Pierre Garnier's massive pay package led to an embarrassing defeat at the AGM and a public perception that all pharmaceutical executives are 'fat cats.' 'I'm not Mother Teresa' was his calm response to the situation, which prompted ridicule from areas as diverse as AIDS charities worldwide and popular news quiz Have I Got News for You." *Are the drug giants in danger of bleeding themselves dry? The pharmaceutical sector is beset by rising costs and bad PR* THE DAILY TELEGRAPH (LONDON), October 09, 2004.

2. See presentation by Dr. Ramesh Mashelkar (Council of Scientific and Industrial Research, India), *Human Development and Pharmaceutical Development, with special reference to TRIPS and India,* National Institutes of Health, Globalization, Justice and Health Conf., Wash., D.C., Nov. 4–5, 2003.

3. Novartis Media Release, *Novartis announces USD 1 billion investment to build largest pharmaceutical R&D Institute in China,* November 3, 2009. See also *Novartis Institute of Biomedical Research, Zhangjiang Hi-Tech Park, Pudong New Area, China,* http://www.pharmaceutical-tecnology.com/projects/novartis-institute (accessed December 12, 2009).

4. Ceci Connolly and Mike Allen, *Medicare Drug Benefit May Cost 1.2 Trillion, Estimate Dwarfs Bush's Original Price Tag*, Wash. Post, Feb. 9, 2005.

5. Competition among generic producers drives down price, and this effect becomes more pronounced as a significant number of producers compete in the supply of the same product.

6. See Frederick M. Abbott, *Are the Competition Rules of the WTO TRIPS Agreement Adequate?*, 7 J. Int'l Econ. L. 682 (2004).

IV

War

11

The Flow of Information in
Modern Warfare

Jeremy M. Kaplan

INFORMATION HAS ALWAYS BEEN IMPORTANT at the strategic level in warfare, whether to defeat the plans and disrupt the strategic alliances of adversaries as espoused by Sun Tzu,[1] to deliberately mislead enemy spies and make use of a carefully concealed ability to intercept plans— as the allies did in WW II[2]—or to galvanize and maintain public support through the presence of embedded reporters, as the United States did during its 2003 invasion of Iraq.

However, the free and rapid flow of information at the tactical and operational levels is currently causing a revolution in the very nature of warfare—a revolution in which the United States far outpaces the rest of the world. This revolution, while fueled by advancing technology, is heavily driven by the willingness and ability to implement the social and organizational changes needed to use that technology. The United States' recent successes in the use of net-centric information in Afghanistan and Iraq have been a wakeup call to the militaries of the rest of the world, which are now scrambling to join in this revolution.

This chapter focuses on information flow in modern war fighting at the tactical and operational levels—on the needs, issues, and challenges. One of the most fundamental of these challenges, that of protecting an organization from attacks on its information systems, is shared by our networked society and may require a common commercial/Department of Defense (DoD) solution.

This chapter does not address the global war on terrorism, which may not be a war in the same sense and may be more societal in nature. It also does not address peacekeeping operations and the challenges of rebuilding a society in the face of factionalism and terrorism. While those topics are both current and important, the challenges of tactical and operational combat are likely to continue as long as nations have armed forces.

Information Flows

Although there has been much recent discussion about effects-based operations, modern combat is dominated by information, mobility, and stealth. This is because the extreme lethality of modern precision weapons means that if you can find a target and get the information to an appropriate weapons platform, you can kill it. Thus the challenge has become to find targets quickly and to get information about them to the right weapons platforms in a timely manner. The targets' challenge is to move or hide while finding and directing weapons at you, your sensors, and your weapons platforms.

This is true for engagements across a broad spectrum of domains, from undersea warfare to air defense, ballistic missile defense, and, to a great extent, land combat. It formed the basis of U.S. successes in Afghanistan and Iraq, and it will become increasingly true for the combat engagements of other nations in the future.

Thus emerging U.S. doctrine increasingly stresses net-centricity—a group of operational concepts and technologies for getting the right information to the right users fast enough to give them information superiority over the enemy. These concepts have their roots in the vision of information superiority originally laid out in the Joint Staff's "C4I for the Warrior"[3] and "Joint Vision 2010"[4] in the early to mid-1990s, in many instances in advance of the technologies needed to achieve them.

Net-centric doctrine generally involves the free flow of all the information needed to plan and execute a campaign. This includes the intelligence information on the disposition of the enemy's supporting infrastructure; the logistical information that enables forces to travel light to theater and be met by the right equipment and supplies at the right locations and times to engage the enemy and continue the fight; the intelligence, surveillance, and reconnaissance (ISR) information that allows a war fighter to know where his enemy is and destroy him before that enemy knows where the war fighter is and can fire or move; and the information to do battle damage assessment, and re-strike insufficiently damaged targets. Finally, it includes the information-handling capabilities that enable forces to collaborate during execution and adjust their plans as the enemy tries to respond.

Networked Information Age

In the industrial age, the information needed to conduct operations flowed down from the top, along the chain of command. Status information on one's own forces and contact information on enemy forces flowed back up. Information flowed through independent or "stove-piped" channels and was often compartmentalized (available only on a need-to-know basis). This slowed planning and caused rigid execution that could not adjust for rapid changes in the disposition of enemy forces.

In the information age, a commander's intent and major resource allocation decisions still flow down from the top, but coordination takes place horizontally on a network that allows everyone engaged in combat, combat planning, and combat support to discover relevant information and collaborate with the other elements needed for the success of the operation. This enables dispersed, massively parallel combat operations at an unheard-of pace. Dispersed war fighters, across echelons, may hear the decision briefings and the commander's intent via networked conferencing and plan in parallel to execute their operations. Logisticians have access to shared databases with current data and understand the competing needs and demands on their resources. Forces self-synchronize their plans for attack and pull the information they need from all available sources. Their operational tempo is increased by globally networked communications that enable coordinated activities and work flows across units and people that are not co-located or even working at the same time.

Networked information flow concepts, like the open posting and pulling of information, are fundamental to hypermodern warfare. They enable organizations (such as supply units) that would not normally have the ability to task assets (such as intelligence, surveillance, and reconnaissance resources) or have access to data to have the ability to search databases (e.g., Web searches of previous reconnaissance imagery) and to locate information no one ever thought to send them because no one ever anticipated their need for that information. DoD has called the concept of open networked information flow "power to the edge," because more people "at the edge" can directly perform mission and mission support, empowered with the information they need, and fewer people are "in the middle," involved with organizing information flows and pushing paper.

Networked Operations

Open information flows and global networks are also driving a decrease in the number of echelons of command needed, and a merging of the strategic, operational, and tactical levels of warfare. An extreme example of this is the ability of a flag officer in the continental United States (CONUS) to direct the flight of an armed Predator unmanned aerial vehicle that is flown by an operator in another part of CONUS and is flying in a theater of operations half a world away.[5]

Globally networked information flows allow some information support units (e.g., some intelligence and logistics personnel) to remain in CONUS and still be effective. This has the added benefit of lowering the footprint in theater (thus fewer forces to support), increasing the speed with which forces can reach theater (fewer forces to transport), and improving the safety of some forces (which do not have to be protected in theater).

Fully networked operations can involve worldwide platforms and people from all four military services working in tandem with analysts from the intelligence community and with the industrial support base and can involve complex operational information flows to and from units around the globe.

To get a feeling for how information flows have changed warfare, first imagine a World War II–era soldier without precision weapons or networked support. He sees a target (perhaps a tank), fires an unguided weapon at it, and probably misses.

Fast-forward in time. Given a precision weapon, the soldier probably hits and does damage if he has the right look angle and enough time to guide the weapon, and if he is not taken out by the enemy's suppressing fire. The soldier's chances of success improve further if he can communicate target information to an airborne platform with a better attack angle, lower vulnerability, and a greater supply of heavier and more powerful precision weapons than the soldier can carry. His chances of success improve still further if he can combine his local target position information (perhaps from a laser rangefinder) with global position information (perhaps from a GPS satellite) and give that to the airborne platform. The likelihood that the target will be hit before it can respond or move improves still further if the soldier can put that information directly into the targeting system of a precision weapon (perhaps a GPS-guided bomb) on board the aircraft—thus making the aircraft merely transportation for the soldier's extended weapon system.

Now imagine doing this across an entire theater, with networked sensors, soldiers, and aircraft designating and attacking hundreds of targets simultaneously, and with a networked, just-in-time, total asset visibility logistics system to supply them. You start to get an inkling of hypermodern, net-centric warfare.

DoD calls the networked information system it is evolving to support these concepts the Global Information Grid. It is composed of sensors and weapons platforms, command and control, communications, and an incredible supporting (and increasingly net-centric) infrastructure.

Issues and Challenges

The movement toward power to the edge through the creation of these net-centric capabilities involves immense questions and challenges that are the subjects of ongoing work. Broadly speaking, are there dangers to the war fighter in overreliance on the net? Will war fighters lose access to essential information or processing functionality at key moments or, still worse, receive information deliberately corrupted by the enemy? Will net-centric forces become vulnerable? As nations increasingly depend on networks to bring vital information to lighter, more mobile forces, can the networks be made secure? Will necessary information be available, timely, reliable (not tampered with), authentic (from the attributed source), and protected from enemy eyes?

Users always stretch resources to the limit. Will they be able to manage scarce resources to support the most pressing missions in the face of competing demands for networks and networked services (data and processing capabilities)?

Every movement in warfare creates a countermovement. How will the branch of cyberwarfare that attacks net-centric services (the networks, databases, and information processing platforms) evolve? From where (inside or outside the theater of operations) will attacks be launched? How will they be defended?

In addition to these broad challenges, the development of a net-centric force requires that very specific system-of system challenges must be addressed in the areas of interoperability, security, information sharing, and supply chain vulnerabilities.

Interoperability

DoD systems are built in parallel by multiple, independent, and competing developers. While this provides rapid modernization and other competitive advantages, it raises the significant challenge of systems interoperability across the DoD Global Information Grid. This interoperability challenge is a far greater challenge than is faced by Internet users because the complexity of the DoD system of systems is greater, and because DoD often needs a more speedy and reliable service that is protected from threats in a hostile environment.

Security

Greater effectiveness in warfare requires greater sharing, openness, and availability of information. Modern information systems are always in a state of flux (nodes are added, moved, and deleted; new software is installed, and existing software is patched). The heterogeneous Global Information Grid will be modified too frequently for any rigid security certification processes to be effective. How will we assure that the system has not been compromised? How will we balance the war fighter's need for access to information against the need to protect information systems, information, and sources?

Information Sharing

Warfare in the future will almost certainly involve coalition forces. If the United States wants its coalition partners to be effective and work at its operational tempo, it will have to do more than give them access to selected and screened information—it will have to put them on the DoD net, so that they can determine and access the information they need. This raises immense information protection and assurance issues, especially with coalition partners who are not long-term allies. Will the United States need to protect information about its operations from less trusted partners? Will it need to protect its information sources and methods? Will it need to protect its operating systems, data, combat applications, and combat-support applications from tampering? How can it provide these levels of protection, given the current precarious balance between computer network attack and defense? Should the United States decide, as it has already done in other areas (e.g., in the open publication via the Joint Technical Architecture of the information technology standards used for interoperability) that its military competitive advantage lies in openness, speed, and interoperability, and not in secrecy? Of course, the foregoing discussion applies to coalition partners who are already interoperable with the United States or use systems it supplies. Coalition interoperability faces additional technical challenges if the coalition partners have their own systems and networks built by their own vendors to different sets of standards.

Supply Chain Vulnerabilities

Software and hardware are inherent in all information technology products—from mobile phones to networked computer services. DoD is now a minuscule portion of the information technology market, so future generations of military information systems will come increasingly from industry—which values market share and frequently achieves it through cost-competitive strategies that do not account for potential vulnerabilities. In addition, as software and hardware are increasingly developed globally, can one ever be assured that they are free from designed-in and built-in vulnerabilities? Of course, with the advent of chat, mobile computing, file sharing, the convergence of voice and data, cloud computing, and software agents, information assurance problems will only get worse.

U.S. military strength comes, in good part, from its net-centric doctrine and ability to exploit, both socially and technically, the information revolution: its ability to collect and fuse data; its ability to network-enable services to achieve interoperability; its use of collaborative tools; and its ability to manage networks, information, and information security. As the pace of innovation quickens, it may become increasingly difficult to balance the benefits of adoption of new capabilities against the growing potential risks.

Conclusion

As a final note, society as a whole currently faces and will increasingly have to deal with most of the problems that DoD faces now.[6] Malicious computer hacking, spyware, identity theft, potential sabotage of infrastructure by persons located anywhere in the world—these are just a few of the growing problems of the commercial networked world. Most of our current information assurance problems (especially those arising from viruses, malware, and information attacks) are the result of weaknesses inherent in modern operating systems, computer languages and software, and the Internet protocol suite. Strong economic incentives (e.g., the advantages of being first to market, and the use of embedded freeware to cut development times) encourage software developers to continue these weaknesses. Can current information assurance approaches, with their heavy emphasis on signature recognition, ever provide adequate protection? Will it take a national disaster for us to put significant resources into research and development of a commercially viable and inherently secure architecture for networked computing? The current Internet is the result of an enormous investment made by the federal government, first in DoD and then in NSF-sponsored university research in advance of the current economic incentives. Perhaps it is time to reinvigorate this research program, with an emphasis on inherently secure computing paradigms.

Notes

The views expressed in this chapter are those of the author and do not reflect the official policy or position of the Industrial College of the Armed Forces, National Defense University, the Defense Information Systems Agency, the Department of Defense, or the U.S. government.

1. Griffith, Samuel B., Sun Tzu The Art of War, Oxford University Press, 1971, pp 78.

2. Brown, Anthony Cave, Bodyguard of Lies, Bantam Books, New York 1976.

3. The Joint Chiefs of Staff, 1992.

4. The Joint Chiefs of Staff, 1995.

5. General Tommy Franks, American Soldier, ReganBooks, 2004, pp 288–291.

6. DoD has the most significant expertise in the federal government (and perhaps in the country) in securing heterogeneous networks and computer enclaves from attack. Should DoD have a role in protecting the nation's information infrastructure?

12

Information Flows in
War and Peace

James Der Derian

IT'S THE INSTANTANEOUS NATURE of cyberattacks that has rendered defenses against them obsolete. Once an enemy finds a chink in U.S. cyberarmor and opts to exploit it, it will be too late for the United States to play defense (it takes 300 milliseconds for a keystroke to travel halfway around the world). Far better to be on the prowl for cybertrouble and— with a few keystrokes or by activating secret codes long ago secreted in a prospective foe's computer system—thwart any attack. Cyberdefense "never works" by itself, says the senior Pentagon officer. "There has to be an element of offense to have a credible defense."[1,2]

The spread and impact of information technology on global politics have left many a scholar in the dust. Methodologically, politically, geographically, the academic disciplines have been too specialized, parochial, or just not up to speed to comprehend the tsunami-like effects of networked information technology. Bound by a state-centrism, my own area of study, international relations, has been slow to consider the impact of information technology on war and peace. Curiously, law schools have been among the first of university bodies to take up the slack, deploying pragmatic, critical, and cross-disciplinary approaches to assess the global impact of information technology. This development hit home when I was invited to present in a single week at the

Columbia and Yale law schools, respectively, on "internment" and "flow"—or, more specifically, on how the technologies of both were affecting the traditional functions of national boundaries and state sovereignty. The two events highlighted what is often presented as the new global divide between "good" and "bad" information technology. On the one side, the rise and spread of information technology was viewed as increasing global communication, transparency, and productivity, thereby ameliorating the human condition. On the other, darker side, information technology was enabling new forms of Big Brother surveillance, terrorism, and war. So within the Ivies two stark contrasts emerge: new technologies condemned as the electronic prison gates of a new virtual incarceration and celebrated as interconnective switch gates for a new open source society. Rather than take sides or pretend that there might be some happy medium of interpretation, I want to consider both positions as just one more symptom of the *sturm und drang* induced by the information revolution. And as a first step in symptomology, one has to ask what other, more subtle, and less polarized signs are being ignored or neglected by the narrow pursuit of celebrating or denigrating information technology.

To Go (or Not) with the Flow

Any inquiry into the impact of information technology on world politics must address not only an increase in speed and volume but also the change in character and content of global information flows. This is most apparent as the flow of images begins to produce more powerful effects and supplant the flow of words. In the yet-to-be-written history of the transition from the Cold War to the information age, images trumped words over and again in political crises that punctuated shrinking periods of stability and order. We watched, literally and visually, as the dual promises of a peace dividend and information revolution after 11/9/89 were reversed and traduced by the events of 9/11/2001 and the "Long Wars" of counterterror and counterinsurgency that followed. In the process, new grammars of security and terror were produced.

As verb, code, and historical method, "to terrorize" has consistently been understood as an act of symbolically intimidating and, if deemed necessary, violently eradicating a personal, political, social, ethnic, religious, ideological, or otherwise radically differentiated foe. Yet, as noun, message, and catchall political signifier, the meaning of "terror" has proven more elusive. From Robespierre's endorsement to Burke's condemnation during the French Revolution, from the Jewish Irgun blowing up the King David Hotel to the Palestinian Black September massacre at the Munich Olympics, from bin Laden the Good fighting the Soviet occupiers of Afghanistan to bin Laden the Bad toppling the twin towers of New York, terrorism, terrorists and terror itself have morphed into the political pornography of modernity: One knows "terrorism" with certainty only when, literally, one sees it. But in a blink of the eye, the terrorist can become the freedom fighter, and vice versa, for at one time or another nearly everyone, from righteous statesmen who terror-bomb cities to virtuous *jihad*ists who suicide-bomb women and children, seems to have a taste for terror.

Without engaging in nostalgia, one can recognize that the most powerful model of terror, which inscribed the most powerful borders of inclusion and exclusion, mutated at the end of the Cold War. With the decline (if not the total demise) of a logic of deterrence based on a nuclear balance of terror, so too eroded the willingness and capacity to inflict mutually unacceptable harm that had provided a semblance of order if not an actual state of peace or justice to the bipolar system. In its place a new model has emerged, an *imbalance of terror*, based on a mimetic fear and hatred coupled with an asymmetrical willingness and capacity to destroy the other without the formalities of war.[3]

This cannot be reduced, as much as leaders on both sides of the conflict have tried, to merely a post-9/11 phenomenon. Its origins can be traced at least as far back as 1992, with the Pentagon's secret effort written by Paul Wolfowitz to model seven post–Cold War "war scenarios," including the rise by the year 2001 of an "REGT" (Resurgent/Emergent Global Threat).[4] It was publicly established in the 1998 US Defense Policy Guidance, which shifted from a strategy of *deterring* to *destroying* the enemy (subsequently reiterated in the Quadrennial Defense Review). And on the other side of the information divide, in 1998 bin Laden issued his pseudo-*fatwa* that decreed Christian and Jewish civilians legitimate targets of the *jihad*.

As in the older, tidier balance of terror, the doctrine of taking civilians hostage and if necessary killing them still held for both sides, but it now operated as a contingent factor of an asymmetrical relationship. Regardless of nomenclature—"terror" or "counter-terror"—high numbers of civilians would (and continue to) be killed in the process. It might be small solace to the victims whether they were primary targets as opposed to "accidental" or "collateral" victims, especially with casualty rates being terribly skewed in both cases. When one takes into account how war-related fatalities have been reversed in modern times, from a hundred years ago when one civilian was killed per eight soldiers, to the current ratio of eight civilians per soldier killed, then compares the combatant-to-noncombatant casualty figures of 9/11, the Afghan War to the Iraq War and now back again to the Afghan War, the terror/counterterror distinction begins to fade even further.

Ageism

Looking back, it does seem remarkable how the age of terror so easily displaced the information age and other competing descriptors of modernity. Historic moments all too often appear to be speaking for themselves. Think of the "Middle Ages," the "American Century," the '60s. Consider 2001, a year that signified awe for an extraterrestrial future in Kubrick's film—that is, until airplanes piloted by kamikaze Al-Qaeda terrorists brought the year, and the World Trade Center (WTC), crashing to earth. We clearly cannot begin to understand the transformation of the Cold War to the age of terror without studying the fundamentalist religious and political beliefs of the major combatants.[5] But we also need to pay more attention to how the information flow of powerful images acted as catalysts for these transitions.

Fueled by a revolution in the digitization and networking of information, the forces driving the information age spread fast and penetrated deeply. From its embryonic moments in the 1940s (when Claude Shannon wrote the first paper on information theory, transistors were invented, and ENIAC, the first computer, was built) to its accelerated takeoff in the 1990s (when packet-switching, personal computers, HTML, and the Internet produced a World Wide Web), the information revolution outpaced, outlasted, and outperformed all commensurable comers.

However, the information age never warranted the status of a *longue durée*. Although the information age might stretch in the United States from Silicon Valley to Silicon Alley and globally from Bangalore to Singapore, the distinguishing characteristic of the information age is a spatio-temporal *intensivity* rather than a geopolitical *extensivity*—that is, a capacity to intensify global effects through a collapse of time and distance. Developing unevenly within and across nation-states, and beset by rapid cycles of dot-com booms and busts, the information age is short on universality and long on instability. When a revolution stops auguring change and begins signifying an age, it usually means that a regime has been stabilized, a cultural shift codified, predictability restored.

Not so with the information revolution at the palpitating heart of the information age. The only constant is fast, repetitious, and highly reproducible change: a kind of hyperspeed Nietzschean "eternal recurrence" that defies—in spite of efforts by democratic peace theorists (with Thomas Friedman leading the pundits' charge)—the predetermined logic of progressivist teleologies. Modernity in an information age manifests not as a more advanced era succeeding an earlier backward one but as rapid oscillations of message and medium (signal-to-noise ratio), regressive repetitions of images (feedback loops), and phase shifts between order and disorder (or complexity).

Eight Propositions for Studying Infoflows

If not the era, can the promise of the information age be salvaged? Only if one first intellectually confronts and publicly compensates for the dark side of infotech and infloflow. I am sure there are more, but I have eight preliminary propositions for getting beyond 9/11 and back to the best the information age had to offer.

First, the most obvious: Infotech is producing new networks of power in IR that must be managed, regulated, and channeled for the amelioration of global, not national, security. Best defined by Kevin Kelly as "organic behavior in a technological matrix," networks are challenging and changing the nature of state power through new lattices of relatedness and responsiveness.[6] Obviously, the United States has emerged as the dominant military and economic power, and even in the worst-case nightmares of global realists, it is difficult to identify a potential "peer competitor" on the horizon. However, post–Cold War, post-9/11, we have witnessed the emergence of competing sources and mediations of power: what I call a *global heteropolar matrix*, in which different actors are able to produce profound global effects through interconnectivity. Varying in identity, interests, and strength, ranging from fundamentalist terrorists to peace activists, new global actors gain advantage through the broad bandwidth of information technology rather than through the narrow stovepipe of territorially based sovereign governments. Enhanced by IT, nonstate actors have become super-empowered players in international politics. Traditional forms of statecraft have become transformed and in some cases undermined by infowar, cyberwar, and netwar. The technologies of weapons of mass destruction, networked terror, accidental crises, and global media have transformed the meaning and discourse of national security.

Second, networked infotech provides new global actors the means to traverse political, economic, religious, and cultural boundaries, changing not only how war is fought and peace is made but making it ever more difficult to maintain the very distinction of war and peace. The West might enjoy an advantage in surveillance, media, and military technologies; but the rest, including fundamentalist terrorist groups, nongovernmental organizations, and anti-globalization activists, have tapped the political potential of networked technologies of information collection, transmission, and storage. We need to undertake a full-scale investigation of how global political actors force-multiply their influence in war and diplomacy through networked infotech.

Third, new global informational and technological networks of power require new modes of comprehension and instruction, and the social sciences have not been quick to take up the challenge. The virtual nature and accelerating pace of infotech is partly responsible: Actualizing global events in real time across traditional political, social, and cultural boundaries, infotech resists the social-scientific emphasis on discerning rational behavior, applying static models, and conducting incremental research projects. Moreover, the study of infotech requires a dialogue among technological, scientific, military and other nonacademic circles that has been notably lacking in discipline-bound university programs and politically oriented think tanks. Taking into account the heteropolar as well as multicultural nature of global politics, we need a strategy that endorses plural, conceptual, and multidisciplinary approaches to investigate what we consider to be the most challenging issue of the twenty-first century: the global application and management of IT in war and peace.

Fourth, we need to recognize that the impact of infoflow is now largely measured by infotech's capacity to produce a *moving* image of the world. In both senses of the word, this multimedium is *e*-motive, a transient electronic effect conveyed at speed. At the emotional level, this means image-based sentiments of fear, hate, and empathy now dominate word-based discourses of ideas, interests, and power. At the electronic level, the speed of the transmission—with real time currently the gold standard of media—matters as much as the content of the message. Paul Virilio, urban architect and social critic, has spent a lifetime demonstrating how this media-driven acceleration has produced what he calls an "aesthetics of disappearance," in which the political subject, be it the accountable leader, participatory citizen, or the deliberative process itself, is diminished and quickly engulfed by a growing "infosphere."[7]

Fifth, infotech—increasingly, repetitively, unavoidably—not only acts as trigger and transmitter of the global infoflow event but also affects how we respond to the event.[8] From the actual moment to the eventual interpretation—for better or worse—infotech records, relays, represents, and informs our response to global events. Infotech also shapes how we remember or forget their significance: We are back to chronology. We are all familiar with the contemporary production and transformation of multimedia by networked information technologies, from increased CPU speeds and broadband access, to real-time cable news and CNN effects, to embedded journalists and network-centric warfare. The global networking of multimedia that makes up the information flow has become unstoppable, and I believe that its effects may well have accelerated beyond our political as well as theoretical grasp. A public attention deficit disorder leaves little time for critical inquiry and political action by a permanently distracted audience.

Sixth, infotech has become essential for the global circulation of power, the waging of war, and the imagining of peace. Information technology is now an unparalleled force in the organization, execution, justification, and representation of global violence, as witnessed in the first Gulf War, the Kosovo air campaign, and the terrorist attacks of September 11. With the war in Iraq, the global effects of infotech became inescapable. We witnessed how antiwar organizers used the Internet globally to muster millions of protesters in large metropolitan areas; U.S. military commanders leveraged technological superiority to wage network-centric warfare; and embedded journalists provided influential battlefield reports by satellite videophones in real time. A glut of information (if a dearth of knowledge) drew viewers by the millions, not only to prime-time TV and cable news but also to instantly updated online press sites and unofficial war blogs. We witnessed the first, but certainly not the last, networked war.

Seventh, the darker side of infoflow, although freighted in the occasional media spasm, continues to evade the sustained attention of IR theory as well as the concern of international institutions.[9] Networked terror; network-centric warfare; network attacks by the Blaster, Nachi, and SoBig viruses; and a hot summer of electrical network failures had a tremendous transnational impact. Networked technologies merged issues of national, corporate, and personal security (and liberty) into an interconnected global problem. Yet the new global risks of interconnectivity, including negative synergies, unintended consequences, and the pathologies of networks like viruses, worms, and Trojan horses, often failed to make the global political agenda at all.

Eighth, the infotech/flow transformation of global politics requires new conceptual approaches. We need to interrogate as critical pluralists (rather than corroborate as social scientists) the extant knowledge of how information flow operates in international relations. My predilection for multimedia montage over parsimonious rationalist approaches is as much a response to these technological changes as it is a reflection of my earlier critiques of social scientific theory's failure to keep up with the pace of these changes. This is not an antitheoretical position. Rather, it shifts our intellectual priorities from the slow, incremental development of theory to the more supple and strategic application of concepts. Put pragmatically, theory informs, concepts perform.

From Infowar to Infopeace

The signs of rapid change are often pathologically manifested: Information, to paraphrase William Burroughs, has become a virus, and the immune response is often worse than the original contagion; densely networked systems produce negative as well as positive synergies with cascading effects; and everywhere global institutions of governance are failing to keep up with the new global risks of interconnectivity. We must adopt new strategies, concepts, and polices for the new dangers and opportunities presented by IT. As a preliminary step, we need to adapt and update a pair of concepts that capture the full spectrum potential of information flow, to enable the continuation of violence through *infowar*, as well as to provide the means to prevent, mediate, and resolve conflicts through *infopeace*. The concepts provide a sense of the complex, paradoxical, and often contradictory nature of the technologies that convey, generate, regulate, and stop information flows.[10] They emerge from but can also help us decouple information flows from the state of emergency that transforms technologies of security into weapons of mass distraction, deception, and destruction.

Information warfare, or infowar, has become the umbrella concept for understanding cyberwar, hackerwar, netwar, virtual war, and other network-centric conflicts. It has a history that goes back at least as far as Sun Tzu, who considered defeating an enemy without violence to be the "acme of skill" in warfare. From its earliest application in the beating of gongs and drums, to more sophisticated uses of propaganda and psychological operations, infowar has traditionally been deployed by the military as a "force-multiplier" of other, more conventional forms of violence. In this sense, infowar is an adjunct of conventional war, in which command and control of the battlefield are augmented by computers, communications, and intelligence. With the development of mass and multiple media, infowar has taken on new forms and greater significance. As the infosphere engulfs the biosphere; as the global struggle for "full spectrum dominance" supplants discrete battlefields; as transnational business, criminal, and terrorist networks challenge the supremacy and sovereignty of the territorial state, information warfare has ascended as a significant site for the struggle of power and knowledge. Infowar wages an epistemic battle for reality in which opinions, beliefs, and decisions are created and destroyed by a contest of networked information and communication systems.

Infowar couples sign-systems and weapons-systems. Command and control, simulation and dissimulation, deception and destruction, virtual reality and hyperreality—all are binary functions, sometimes symbiotic, other times antagonistic. Networks of remote sensing and iconic representation enable the targeting, demonization, and, if necessary, killing of the enemy. In its "hard" form, infowar provides "battlespace domination" by violent (GPS-guided missiles and bombs) as well nonlethal (pulse weapons and psychological operations) applications of technology. In its "soft" form, infowar includes a virus attack on a computer network or the wiping out of terrorist organisations' bank accounts. In its most virtualized form, infowar can generate simulated battlefields or even create *Wag the Dog* versions of a terrorist event. In any of these three forms, information warfare can be offensive (network-centric war, Trojan horse virus, or intelligence dissimulations) or defensive (ballistic missile defence, network firewall, or preventive media).

In spite of the official spin, infowar is not a precision munition. It might seek to discriminate in its targeting of enemies, but it is as broadcast forms of media that it is likely to produce all kinds of collateral damage, blowback, and newly resentful enemies.

At the other end of the information spectrum lies infopeace: the production, application, and analysis of information by peaceful means for peaceful ends. Starting with Gregory Bateson's definition of information as "a difference that makes a difference"[11]—this is war, that is peace, this war is here, that war is over there, this war is now, that war was then—infopeace seeks to make a difference through a difference in the quality of thinking about the global contest of will, goods, and might. Measuring information in terms of quality rather than quantity, and assessing quality by the difference it makes in the reduction of personal and structural violence, infopeace opens up possibilities of alternative thought and action in global politics. Unabashedly utopian yet pragmatic, it counters a "natural" state of war with an historicized state of peace.

Infopeace seeks to prevent, mediate, and resolve states of war by the actualization of a mindful state of peace. Positing the eventual abolition of violence as a global political option, peacemindedness ranges from the prevention, admonition, and mediation of violence to the outright disavowal of violence to resolve problems in the international arena. It draws on a long tradition of peace-thinking, exemplified in early Christian pacifism and Eastern philosophies, in which the need for peace begins internally and proceeds outwardly. It starts by embracing a wholeness of the individual and expands to families, communities, countries, and beyond. The notion of Gaia as a self-regulating biosphere contributes to the rhetoric of peace-thinking, but it is the networked reality of an expanding infosphere that makes peace an attainable and ever more vital necessity.

Infopeace stresses the actualization of peace through the creative application of information technology and public diplomacy. As a form of critical imagination, infopeace resists a technological determinism that increasingly circumscribes human choices. Further, infopeace integrates a strategy in which difference, conflict, and antagonism are recognized as essential aspects of human relations. It aims to develop an awareness of how these aspects can be addressed by nonviolent means.

The Banality of Terror

Let me conclude by returning to the images that take us to war and that can lead us to peace. As we know from medical pathology, the autoimmune response can kill as well as cure. The response to the most powerful images—the towers toppling, the bin Laden tapes, the Abu Ghraib photos—bears this out. Heinous crimes were revealed, public outrage was expressed, official apologies were proffered, congressional hearings convened and courts-martial put into place. In the case of the Abu Ghraib photos, once established as authentic, they took on a singular significance: a crisis for the Bush administration and America's reputation in the world. Numerous reports of earlier instances of dissimulations, groupthink acts of self-deception, and outright lies by the U.S. government—from claims about Iraqi ties to Al-Qaeda, the presence of weapons of mass destruction, and the likelihood of a swift postwar transition to peace and democracy—all paled in comparative political effect to the digital images of simulated sex, bondage, and mock lynchings. However, the surfeit of images also produced a reverse effect: Overexposed to images of prisoner abuse, Islamicist hip-hop videos, and brutal snuff films of hostages, many preferred to remove the realities of war with the flick of a channel, the click of a mouse. The way was clear for a banalization of terror.

We now see how the infoflow of terror and counterterror produces an iconic, virtual, and, even worse, increasingly banal effect. In her study of the "thought-defying" nature of evil that earmarked the killing machine of Nazi Germany, Hannah Arendt identified the political effects of this banalization. Citing Arendt and the "banality of evil" can, admittedly, be just another way of not really thinking through the pervasive and perverse state of emergency that shapes so much of world politics today. However, a more obscure observation by Arendt, captured during an interview from late in her life, leaves us with a sense of what radical measures are needed when the most destructive information flow takes on a banal character:

> It is indeed my opinion now that evil is never "radical," that it is only extreme, and that it possesses neither depth nor any demonic dimension. It can overgrow and lay waste the whole world precisely because it spreads like a fungus on the surface. It is "thought-defying," as I said, because thought tries to reach some depth, to go to roots, and the moment it concerns itself with evil, it is frustrated because there is nothing. That is its "banality." Only the good has depth and can be radical.

Notes

1. "U.S. Cyberwar Strategy: The Pentagon Plans to Attack," Mark Thompson, Time.com (2 February 2010).

2. "Inter arma silent leges." (In wartime, the laws fall silent.) Cicero, *Pro Milone* (52 BC) Justice Antonin Scalia, *Hamdi v. Rumsfeld* (2004).

3. "The art of deterrence, prohibiting political war, favors the upsurge, not of conflicts, but of acts of war without war." See Paul Virilio, *Pure War*, trans. Mark Polizotti, New York: Semiotext(e), 1983, p. 27.

4. See Patrick Tyler, *New York Times* (February 17, 1992), p. A8.

5. See James Der Derian, *Virtuous War: Mapping the Military-Industrial-Media-Entertainment Network*, Boulder and Oxford: Westview Press, 2001.

6. Kevin Kelly, *New Rules for the New Economy* (London: Fourth Estate, 1999), 31.

7. See Paul Virilio, *The Aesthetics of Disappearance,* trans. Philip Beitchman (New York: Semiotext(e), 1991), and James Der Derian, 'Introduction', *The Paul Virilio Reader* (Oxford: Blackwell Publishers, 1998), 1-15.

8. See *Philosophy in a Time of Terror: Dialogues with Jurgen Habermas and Jacques Derrida,* ed. Giovanna Borradori (Chicago, IL and London: University of Chicago Press, 2003), 85–90.

9. This was borne out at the December 2003 World Summit on the Information Society held in Geneva, at which the techno-optimists, vamping the political, cultural, and developmental promise of technological interconnectivity, had center stage while critics—especially American ones—were marginalized and kept out of the main planning sessions.

10. Even before Sun Tzu wrote his informative study of war, it seems that the Chinese well understood the nature of this contradiction, as demonstrated by the actual Chinese character for "contradiction": a combination of the ideograms for sword and shield.

11. Gregory Bateson. *Steps to an Ecology of Mind* (Chicago: University of Chicago Press, 2000), 459.

V

Power

13

Power over Information Flow

Dorothy E. Denning

INFORMATION FLOWS through a global environment characterized by conflict and competition. One party wants a flow to occur; another wants to block it. To illustrate: Users want to freely exchange information, while governments and businesses seek to block information harmful to their interests. Spies try to infiltrate the networks of their adversaries and competitors to gather intelligence, while their targets employ security mechanisms to prevent network exploitation and attack. Hackers and identity thieves send e-mails loaded with viruses and other forms of malicious software, while users employ antiviral tools to block the same.

Conflicts over information flow are at the heart of information operations and warfare, to include cyberwarfare, cybercrime, and cyber conflict in general. One party sends packets or streams of information that aim to attack, exploit, or influence a target, while the opponent employs measures to stop the flows. The cyber assault against Estonia in 2007, for example, was launched by patriotic Russian hackers who were incensed by the relocation of a Soviet-era war memorial in Estonia's capital, Tallinn. To express their outrage, they flooded select Estonian Web sites with Internet packets, exploiting at least one "botnet" of compromised computers to create a massive amount of traffic. Their distributed denial-of-service (DDoS) attack shut down the sites until the Estonians could effectively block the traffic and the hackers backed off. Russian hackers launched similar attacks against Georgian Web sites in 2008, this time in conjunction with a military confrontation between Russia and Georgia over South Ossetia.

Not all information-related conflicts center on cyberattacks. Following the 2009 presidential election in Iran, for example, protesters used various cybermedia, including Twitter, Facebook, YouTube, and text messaging, to distribute information and videos about the protests. In response, the Iranian government took steps to block access to certain Web sites and media. The government's efforts were only partially effective, however, as Iranians shared information and tools for circumventing the censors. Some of the protestors also launched a DDoS attack against President Mahmoud Ahmadinejad's Web site, but this was short-lived and played only a minor role in the overall conflict.

This chapter examines the global flow of information in terms of a power struggle between efforts to cause flows and efforts to block them. It analyzes the nature of this power, how it is exercised, and the objectives served. Although a variety of information media are considered, emphasis is placed on flows enabled by computer networks, including the Internet and mobile phone networks. Whereas information flows were at one time dominated by human interactions within small localities, today they are facilitated by global networks of hardware and software systems. The software itself is data, allowing it to flow like other information. But unlike other forms of information, which are effectively inert, software causes things to happen, including information flows. Spyware, for example, captures data on one computer and transmits it to another; computer worms spread their damaging code to other vulnerable hosts.

In viewing the global flow of information as a power struggle, the chapter does not mean to imply a lack of cooperation and collaboration in the information environment. Indeed, people frequently cooperate to share information and promote flows, as well as stop them. The world's largest encyclopedia, Wikipedia, is the product of widespread collaboration on the Internet. But even there, conflicts are common over specific content, as users edit and delete material to serve their interests.

After examining the power of flow and the power of blockage, the chapter looks at the characteristics and challenges of flows that are covert in nature. It then examines how laws and regulations support blockage power and, to a lesser extent, flow power. With this background, the chapter considers the issue of information control, and whether such control is even possible. Finally, it turns to the question of what power over information flow means in terms of influence. Ultimately, it is not the ability to control flows that matters as much as the ability to influence decisions and actions.

Flow Power

Information flows arise when information is transmitted from a source (or sender) to a destination (or receiver) over some channel. The source can be a human; a device such as a computer, sensor, or broadcast station; or some combination, as when a user sends an e-mail message from a laptop or places a call from a mobile phone. Similarly, the destination can be a human, a device, or both. The information channel may be provided or mediated by third parties, including communication service providers and governments. Further, the channel itself may be the source or target of additional flows, as when it is wiretapped.

Flow power is the ability to cause a flow of particular information from a given source to a given destination within a specified time. Time is an important element, because information can become stale and irrelevant.

Flow power can reside at the source, destination, or channel. At the source, power is characterized by an ability to *push* information to the destination. The means vary and include sending an e-mail, text, or instant message; talking in person or on the phone; transmitting a fax; broadcasting a television or radio program; and uploading information to a Web site or file directory.

Power at the destination is characterized by an ability to *pull* information from the source. A principal means is downloading information from a Web site or file server.

Many, perhaps most, information flows result from a combination of push and pull. Radio and television broadcasters push their programs onto the airwaves; viewers pull the ones they desire by tuning their receivers to the specified channels. Owners of Web sites push information onto their sites; interested users visit the sites and pull the information they want; they may also push new information onto the site by filling in a form or adding comments to a discussion thread. Even e-mail, which is predominantly a form of push, requires some pull from the recipient, namely to select, open, and read a message in the inbox. The result is that flow power may be shared by senders and receivers, with neither party being in full control of the flow. Still, the balance of power may not be even. E-mail and postal mail seem to favor senders, as illustrated by junk mail.

In some cases, the sender or receiver can execute a flow without help from the other party, or at least a human party. For example, pop-up ads are essentially pushed onto a user's computer, although facilitated by software running on the user's machine. Fax is another example that puts virtually all of the power in the hands of the sender. As an example where the receiver of information has the power, consider a hacker who breaks into another computer system. The hacker can pull information from the compromised machine without the owner's cooperation or consent, assisted only by software on the computer (possibly even pushed there by the hacker).

Third parties who provide or control the information channels also have power over information flows. These include Internet service providers and the owners and operators of network routers and name servers. E-mail and Web traffic cannot flow without this basic infrastructure. In addition, much of what people access on the Web is mediated through search engines, which control the order of entries in "hit" lists and which sites on the Web are indexed. The authors of blogs and other types of Web pages also facilitate flows by linking to other pages.

Receivers of information can serve as intermediaries for additional flows by forwarding the information to others, thereby facilitating flows from the originating source to downstream recipients. Indeed, information often flows through social networks via e-mail and other channels, reaching people not even known to the originator. In the process, intermediaries serve as brokers or gatekeepers to further flows.

In general, flow power is increasing across the board. One reason is that the volume of information is increasing, so there is considerably more information to push and pull. But technology has played an even larger role, reducing human effort at both the sending and receiving ends and reducing transmission times and costs. Software performs many tasks that once required considerable human effort, such as sending mass mailings and regular news updates, and managing distribution lists. Today's messaging environment has made it virtually effortless to send new and forwarded information across the globe in practically no time and at practically no cost. The Web, together with powerful search engines that comb it, has become an enormous library and marketplace, empowering those who want to find and acquire information as well as those who want to publish and disseminate it. The benefits are enormous, but they are partially offset by numerous problems: spam, pop-up ads, computer viruses, hackers, and so forth.

Blockage Power

Blockage power is the ability to prevent particular information from flowing from a given source to a given destination. It is the opposite of flow power and serves to undermine it by denying, degrading, and disrupting information flow.

As a rule, blockage power is selective. The goal is not to prevent all information flow, only that which is deemed harmful. Blockage power is directed at a range of information, including spam; malicious software such as computer viruses, worms, Trojan horses, and spyware; sensitive information sought by spies; intellectual property transmitted in violation of copyrights; information contraband such as child pornography; and information censored by governments.

Like flow power, blockage power can be exercised at the source or destination, or by third parties along the way. At the source, it takes the form of security measures, including access controls, filters, encryption, and digital rights management. Access controls deny unauthorized persons the ability to transmit information from the source. They typically depend on a system of user identification and authentication, such as user names and passwords. However, they can be based on other factors such as location. *Jihadist* Web sites, for example, have been known to prohibit access to visitors from certain countries. Filters, including firewalls and antiviral tools, serve to block certain information from leaving the source, including packets and messages with malicious code. Encryption protects data both in storage and in transit. Even if the bits flow, the information conveyed by them will be inaccessible to those without the key or the means to crack the code. Digital rights management (DRM) uses a combination of access control and encryption to protect intellectual property from flowing in ways that violate a licensing agreement.

Security is also essential to block flows at the receiving end. Access controls deny unauthorized persons the ability to deposit information at the destination. Filters block incoming information deemed harmful, including packets associated with computer intrusions. They stop malicious software and spam that arrive via messaging systems or Web browsing.

Intermediaries also have the power to block flows. Infrastructure operators can filter out spam, malicious code, and information that violates policies and laws. Web-hosting services in the United States and elsewhere have taken down thousands of Web sites containing child pornography, pirated software and music, and scams. They have also removed *jihad*ist Web sites supporting terrorists. In China, where information is heavily censored, Internet service providers are required to filter out and remove banned information. Information entering the country is filtered at border routers implementing China's "great firewall."

Third parties can block flows even if they do not own or control the infrastructure. For example, they can keep information from flowing in or out of a Web site by bombarding the server with worthless traffic, as was done in the Estonian and Georgian cyberattacks. Even if the channels are not fully blocked, these denial-of-service attacks can substantially degrade legitimate flows. Such attacks have driven some e-commerce sites and Internet service providers out of business, because they could not sustain the losses. Others have given in to extortionists, paying perpetrators to stop their attacks.

Unscrupulous businesses have also engaged in "click fraud" in order to get their competitors' click-through ads off the Internet. For example, by repetitively clicking on prepaid ads that are limited to so many clicks, they can drive the clicks up to the limit, whereupon the ads are removed.

Just as information technology has increased flow power, it has increased the power to block those flows. Information security and content filtering tools, for example, continue to improve, making it possible to block traffic that at one time flowed freely. As bad as spam is, at least it is susceptible to blockage, whereas postal junk mail is not. However, considering the rate of increase in information flow, it is not clear that advances in blockage power have kept up with flow power. Part of the reason is that improvements in blockage motivate those who wish to move information to find new ways of doing so. Often, the new methods are covert and distributed, making them much harder to observe and stop.

Covert Power

Covert power is a form of flow power wherein the information flow is hidden. The objective is to conceal the source, destination, or content from an adversary who might observe or obstruct the flow.

A wiretap or other type of hidden communication intercept is an example of a covert flow wherein a copy of the intercepted message stream flows secretly to a hidden receiver. However, although the communicants may not know that their messages are being read or heard, they can effectively block the covert flow by encrypting their communications, as noted earlier.

Most computer attacks involve covert flows. Hackers, for example, secretly plant malicious software, including spyware and hacking tools, on vulnerable machines. The software allows the hackers to secretly exfiltrate sensitive information from the systems. In addition, the compromised machines may be employed in botnets that send out spam and launch DDoS attacks, all without their owners knowing. Likewise, computer viruses and worms spread secretly from one machine to another without the owners even realizing that their machines have been infected.

Some covert flows circumvent security controls at a destination by pretending to come from a trusted source. Packets get through firewalls with fake IP source addresses, and malicious e-mail arrives with spoofed headers. Users unwittingly open e-mail attachments and click on links to malicious Web sites thinking the e-mail came from their bank or other trusted party. In a typical "phishing" scenario, the user is duped into entering personal information such as a username and password or Social Security number.

Initiators of flows can also hijack channels in order to take over a network connection or broadcast medium. Israel, for example, hijacked live broadcasts from Hezbollah's Al-Manar television station in order to supplant the station's regular programming with its own messages.

In some cases, the source and destination of a flow collaborate in order to hide a flow from third parties such as wiretappers. An example is the use of steganography, which attempts to hide the transmission of information. By hiding the message within a cover medium such as an image or video, the communicants can conceal the flow of the message from third-party observers. However, a third party may observe the flow of the cover message and thereby learn at least that something is being communicated. Encryption is similar, but in this case the message is hidden by scrambling the bits rather than trying to conceal its transmission.

Third parties can facilitate covert flows. Proxy servers, for example, allow users to browse the Web while concealing their IP address from a visited Web site, and the Web site's IP address from intermediaries (e.g., governments) watching what flows in and out of the user's computer. They provide one means whereby users in China, Iran, and other countries that censor the Internet can get around the filters that prohibit access to certain foreign sites. Banned information can also slip past the filters of these countries through the use of encryption and steganography. Software tools have been developed explicitly to support these covert flows.

Laws and Regulations

The preceding discussion illustrates how technology enhances both the power of information flow and the power of blockage. This power is also strengthened through laws and regulations. Those that support the rights of free expression and access to information strengthen the power of flow, while those that restrict those rights strengthen the power of blockage.

Most if not all governments have regulatory authority over their information environments. Authoritarian governments generally restrict more information than democracies, but even democracies prohibit certain types of information such as child pornography, defamatory speech, fraudulent advertising, and speech that incites violence. In addition, governments have laws protecting classified information from disclosure and intellectual property from piracy and theft. When these laws and regulations are broken, infrastructure owners are entitled to block offending information flows. They can take down Web sites or remove files from them, block broadcasts and individual messages, and deny access to perpetrators. At the same time, free speech laws ensure that public providers cannot block information flows just because they find them offensive. In addition, the Freedom of Information Act (FOIA) and corporate disclosure laws ensure that government agencies and corporations release certain information even when they would prefer to withhold it.

Regulations do not provide absolute power over information flows, as laws can be violated and information can flow covertly. Further, enforcement across borders can be difficult. Information prohibited in one country may not be prohibited in another, and monitoring information flows over borders is difficult at best. Denizens of a country where information is prohibited may be able to acquire it from foreign sources by covert means, as noted earlier.

Still, laws and regulations matter. Most Internet service providers in China abide by the regulations to censor, lest they risk heavy penalties or closure. This is equally true of Western companies operating within China, leading to criticisms of Google, Cisco, and others for supporting the censors instead of demanding free speech. In addition, most Chinese accept the legal regime and self-censor. Relatively few flagrantly violate the law, and many who do end up in prison.

Although intellectual property laws have certainly not prevented the flow of software, music, and other files in violation of copyrights, they have arguably reduced their flow. Lawsuits against businesses found to have unlicensed software motivated companies to make sure the software on their computers was licensed. Similarly, those against Napster and other services that promoted unfettered music sharing led to the launch of new services that better support the protection of intellectual property, while enabling its flow. Had these and lawsuits against individual violators not been filed, copyrights might be meaningless in today's information environment.

Control

Control over the information environment is usually regarded as the ability to prevent certain flows, including downstream flows following the limited release of information. The general consensus is that these flows cannot be controlled. Once information is out there, especially on the Internet, it cannot be retracted or restricted to particular parties. It can go anywhere, assisted by covert means or even overtly. Moreover, anything can be put on the Internet, in defiance of government and corporate censors.

This chapter takes the view that the issue of control is more nuanced. Although the ability to block flows is never complete, steps can be taken to reduce considerably the likelihood or extent of particular flows. These steps can draw upon both technology and the law. In China, the information environment is strongly affected by laws and regulations governing users and service providers, by the products that block and filter flows at the border routers and internally, by the thousands of cybercops who enforce the laws, and by the severe penalties imposed on violators. Chinese users can circumvent the filters using encryption and steganography, but most do not bother.

Information placed on the Internet may seem impossible to take back, yet it happens all the time. News sites remove stories from public view, organizations pull documents, and entire Web sites disappear. In some cases, the information may still be on the net, but hidden on a page that is password controlled or not seen by search engines. Unless the information has been copied to a public Web site that is scanned and indexed by major search engines, it will be as good as gone, as far as most users are concerned. That the information may exist somewhere will be of little value. The Internet archive (www.archive.org) is an ambitious attempt to keep a record of information posted on the Internet, but it is far from complete, and information has been removed from there as well.

Still, there are many situations where people lose control over their information. Internet users give their personal information to a Web site, only to learn that the site has been compromised by hackers or sold to a third party. They find out that sensitive information sent in a private e-mail was forwarded to others or posted on a Web site. They discover that their search queries are logged and potentially available to the government. They find out that a software product installed on their computer has hidden spyware, which has been sending information from their machine to the vendor's. Government officials post redacted documents on their Web sites, only to learn that the "deleted" information was inadvertently exposed and published on a site outside government control. Information security mechanisms protect against some of these flows, but not all.

In general, it is easier to control information the closer it is to the source. If the photos taken at Abu Ghraib had never been taken or entered the public domain, whence they quickly spread around the world, the impact would have been far less. Better still, had the prisoners never been abused, there would have been no story of mistreatment to report in the first place. Even if we cannot completely control the downstream flow of information, we can control our actions, which in turn affect the information generated about us and disseminated to other parties. However, we are still not in complete control, as people can concoct and propagate conspiracy stories and other falsehoods. These stories will coexist with accurate ones in a sea of information where perception can matter more than truth.

Overall, governments have greater control over the information environment than other entities, because of their ability to censor information within their borders under national laws, however limited that power may be. But organizations are not powerless, as they can fire their own personnel for accessing or posting inappropriate information, and they can sue those who steal their intellectual property.

In addition to blocking information, governments and other entities can attempt to shape the information environment through information flows. They can flood the information environment with carefully crafted messages, submit stories to the press faster than their opponents, and post messages on venues that draw large audiences. Indeed, it may be more effective to post information on a popular Web site than on one that is rarely visited but under its publisher's control. Chinese authorities, operating undercover, reportedly post commentaries defending the government on Internet discussion sites to counter negative comments on those sites, finding this to be more effective than posting to official government sites.

Influence

Ultimately, one's goal may go beyond simply causing or blocking flows, or even controlling the information environment. It may be influencing the opinions, decisions, and actions of target audiences. Governments are interested in promoting their national and international agendas; political parties seek votes for their candidates; and businesses want consumers to buy their products.

For information to influence people, it must first reach them. This can be easier said than done. Simply publishing information on a Web site or broadcasting it over the airwaves does not guarantee it will reach a target audience. The audience may never visit the site or tune its stations to the desired content. As noted previously, posting information to already popular Web sites and other media can help. In the Arab world, one can reach a much larger audience through Al Jazeera than CNN.

Sending information directly via e-mail or other messaging systems is also problematic, as the messages may be viewed as spam and discarded. These systems generally work best when the receivers knows the senders and are favorably disposed toward them or have asked for information from them, for example by subscribing to an e-mail newsletter or "following" someone on Twitter. Another strategy is to relay the message through a trusted relationship; instead of contacting the target directly, the message is sent to a trusted friend or colleague of the target. Internet services such as LinkedIn give users the ability to construct, manage, and use trusted networks to reach people they do not otherwise know.

Assuming a message has reached its target, how the target responds will be a function of the message's perceived credibility; the target's psychology, experiences, social communities, and culture; the target's relationship to and views of the source of the information; and the context in which the message is received. A message that appeals to a government's own citizens might be found repugnant to a foreign audience.

The ability to influence another party can be based on different types of power relationships. John French and Bertram Raven identified five in their seminal paper "The Bases of Social Power" (*Studies in Social Power*, 1959): reward, coercive, legitimate, expert, and referent.

With reward power, influence is achieved by mediating rewards to the target of influence, where the granting of rewards is contingent on the target's taking a desired action (or inaction). Con artists exploit reward power by promising benefits that are never delivered. With the Nigerian 409 scams, victims believe they will receive millions of dollars after putting up a few thousand; instead, they find that they have been duped. Enough people fall for such scams that a considerable portion of the global e-mail traffic contains fraudulent messages.

With coercive power, influence is achieved through threats or acts of punishment.

By serving lawsuits against file-sharing services that facilitated music sharing in violation of copyrights, the music industry influenced the development and deployment of products and services that support copyrights. Extortionists have also used coercive power, threatening to disclose secrets acquired by hacking or to launch a DDoS attack against a critical Web site unless the victim pays.

Legitimate power refers to the power that comes from the authority vested in roles and social norms. The target of influence accepts that the source has the authority to prescribe certain actions. As noted earlier, most Internet users in China accept the rulings by their government about posting certain types of information on the Internet. Similarly, employees accept certain restrictions imposed by their organizations on Internet use. In many cases such as these, the legitimate power is also backed up with coercive power, for example the threat of being fined, imprisoned, or fired.

With expert power, one's influence on another party is based on knowledge and expertise that has value to the other party. The information supplied by experts is generally more likely to receive widespread distribution and be acted upon by recipients than information from non-experts.

Referent power, one of the strongest forms of social power, is based on a feeling of attraction to and identification with the influencer. The target of referent power will take actions to please, imitate, or support the source, for example by buying a product or donating to a charity promoted by a celebrity. The source may not even be aware of the power held over the target. Referent power is similar to the soft power described by Joseph Nye in his book by that title. As with the other forms of social power, people with referent power have an advantage when it comes to reaching and influencing others.

Intermediaries also play a role in influence. Consumers consult product ratings and reviews before making purchasing decisions; voters talk with family and friends before filling in their ballots; and government leaders examine intelligence reports before making certain decisions. In some cases, the value of intermediaries can be subverted. For example, book authors can improve their ratings on Amazon.com by posting anonymous five-star reviews of their own books. Similarly, they can lower the ratings of competing books by posting anonymous one-star reviews of those books. With the submission of numerous reviews from phony reviewers, both scores can be further affected.

Conclusions

The global flow of information is competitive, with the power of flow frequently bumping up against the power of blockage. While no player has complete control over the information environment, each has limited power to cause or support certain flows and block others. However, there is a constant tension between the power of flow and the power of blockage. Channels that seem to be blocked may be circumvented through covert flows; yet, at the same time, flows that seem impossible to block technically may be sharply reduced through laws and regulations.

The competition between flow power and blockage power is manifest in both domestic and international conflicts. In addition, it has given rise to several information-related conflicts, including the free flow of intellectual property versus copyright protection, free speech versus government censorship, spam versus e-mail control, hacking and malicious software versus security and privacy, and government and corporate surveillance versus privacy. None of these have or are likely to have clear winners and losers, as technology continually advances to support new means of flow and new means of blockage. At the same time, the legal environment adapts to better empower certain actors.

In at least some of these conflicts, the ultimate question is not who wins the flow wars but who wins at influence. Which companies succeed in the market? Which governments realize their policy agendas? Do individuals retain their civil liberties? Still, the global flow of information plays a critical role in determining influence and is fundamental to it. As long as there are competing agendas, there will be power struggles over the information environment.

14

Information Power

The Information Society from

an Antihumanist Perspective

Jack M. Balkin

WHEN WE THINK ABOUT INFORMATION as power, we usually think about individuals, groups, and nations using information and information goods as a resource that helps them gain advantages over others. In this chapter, however, I am interested in how the globalized information networks create new forms of power that transcend people's conscious design. Digital information technologies, I shall argue, enmesh individuals, groups, and nations in proliferating networks of power that they neither fully understand nor fully control, and that, in fact, are controlled by no one in particular.

To explain this phenomenon, I offer three portraits of our current situation, which I call the *memetic* model, the *Gaia* model, and the *proliferation of power* model. Each model focuses on forms of power that shape human beings, exercise control over them, and reshape their attitudes, their self-conception, and their modes of behavior. Each perspective suggests that larger forces are reshaping and even sacrificing human values and human interests to serve goals that no human being in particular is seeking. And in these models, the choices people make are consequences of the way these larger forces play out. Thus, these models take human agency as both an input and an output of the global information system. For this reason, they are all antihumanist approaches—that is, they treat human beings as the constructions and unwitting agents of larger forces produced by the concatenation of individual human belief, desire, and action.

The point of this analysis is not to deny the role that human agency plays in making the world we inhabit. All of the mechanisms I describe in this chapter are produced by the actions of individuals, working either separately or collectively in groups. Nor is it to reject the importance of human values and interests as goals of information policy. Quite the contrary: I hope to identify features of our current condition that we might otherwise overlook. If we care about promoting human freedom and human flourishing in a globalized information society, we need to think about all the various forces that might affect them.

The Internet from a Meme's Point of View

The memetic model, as its name implies, asks how the evolution of the Internet looks from a meme's point of view. Memes are bits of information that replicate themselves in human minds and in human-created methods of information storage and retrieval.[1] (In fact, there is some dispute about whether the latter should properly be called memes, but for ease of discussion I shall include them in what follows.) Memetics holds that culture, knowledge, and information consisting of complexes of memes replicate themselves by spreading from mind to mind through communication, imitation, and social learning. Replicating memes compete for space in limited human memory and human attention, evolving in a Darwinian process. Human beings are hosts for memes; we use memes to think with, but memes use us to communicate and spread them, in the process generating cultural evolution.

Memetics studies how culture evolves as memes employ their human hosts to proliferate and compete with other memes for limited space in human minds and methods of information storage. Like genes, memes survive to the extent that they successfully propagate; therefore we may talk about them *as if* they were seeking to ensure their own copying and survival. But that conceit is largely metaphorical. For the memetic perspective to be useful, it isn't necessary that there actually be roaming around our heads little bits of culture that are secretly working to further interests of their own. All that is necessary is that features of culture reproduce and develop as if this were the case.

How do the Internet and globalization look from a meme's point of view? Daniel Dennett once quipped that "a scholar is just a library's way of making another library."[2] He meant that successful memes use human beings as their witting or unwitting vehicles for reproduction and spread. Human beings use memes to think with, so from our perspective memes are just tools for our understanding—they form part of what I call our "cultural software."[3] But from a meme's perspective it is we humans who are a means to an end—that end being the replication and propagation of memes.

To survive, memes must either win a competition against other memes for limited space in human memory or attention, or they must create additional space for themselves. Hence memetic competition favors ideas and behaviors that promote communication and increase the number of places where memes can propagate and be stored. Note once again that if we define memes as brain states, bits of information stored in books or sent through telephone wires aren't memes in that narrow sense. But the forces of cultural evolution might generate new kinds of informational entities that can exist in formats outside the human mind. Indeed, that is precisely what a memetic perspective might predict.

New forms of memory storage and communication benefit many different types of memes. Although memes compete with one another, some memes assist one another's survival (just as some genes do). Hence many memes would welcome the spread of ideas that lead human beings to develop ever more powerful methods of communication and information storage. A memetic perspective would predict that, over time, human beings would generate and spread many ideas and behaviors that would lead people to expand communications and information technologies and facilities for information storage and retrieval. These might include (1) ideas promoting education, literacy, and the spread of knowledge; (2) ideas for technologies that let people send information and ideas to one another easily, quickly, and cheaply; and (3) ideas for technologies that make it possible to store vast amounts of information easily, quickly, and cheaply. Eventually these ideas and behaviors might lead to something like the Internet, which connects billions of people around the world and—in conjunction with the world's computers—can store and transmit enormous amounts of information and ideas. To vary Dennett's aphorism, we might say that the Internet is a device made by memes for making other memes.

From a meme's point of view, the Internet is little short of paradise. It greatly amplifies the spread of ideas, knowledge, and bits of culture. In fact, all communication on the Internet occurs through copying, which is how memes reproduce. If cultural reproduction is a meme's version of sex, then the Internet is just one big orgy, an endless informational bacchanal. The Internet copies information from everywhere and then transmits it in redundant copies to millions of places around the world. From a meme's perspective, the Internet is not a great achievement of human liberty. It is the most powerful technology yet devised for memes to reproduce themselves in perpetuity. The glut of information produced by the Internet leads to increasingly powerful technologies of search and retrieval—like search engines—that become central to the network because they lower the costs of finding information. These new search and retrieval technologies, in turn, produce and propagate vast amounts of metadata—information about information—thus spewing ever more memes into the global information environment.

Memetic reproduction isn't concerned with whether human beings are making wise choices or bad choices in how they globalize the flow of information. Rather, the globalization of information and the push for ever more efficient methods of information transfer and storage arise from a memetic imperative. Memes use us to create an ever more suitable environment for their replication and spread. The memetic imperative isn't interested in what is good or bad for human freedom or human flourishing. It cares about what is good and bad for memes. Some things that help memes spread may assist human freedom and human happiness. But some may be indifferent or even hostile to them. Two obvious examples are the spread of hate speech and the self-replicating informational entities we call computer viruses. The proliferation of information can make human life more complicated and hectic; it can also threaten our health and even our survival when dangerous or harmful information proliferates.

The point of viewing globalization from a meme's point of view is not to get you to believe that tiny, inanimate bits of information are secretly in control of your life. The point, rather, is that although we may think that we are promoting the growth and spread of information technology to serve the goals of human enlightenment, the story is far more complicated. The memetic perspective helps us see that the proliferation of information and information technology takes on a life of its own, and that thinking in terms of memetic imperatives, and not human values, will help us understand why this is so.

Mother Earth Thinks about Herself

The Gaia model offers a second perspective on the global spread of information networks. It takes its name from the Gaia hypothesis, which proposes that the Earth's biosphere, atmosphere, oceans, and soil form a single entity that evolves over time and produces and maintains the conditions necessary for life. James Lovelock formulated the Gaia hypothesis in the mid-1960s; he sought to promote environmental values, and he emphasized the complexity of the global ecology and the necessary interdependence of all life on the planet.[4] Robert Wright offered an informational version of the Gaia thesis, arguing that the development of human intelligence is the next step in the evolution of the planet's biosphere and that globalization is a largely positive force that will draw human beings into increasingly interconnected economic, political, and informational cooperation, leading ultimately to a "global brain."[5] Wright was influenced by the work of the Jesuit philosopher and theologian Pierre Teilhard de Chardin, who argued that the "noosphere" of human thought would evolve toward a maximum level of complexity and consciousness, which he called the Omega Point.[6] In the Teilhard version, the world is not just a single organism evolving; it is also becoming more conscious of itself over time. There is an obvious analogy between Teilhard's model and the Hegelian notion of a world Spirit that comes to understand itself through history.

As in the memetic model, human beings in the Gaia model are a means to a larger end. We are information-processing nodes in a developing central nervous system. We are parts of an emerging world brain that increasingly makes new neural connections and, in the process, becomes more aware of itself. Individual human beings are neither the beginning of this story nor its end. They are merely a historical stage in the world's development from relatively primitive forms of ecological feedback and information exchange to an ever more complex and sophisticated system of information flows and information potentials.

In the Gaia model, the world is a self-organizing computing system that collects and distributes increasing amounts of information about itself to itself, so that, in the end, the world becomes fully aware of itself and its own operations. Hence every new bit of information and every new mechanism for collecting, distributing, and analyzing information, even if pursued by human beings for completely selfish ends, increases the world's awareness of itself. Technological advancement creates ever new methods of informational feedback; the Internet draws ever more connections and pathways of informational flow; every new information collection and storage device increases the possibilities for information and feedback about the states and functions of the world and its elements. At this stage in the world's history, we are its neurons, and every bit of technology we develop helps the planet create new connections and promote new information flows, spurring the system onward toward intelligence and sentience.

Like the memetic analogy, the Gaia hypothesis of a single organism increasingly able to think about itself may be no more than a helpful metaphor that helps us to see historical processes from a different perspective. Yet there is some truth in the notion that increasingly complex self-organizing entities spontaneously produce new feedback mechanisms, so that they respond in ever more nuanced ways to signals and changes in information potentials flowing through the system. In this sense we can say that self-organizing entities "know" about themselves and respond to that knowledge.

Over time, such feedback mechanisms can be multiple, increasingly complex, and highly differentiated. Markets, to take only one example, are a kind of self-organizing system that produces continual informational feedback with powerful real-world consequences. We already live in a world of globalized markets in which the unexpected frost of an orange crop in one part of the planet has ripple effects throughout the world economy. Globalized economies not only make different parts of the world more interdependent, but they also create incentives to collect and transmit ever more information from one part of the world to another, so as to anticipate the economic causes and effects that come with this interdependence. Similarly, globalized financial systems require elaborate network surveillance to ensure security and trust and to forestall attacks on the system.

The Gaia hypothesis suggests that the globalization of information technology represents the latest stage of a far more complex self-organizing system that collects information about what happens on the planet and combines it with multiple mechanisms of feedback and control. Before human beings evolved, ecology itself was the major carrier of informational feedback, but now human beings and human technologies do an increasing share of the work. Imagine a world in which every street corner has multiple cameras that collect visual information from every angle; every street has multiple sensors that monitor traffic flows; every house is a "smart" house that collects and analyzes information about what happens within it; every market transaction is dutifully recorded, collated, and analyzed by computers around the world; every computer network continuously monitors its security and tests its vulnerabilities to attack; every search engine perpetually sends out bots seeking new connections and new information to copy; every Internet service provider keeps continuous tabs on what information is being requested and where it is being sent; and that various entities, some public, some private, some human, some automated, continuously gather all this information, sifting it and analyzing it for patterns to predict future behavior and forestall future problems. Such a world would indeed begin to approach a global information processing system, if not a world brain.

The twin forces of globalization and Internet penetration have accelerated this process. We are still at the beginning of a fully globalized network that collects information from around the world, collates it, analyzes it, and sends it to anywhere and everywhere. In this sense, it is not so strange to say that the world is becoming increasingly "aware" of what is happening within it. Perhaps more important, in this emerging world we are not necessarily the central characters. Although these systems of informational feedback grow through the motivations and actions of individual human beings, they do not necessarily evolve to benefit us; rather, our interests, expectations, values, and desires will increasingly be shaped to mesh with the imperatives of this self-organizing world. We will become the sort of beings who are fully immersed in global information flows; who are continuously tracked, traced, and monitored; who can send and receive information from anywhere to anywhere anytime; who have at their disposal multiple methods of communication and infinite sources of information from around the world; and who can no longer imagine what it would be like to live otherwise.

The Proliferation of Information Power

This brings us to the third perspective for understanding informational globalization—the proliferation of power model. The idea of proliferating power is inspired by the European social theory tradition of Karl Marx, Max Weber, and Michel Foucault. Marx pointed out that the evolution of economic forces drives people to make history but not as they intend, creating ever new forms of economic subordination that are repeatedly justified under the name of increasing freedom (although Marx believed the story would conclude with the happy ending of a proletarian revolution). Weber argued that modernity produces an iron cage of increasing bureaucratization in which individuals are subjected to expanding forms of rationalized organizational power. Foucault heralded the age of a disciplinary society in which surveillance and professional knowledge increasingly normalize and regiment human behavior; he imagined new forms of power that, rather than being controlled by any single group or agent, disperse themselves in ever finer webs throughout society.

A proliferation of power perspective argues that the information technologies which human beings implement to transfer, store, and analyze information do not necessarily bring a net increase in either human freedom or human empowerment. Rather, the rise of the global information economy enmeshes human beings ever more tightly into digital information networks, while simultaneously monitoring, shaping, directing, and controlling human beliefs, values, behaviors, and actions. Power does not disappear in a digital networked world. Power shifts from the arbitrary will of specific individuals and the imperatives of large bureaucratic organizations to the channeling effects of software code, surveillance technologies, and information networks. Increasingly, software architectures and information networks direct, block, filter, categorize, monitor, and normalize behavior; they drive the pace and possibilities of human interaction, the scope of human imagination, and the search for and realization of human desires.

Information, information filtering, and information transfer become central to everyday human life, shaping human expectations and possibilities while they expand our powers. Although we are increasingly integrated into information networks in some ways, we are also alienated from them in others. Information in the form of computer code, databases, information-collection systems, and data analysis turns information into a thing and a tool that does more than empower human beings. The proliferation of power model predicts that digital information flows will increasingly monitor and control human beings, reshaping their activities, intentions, hopes, and desires. Instead of being subjected to the arbitrary will of another, human beings will be subjected to the distributed power of networks. Digital networks tie people together and, in tying them, bind them in ever new ways. Power, instead of being increasingly concentrated in individuals and organizations, is increasingly diffused, so that its effects are felt everywhere.

People routinely praise the Internet for its decentralizing tendencies. Decentralization and diffusion of power, however, is not the same thing as less power exercised over human beings. Nor is it the same thing as democracy. Consider technologies that trace position and identity, such as global positioning systems, radio frequency identification tags, and biometric readers. These devices are widely diffused throughout the system, collecting information from anyone who interacts with them. Or consider digital rights management systems, technical protection measures, and digital watermarks. These forms of control travel wherever files go, carrying their instructions and controls with them. Finally, consider search engines and related systems of categorization and accreditation. Millions of people contribute to the results that search engines provide, but search engines are not a form of democracy. Rather, they are a form of normalization. Individuals do not vote for links in the way they vote for candidates who will represent them and who are accountable to them.

Links construct a regime of norms and expectations. The same is also true of network services that provide accreditation and relevance, filter, collate, and categorize. We can design these systems so that no single individual controls them. But this does not eliminate their power over human beings. It simply enables power to flow everywhere through the system. The fact that no one is in charge does not mean that everyone is free.

An Antihumanist Perspective on Internet Regulation

Familiar issues of Internet regulation look quite different from these three perspectives. Consider pornography as an example. From a memetic perspective, pornography is a "killer app"—that is, an application that motivates people to invest in new technologies or more powerful versions of existing technologies. Pornography harnesses human sexual desires to push human beings to use and develop ever more powerful ways to deliver sexually explicit content. Once the informational pathways have been created, however, they enable many more memes to flow through digital networks and gain storage space on computers. It is possible, even likely, that the Internet as we know it would not have grown so far or as fast had it not been for pornography. Pornography is still driving new markets and new innovations for video phones, portable video players, and virtual worlds. Moreover, each new advance in information technology becomes both a delivery device and a magnet for pornography.

The Gaia model views pornography in similar terms. Pornography drives human beings to create ever more powerful communications networks. It facilitates and fosters the creation of the global neural network that helps the world become more conscious of itself. The proliferation of power model adds an additional wrinkle: The proliferation of pornography not only drives the creation of informational networks that people eventually cannot do without, and which eventually control their lives, it also proliferates forms of sexuality that rob people of their dignity and keep them preoccupied with sexual entertainments and therefore docile and more easily controlled.

From a standard policy perspective, pornography is a problem of public morals let loose by the Internet, or it is a necessary consequence of the freedom of expression that the Internet offers individuals. From the Gaia perspective, however, pornography multiplies neural connections in the world brain. From the proliferation of power perspective, it drives people to communicate incessantly about sex. And from a meme's perspective, pornography is a collection of good (i.e., successful) memes. Pornography not only thrives in existing information environments, but it also drives the creation of new information environments that benefit its survival and propagation. The closest analogy in the natural world might be the genes that cause beavers to alter their environment—through building dams—to help ensure their continued reproduction. In fact, pornographic memes are not only incredibly successful, they are also altruistic—because the new environments they drive humans to create work to the benefit of many other memes as well.

Spam offers a second example. As with pornography, new information environments both proliferate and attract spam. In fact, a very significant percentage of e-mail traffic is spam, which suggests that spam, no matter how annoying it may be to human beings, involves very successful and adaptable memes. From the perspective of public policy, of course, spam is objectionable content. We either work to eliminate it or else we must accept it as an inevitable by-product of the benefits of the digitally networked environment. But consider spam from the antihumanist perspectives offered in this chapter. Objectionable content—and the reaction to this content—drives technological advancement in information technology, which serves the propagation of memes, increases the number and the power of the neural connections in the world brain, and promotes the proliferation and diffusion of ever more finely grained forms of power. Spam, like porn, drives human beings to build, design, and implement information controls that later can be used for other tasks.

Objectionable content—like pornography or spam—leads to new investments designed to control its flow and propagation, in addition to laws that prohibit its spread. These include elaborate filtering systems and devices for tracking and locating the source of objectionable content. Legal and technological measures, in turn, lead to an arms race between pornographers or spammers and those determined to limit or stop them. The same is true of other types of objectionable content, including fraudulent advertising, phishing schemes, and, in those countries determined to control it, political dissent and blasphemy. The arms race between those who promote content deemed objectionable and those who try to control or block it, in turn, produces ever new investments in technology and inventive ingenuity—including, for example, encryption technologies (and methods of breaking them), routing and control technologies (and methods of evading them), and devices for anonymization (and devices to unmask identities). Each of these information control technologies, once implemented, has multiple uses beyond its original purposes, thus driving the increasing power and complexity of global information networks.

Once put in place, the digitally networked environment attracts an increasing share of commercial and government operations. Eventually it becomes indispensable to support the world banking system, the delivery of health care services, everyday commercial transactions, and national security. Its centrality to our lives attracts new forms of cybercrime and new forms of attacks on the network. In order to protect their interests, governments and private businesses must invest ever more heavily in computer security technologies and information collection and analysis methods that can identify security threats and prevent them before they happen. The arms race set off by the digitally networked environment produces ever more surveillance of the system, ever more collection of analysis and data to predict and head off potential dangers, and ever more powerful technologies of control over information flows.

We can view the current struggles over privacy and intellectual property rights similarly, not as problems in their own right but as spurs to innovation and the proliferation of information technologies. Digital networks undermine intellectual property rights in familiar ways: They allow unlimited copying and transmission of digital content at vanishing costs and undermine the rights holder's legal monopoly over reproduction and expression. This leads to technical measures to protect intellectual property interests, which leads in turn to new devices to route around these measures or disable them, producing an arms race that enhances technological advancement and proliferation. The need to protect profits in intellectual property drives increasing surveillance of digital networks and attempts to establish more finely tuned control over bits of digital information wherever they travel through the network.

The contemporary fight over digital privacy provides the flip side of the coin, because many of the same technologies and strategies protect both privacy and intellectual property. Digital technologies undermine privacy because they allow new ways of collecting, collating, and analyzing information. The loss of privacy leads to technical and legal measures that attempt to control information flows, producing its own version of the technological arms race.

This story makes particular sense in the Gaia and proliferation of power models. Technological arms races produce ever more finely grained and powerful methods for collecting information about the information that flows through the network. The spread of technologies and countertechnologies enhances flow control and feedback in the global information system, as well as ever new methods for proliferating power over human beings from everywhere in the system. The memetic story, by contrast, is more complicated: Although memes do not benefit from technological environments that prevent their transmission and limit their flow, they do benefit from environments that produce a net increase in their spread and propagation. To the extent that intellectual property protection promotes propagation of ideas, some memes would favor it. Nevertheless, if we see our current struggles over intellectual property and privacy from a meme's point of view—rather than from the perspective of what benefits individual rights and existing business models—we can guess at the long-run result: far less privacy and fairly limited effective protection of digital content (whatever the law may say), combined with increasing amounts of metadata and greatly increased surveillance of digital networks.

Conclusion

Many Internet theorists—including me—have seen the key struggle of the digital era as one between centralization and decentralization, between open and closed systems of innovation, between a culture dominated by a relatively small group of powerful corporations and a truly democratic culture in which ordinary people are producers as well as consumers of informational goods. These theorists argue for increasing decentralization, for increasing connectivity, for increasing democratization of culture and information technologies, for putting more powerful information production tools in everyone's hands and making information cheaper and more easily accessible to everyone.

I support these goals. I do not offer the argument in this chapter to suggest that we should abandon them. Instead, I offer this analysis to suggest that we face other issues as well. If we are interested in promoting *human* rights, we must also be interested in how human beings will change in response to changes in information technology and information flows. Culture reshapes what it means to be human. As the network changes, and as we become increasingly subjected to it, we will become human in different ways.

Ironically—or perhaps not—human beings will use the language of liberal individualism to justify and legitimate the world we are entering. We will defend the spread of memes, the deployment of new global neural connections, and the proliferation of information power in the name of freedom—to speak, to innovate, to buy and sell—and in the name of security—from crime, from terrorism and from the theft of intellectual property. But our model of individual liberties and rights—and our political struggles over the same—does not fully capture how power changes and spreads with the evolution of global information architectures and global information flows. That is because the forces of global information evolution are orthogonal to the pursuit of human freedom. Our goal is to divert this new form of power toward human ends. It will proliferate in any event. The real question is how it proliferates.

Notes

1. See Richard Dawkins, The Selfish Gene (Oxford: Oxford University Press, new ed., 1989), 192; Daniel C. Dennett, Darwin's Dangerous Idea: Evolution and the Meanings of Life (New York: Simon and Schuster, 1995); J. M. Balkin, Cultural Software: A Theory of Ideology (New Haven: Yale University Press, 1998).

2. Daniel C. Dennett, Consciousness Explained (Boston: Little, Brown, 1991), 202, 206.

3. Balkin, Cultural Software.

4. James Lovelock, Gaia: A New Look at Life on Earth (New York: Oxford University Press, 1979, 2000).

5. Robert Wright, Non-Zero: The Logic of Human Destiny, 297, 316 (New York: Pantheon Books, 2000).

6. Pierre Teilhard de Chardin, The Future of Man (New York: Harper Torchbooks, 1969).

About the Contributors

FREDERICK M. ABBOT is Edward Ball Eminent Scholar at the Florida State University College of Law. His most recent books are *Global Pharmaceutical Policy: Ensuring Medicines for Tomorrow's World* (with Graham Dukes) and *International Intellectual Property in an Integrated World Economy* (with Thomas Cottier and Francis Gurry).

C. EDWIN BAKER was Nicholas F. Gallicchio Professor of Law at the University of Pennsylvania. He was the author of many books, including *Media Concentration and Democracy: Why Ownership Matters*. He died December 8, 2009 at the age of sixty-two.

JACK M. BALKIN is Knight Professor of Constitutional Law and the First Amendment at Yale Law School and the founder and director of Yale's Information Society Project, as well as the director of the Knight Law and Media Program at Yale. His books include *Cultural Software: A Theory of Ideology*; *The State of Play: Law, Games and Virtual Worlds* (with Beth Noveck); *Cybercrime: Digital Cops in a Networked Environment* (with James Grimmelmann et al.); *What Brown v. Board of Education Should Have Said*; *What Roe v. Wade Should Have Said*; and *The Constitution in 2020* (with Reva Siegel).

DAN L. BURK is Chancellor's Professor of Law and a founding faculty member at the the University of California, Irvine, School of Law. He is the author, with Mark A. Lemley, of *The Patent Crisis and How the Courts Can Solve It*.

MIGUEL ANGEL CENTENO is Professor of Sociology and International Affairs at Princeton University. From 2003 to 2007, he served as the founding director of the Princeton Institute for International and

Regional Studies. He has published many books as author or editor, including *Democracy within Reason: Technocratic Revolution in Mexico* and *Blood and Debt: War and Statemaking in Latin America.*

DOROTHY E. DENNING is Distinguished Professor of Defense Analysis at the Naval Postgraduate School in Monterey, California, and the author of *Information Warfare and Security.*

JAMES DER DERIAN is Watson Institute Research Professor of International Studies at Brown University, where he directs the Innovating Global Security and Media Project. His most recent books are *Virtuous War: Mapping the Military-Industrial-Media-Entertainment Network* and *Critical Practices in International Theory.*

DANIEL W. DREZNER is a professor of international politics at The Fletcher School at Tufts University. His most recent publications are *All Politics Is Global: Explaining International Regulatory Regimes* and *U.S. Trade Strategy: Free Versus Fair.*

JEREMY M. KAPLAN, now a consultant in private practice, was previously a professor at the Industrial College of the Armed Forces and the deputy director for Technical Integration Services at the Defense Information Systems Agency. He is the author of *A New Conceptual Framework for Net-Centric, Enterprise-Wide, System-of-Systems Engineering.*

EDDAN KATZ is International Affairs Director for the Electronic Frontier Foundation. Before EFF, he was the executive director of the Yale Information Society Project and Lecturer-in-Law at Yale Law School. He is the editor of *Cybercrime: Digital Cops in a Networked Environment.*

STANLEY N. KATZ is director of the Center for Arts and Cultural Policy and lecturer with the rank of professor at the Woodrow Wilson School of Public and International Affairs at Princeton University. The author or editor of several books, he is the editor most recently of the *Oxford International Encyclopedia of Legal History.*

LAWRENCE LIANG is a legal researcher and co-founder of the Alternative Law Forum in Bangalore. He is the co-author of *The Public Is Watching: Sex, Laws and Videotape.*

ELI NOAM is a professor of economics and finance at the Columbia Business School and the director of CITI, the Columbia Institute for Tele-Information. He is the author or editor of twenty-eight books, including *Media Ownership and Concentration in America.*

JOHN G. PALFREY JR. is Henry N. Ess Professor of Law and Vice Dean for Library and Information Resources at Harvard Law School. His books include *Born Digital: Understanding the First Generation of Digital Natives* and *Access Denied: The Practice and Politics of Internet Filtering.*

VICTORIA REYES is a graduate student in sociology at Princeton University. Prior to coming to Princeton, she conducted research in the Philippines as a 2006–2007 Fulbright Fellow and worked as an education associate at a reproductive health nonprofit in Washington, D.C.

RAMESH SUBRAMANIAN is Gabriel Ferrucci Professor of Information Systems at Quinnipiac University and Visiting Fellow at the Information Society Project, Yale Law School. He is the editor of *Computer Security, Privacy and Politics: Current Issues, Challenges and Solutions* and *Peer-to-Peer Computing: The Evolution of a Disruptive Technology.*

Index

www.ingramcontent.com/pod-product-compliance
Lightning Source LLC
LaVergne TN
LVHW042136040326
832903LV00010B/269